rude®

RUDE®

LOVE IS BLIND

LETS MAKE T-SHIRTS

rude® www.thisisrude.com

rude® xxxxxxxxxxx

rude®
RUDE®
rude
www.thisisrude.com
xxxxxxxxxxx
LOVE IS BLIND
LETS MAKE T-SHIRTS

Time flies when you're being Rude

1999 – 2008

RUDE®

A small word of huge thanks

Hopefully not as long, boring and turgid as the thank you's at a wedding, but just as heartfelt.

We are truly indebted to the designers, printers and paper suppliers who have made this book possible. Without their support and dedication this project would still be sitting on the hard drive. So much passion and determination has come from our friends at ico Design, the London design studio that has championed this project from the beginning. They have dedicated their time, energy and creativity to the design of this book, keeping the momentum going right to the end and giving us something way beyond our expectations.

L&S Printing are also old friends of Rude whom we've worked closely with on many projects. We've been fortunate for them to apply their expertise and turn our vision into a beautifully printed and finished book. Likewise our friendship with G.F Smith has lasted many years and we'd like to thank them for having such great paper to print onto.

Published by Rude Limited
© Rude 2014

First edition, August 2014

ISBN 978-0-9930161-0-3

Design
ico Design
icodesign.com

Editor
Caitrina Cody
caitrinacody.com

Printing
L&S Printing
ls-printing.com

Paper
G.F Smith
gfsmith.com

Cover Illustration
Rude
thisisrude.com

Rupert + Abi

We'd like to dedicate this book to our two sons Billy and Herbie Meats whose lack of physical input is understandable but whose life input is immeasurable.

Rude Ups and Downs

6–7	Why make a book?		54–57	Family Clothing Collection Rude
8–9	**1999**			**2001**
10–11	Lookbook Rude		64–65	
12–15	First Samples Rude		68–69	Rude World Urban Outfitters
16–17	Our Mugshots Rude		70–71	Rude Go to Japan Style
18–21	Samples and Lookbook Rude		72–77	Rude School Rude
22–23	First Collection Rude		78	Promotional T-shirt Marie Curie Cancer Care
24–25	Premier Collection Rude		79	Closer to Heaven The Pet Shop Boys
26–31	First Advertising Campaigns Rude		86–87	**2002**
32–39	Press Clippings Rude		88–91	Things aren't always what they seem Rude
44–45	**2000**		92–97	Keep Smiling with Dwayne and Eileen Rude
46–47	8 Hole Cherry Red Dr. Martens		104–105	**2003**
48–51	San Miguel & Café del Mar San Miguel		106–111	Let's Make T-shirts Rude
52–53	Homeware Rude		112–117	Kruel Summer Collection Rude

118–121	Playstation Experience Sony Playstation	160–161	Hello World Merchandise Travelocity	207	Do You Want to Escape Rude
122–125	Geoff Capes Advertising Campaign Geoff Capes	162–163	I Love London Rude	208–211	Invites and Promotional Artwork The Chocolate Factory N16

130–131	**2004**	168–169	**2006**	216–217	**2008**
132–133	Rude Portrait Spitalfields Regeneration	170–175	Icons Homeware Collection Joseph Joseph	218–219	Credit Crunch Collection Rude
134–135	Eyetoy Merchandise Sony Playstation	176–177	Window Blinds Love is Blind	220–221	Eat Me Now Tour Poster Campaign Cadbury Creme Egg
136–137	Edward Hopper Merchandise Tate	178–179	Rude for Topshop Womenswear Collection Topshop	222	Nokia TV Advert Weiden Kennedy
138–139	Health, Wealth & Happiness Rude	180–187	T-shirt Graphics No Added Sugar	223	Ear to the Underground Capital Radio London Paper
		188–189	Wonderful Collection Rude	224–225	Pop Promo John Power
148–149	**2005**	190–191	Christmas Poster Polydor	226–227	Print Exhibition Print Club
150–151	More Legroom to Moscow BMI	196–197	**2007**	228–229	Poster Campaign Rakish Heels
152	Just Ask Jamie Ace Magazine	198–199	TV Advert Homebase		
153	Montag DDB Advertising	200–205	Exhibition Rude		
154–155	Coca Cola Campaign Weiden Kennedy	206	Below the Line Advertising Campaign Transport for London		
156–159	Dumb Menswear Collection Nickelodeon				

5

Why make a book?

It seems to be a recent phenomenon that starting a creative business in the age of advanced technology is easier than ever. In some respects I believe this is true; we certainly have more tools at our disposal and direct access to decision makers. However the stand-out you need to achieve in such a crowded market makes the competition tougher and more aggresive than ever. So the telling of our story is meant to encourage designers whose only dream is to create work they believe in and earn a crust at the same time.

Rude started when boo.com collapsed and internet shopping was over before it had begun, when ASOS was a start-up and dial up internet connection was cutting edge. Rude's journey highlights the good times, creative output, over expansion, going bust and revival of a small creative agency, whose only desire is to make good stuff.

With sketchbooks, a borrowed Mac and no clue as to how to start a fashion label, Rude was born. Rupert and I met at a London design agency in the late 1990s and quickly realised that our design aesthetic and attitude perfectly aligned. Our desire was to start something new and experiment with different mediums to create our own unique products.

Over a few pints in the pub we decided to join forces as a small start-up and combine my meagre client list with Rupert's handful of recently secured clothing accounts. We registered the name Rude (which is an abbreviation of RuDesign) and split our shares 50/50. We pooled our limited funds to fulfil the handful of orders we had taken and our life as a brand had begun.

1 9
9 9

9 . 1999

Rude

Project
Lookbook

Discipline
Graphic Design and Photography

The beauty of being a graphic designer is the ability to project a perception of who you'd like to be. In this instance we were a tiny start-up with a vision to be taken seriously as a major new street brand.

Immediately we turned our collection into a visual format, a lookbook that featured the clothing, and more importantly a vibe that captured the essence of Rude. We dragged friends onto Rupert's rooftop to model our first samples and create our first catalogue.

Our stylist Jackie knew exactly how to make the clothes look good and create the right image for the brand.

1999.10

rude®
catalogue issue four*

11.1999

Rude

Project
First Samples

Discipline
Applied Graphics

'Map of London' was one of our first designs, which we applied onto a small range of clothing including ties, knickers and T-shirts for both men and women. Essentially, printing onto a garment should be an easy thing to do, however if you're not sure what you're doing there are some obvious pitfalls. Straight off, we ordered 3000 pairs of jersey knickers from China. When we unpacked our goods we realised that they were made for children and even the smallest women had their blood supply cut off after five minutes of wearing them. Lesson one learnt, make sure your spec sheets are correct.

1999.12

13.1999

Rude   First Samples

1999.14

15.1999

1999.16

Project
Our Mugshots

Discipline
PR

This is Rupert and I on one of our first photo shoots.

On the advice of a friend we hired an excellent PR company called Surgery. We were clueless about what a PR should do but felt it right to invest any money we had in people who believed in what we did and who would shout loud and hard to the right audience on our behalf.

This image was taken with the view that editors and readers want to see who is behind a brand. It was an excruciating experience, especially with Baldrick inspired fringes.

Rude

17.1999

Rude

Project
Samples and Lookbook

Discipline
Sales

Finding the route to market was one of the first challenges we had after we'd designed our collection and sales material. In the first instance this was simply Rupert and I with suitcases of clothing and a simple mail order system. After we'd been to the small shops we started contacting buyers of bigger stores with samples and lookbooks.

Along the way we were fortunate to meet someone who worked in sales for a really well known fashion brand.

As he liked what we were doing and was based locally, he brought buyers round to see us. He had fantastic contacts and quickly got us accounts such as Selfridges, Colette and Harrods.

19 . 1999

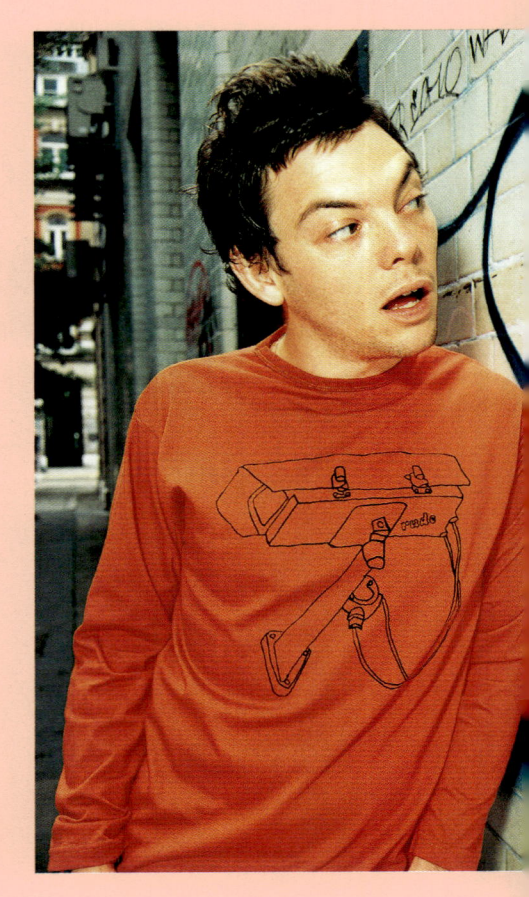

Rude   Samples and Lookbook

1999.20

21.1999

Rude

Project
First Collection

Discipline
Illustration

During a road trip to the USA I made a scrapbook of voyeuristic sketches of American life. These were drawn pre-Rude so I had no intention of using them for anything other than filling time and a book. When I showed the sketches to Rupert he ripped them out of the book, scanned them in and created screens to mass manufacture the drawings onto garments.

'Hanks' was one of several diners we passed, but it was the Fish Fry Fri that caught my attention - we'd never say that in England. 'Man with Fag' is a favourite, I love his gut spilling over his Dickies.

23.1999

Project
Premier Collection

Discipline
Textiles Manufacturing

Unwittingly, we had found ourselves in the garment industry. It was a trade we knew nothing about, so we quickly learned the basics to ensure that our clothes didn't fall apart, stretch out of recognition or lose their print. All of which they did at some point along the way.

Our new language consisted of overlockers, kimballing and interlock jersey. Here's our first collection of tees, vest and skirts.

Rude

1999.24

25.1999

Sales: 020 7636 7371
P.R: Surgery 020 7684 7699
e-mail: sales@rude-products.co.uk
www.rude-products.co.uk

rude LONDON

1999.26

Project
First Advertising Campaigns

Discipline
PR and Marketing

Now that the press and public were becoming aware of us, we were approached by magazines such as i-D about taking out advertising space with them.

It was at this point that we realised that if the images we created were good enough, we could propel ourselves from a two man team with a handful of accounts to a two man team with loads of accounts.

With zero budget we used our good looking friends to model for us in return for beer and sausages. We were fortunate enough to use a young photographer called Flo Kolmer who was willing to create images for free to use in his portfolio.

The series of pictures were really well received and as a result, we managed to obtain many free or seriously discounted ad spaces within publications such as Dazed and Confused, Vogue and Nova.

Rude

Rude — First Advertising Campaigns

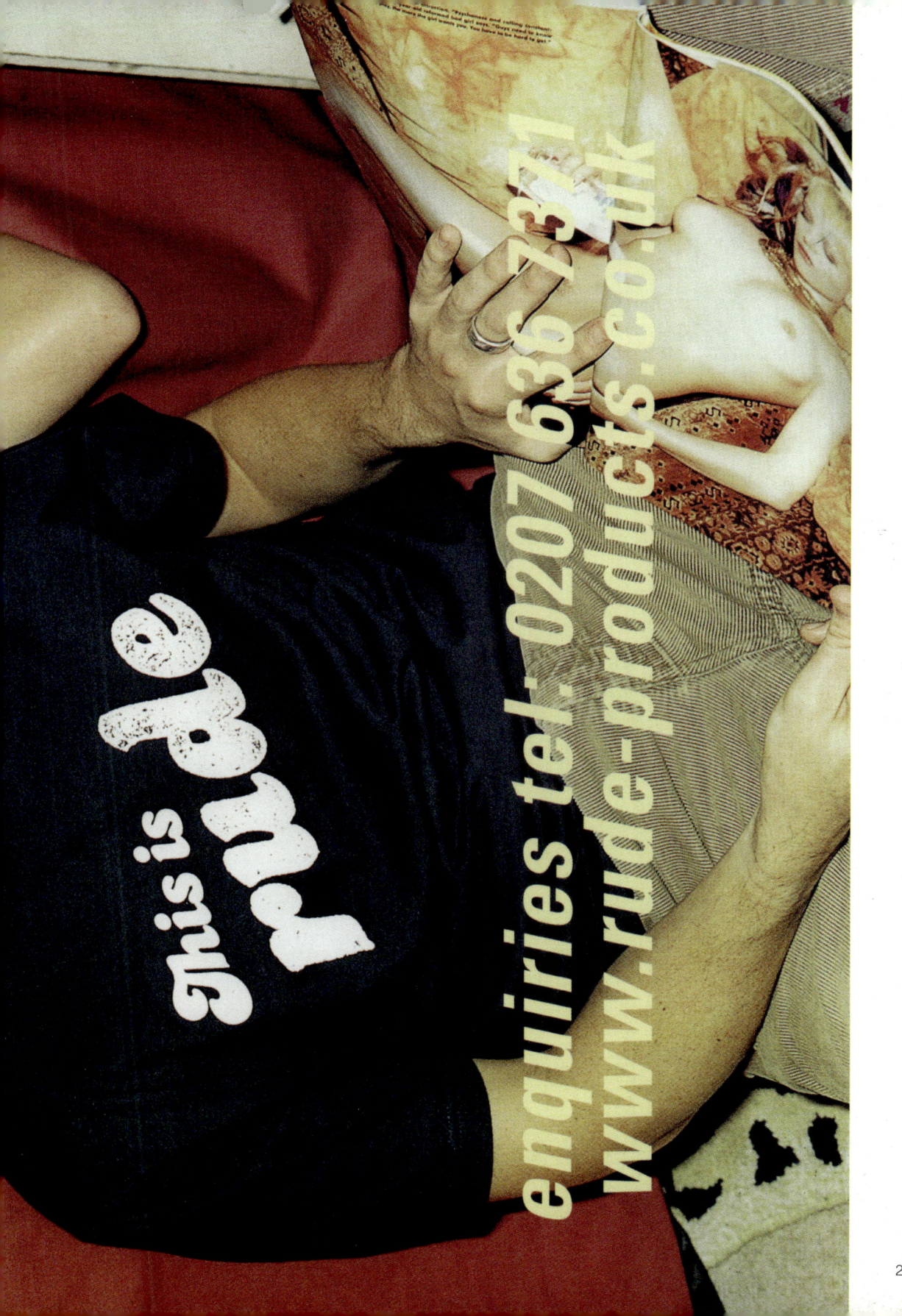

enquiries tel. 0207 636 7371
www.rude-products.co.uk

29.1999

Rude   First Advertising Campaigns

1999.30

rude *LONDON*
TELEPHONE 020 7636 7371
e-mail sales@rude-products.co.uk
rude-products.co.uk

31.1999

Rude

Project
Press Clippings

Discipline
PR

The beauty of sending products out to press is that they come back with fantastic images. These pictures are often taken by great photographers with high production values and access to young creative talent like stylists and models. These particular shots were taken for Mixmag and i-D Magazine.

Having access to this free resource gave us a larger bank of material and the right associations, thus taking our brand to another level.

1999.32

Men's black and pink cotton stretch tank top, £28, Rude Clothing. Black wool trousers (part of men's suit), £209, Nicole Farhi. Silver link bracelet, £250, Tateossian. **Black leather studded bracelet**, stylist's own

Rude   Press Clippings

1999.34

35.1999

Rude   Press Clippings

37.1999

Rude   Press Clippings

THE BIG ISSUE

60p of cover price goes to vendor. Please buy from badged vendors only

£1

ALL SAINTS
BEING GOOD-TIME GIRLS DOESN'T MAKE US BAD

COMING UP FROM THE STREETS
JANUARY 8 – 14 2001 NO. 419

1999.38

...goodness, Natalie recounts that a couple of
...ars ago, her sister spent £10,000 on chil-
...en's toys and took them anonymously to a
...ospital. "There was no press there, and
... the kids were sleeping. She did it
...ecause she wanted to." Last Christ-
...as, Nicole and Liam Gallagher also
...ught £900-worth of toys which
...ey donated to Boots' Pass the Par-
...l Toy Appeal.
   Of all the All Saints, Natalie
...s had it the hardest, raising
...r daughter Rachel as a
...ry young single mother.
... was a kid myself. Her
...ther walked out. Every-
...ing I did was for her
...d I sacrificed a lot,"
... says. Criticism
...om other women
...sets her most. "I'm
...o-women," she
...mes. "It's like, whose
...de are you on?" But
...e's on a very short fuse in
...neral. "I get so angry, I get
... frustrated," she says.
...hank God I don't own a gun."
   Surprisingly, if her life hadn't
...orked out the way it had, she'd
...ve liked to have been a scien-
...t. "I wanted to go back to school,
... study forensic science. I always
...nted to be a doctor. Do a PhD."
   Unlike Shaznay Lewis, whose
...lm and laid-back attitude reflects
...r stable upbringing, Appleton is a
...atile mixture of anger and vulnerabil-
... "I'm madly in love," she enthuses
...out her current boyfriend, the
...odigy's Liam Howlett. "He's *so* not
...at you'd think – calm and quiet –
...rfect for me." She denies that he's
...other 'famous boyfriend'. "When I
...t him," she insists, "I didn't know
...o he was." She isn't about to settle
... carpet slippers, though. "I like to
...ve a good time – we're still young.
...'re not going to become a bunch
...nuns. Never."
   The band seems fractured, and
...hough the Saints make much of
...eir fondness for each other, they

people around me for years," says Lewis. "I'm not very good at being fake. I don't go around thinking, I'm Shaznay from All Saints. The celebrity thing is not a lifestyle I want."
   Melanie Blatt, who made front pages performing onstage with her bump, now has a two-year-old daughter with her musician boyfriend; she always said she didn't want to be a pop-star mum. And as for Nicole, "she'll have to settle down," says Shaznay Lewis. "She hasn't got any choice." She likes Gallagher, though. "He's nice. Quiet. Very polite," she says. And Natalie Appleton hasn't written off having another child, either. "There are times when I get broody," she says. "But not just yet. I want to have a father-figure around."
   So, no one's pretending the All Saints are going to go on forever, or even much longer. That could be why they feel, today, as if they're simply going through the motions with as much grace as possible. "I always said, I'm in it as long as people want me around," says Lewis. She, and Blatt, don't hanker after the high-life. "Our circle is so tight it's hard for superficial people to get in," says Lewis.
   But before All Saints turns into mothercare central, there's still the new single, All Hooked Up – a prime piece of slinky, funky All Saints attitude with a dirty kiss-off chorus, proving that when they do their sulky-angelic thing, they're miles ahead of the rest. "We're all very strong-minded and we sing well together," says loyal, fierce Natalie Appleton. "We're like a rollercoaster – lots of passion, lots of feelings. And we're friends. No matter what happens, there's a magic." ■

All Hooked Up is out on London Records on January 15.

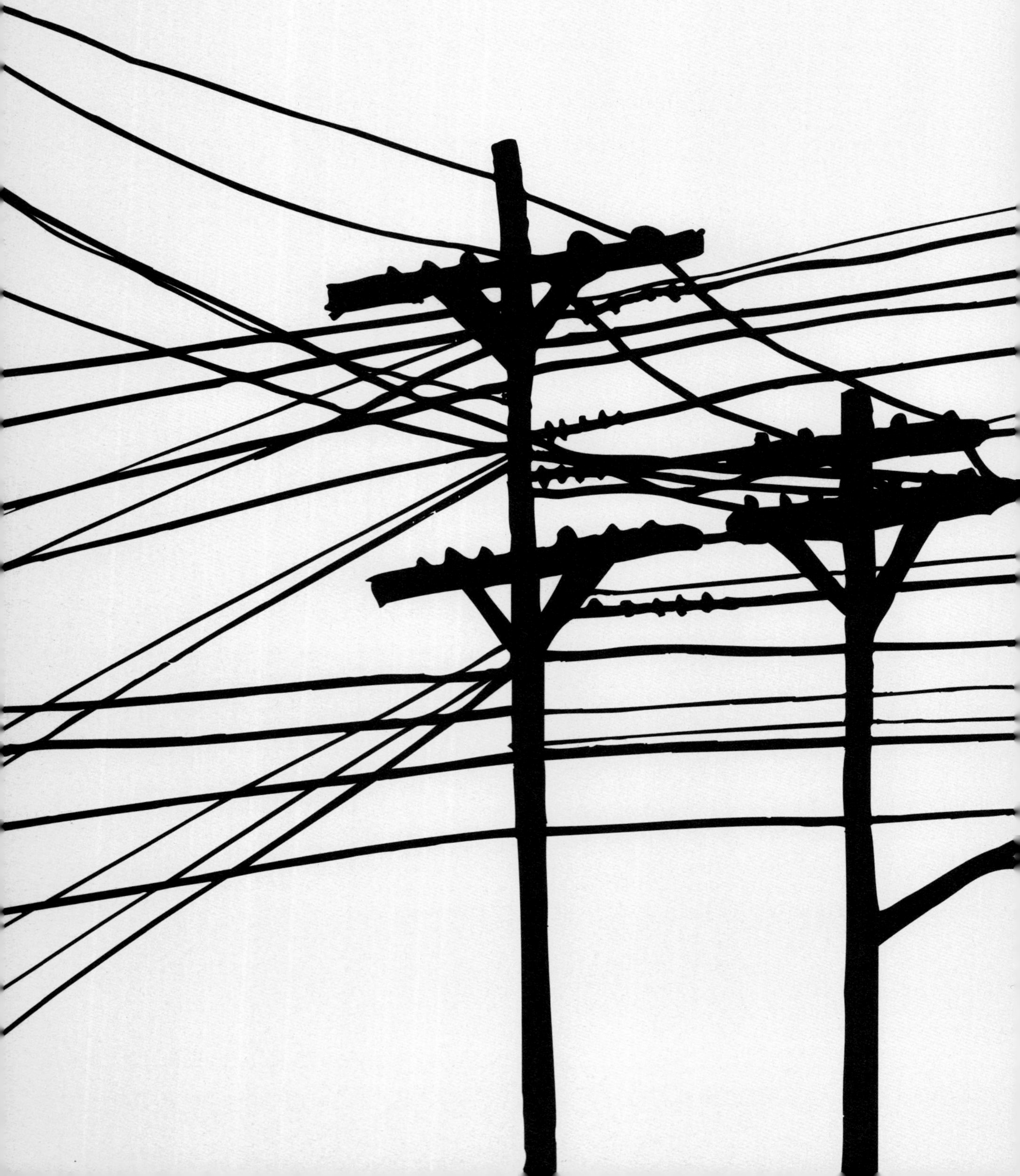

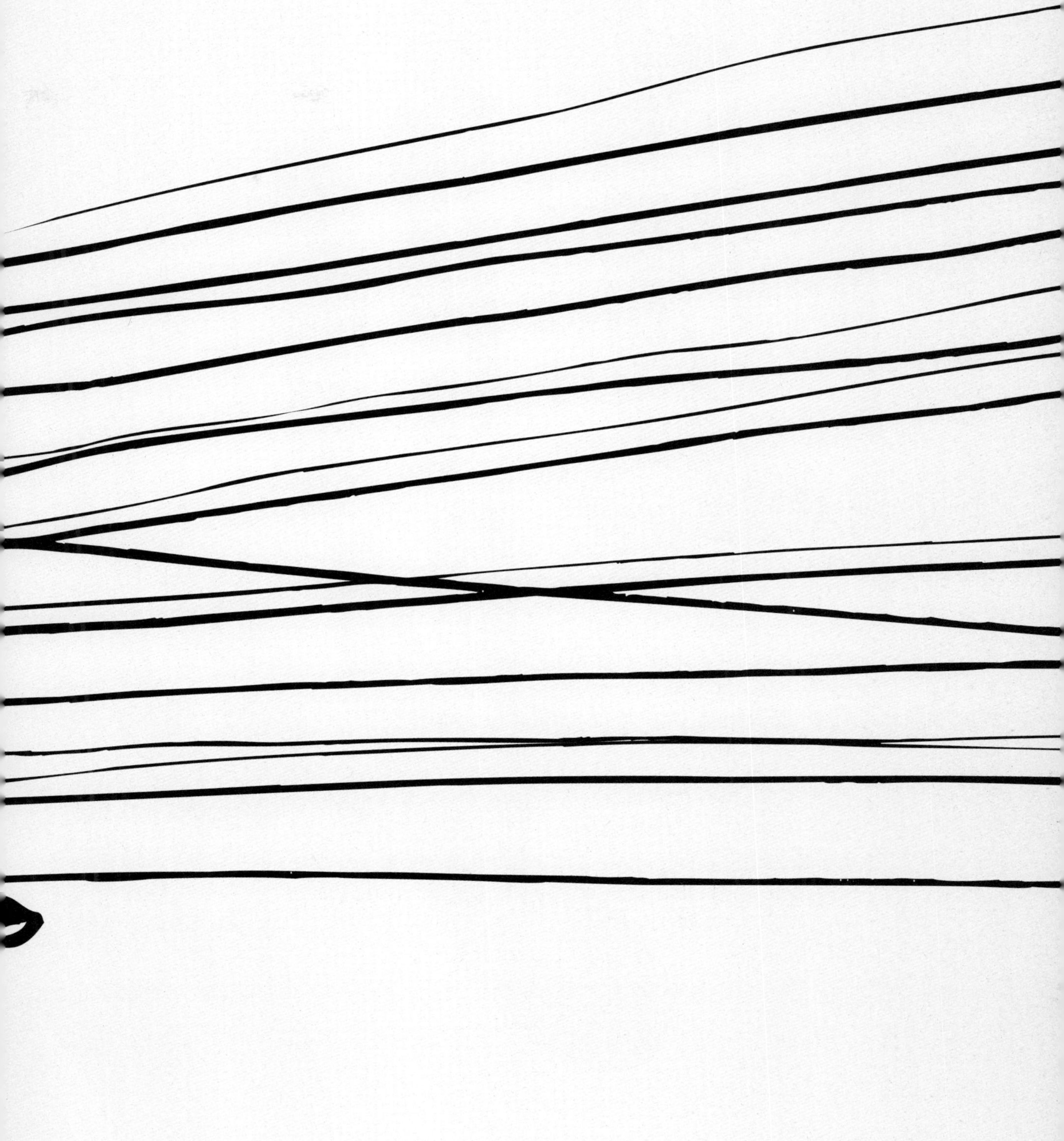

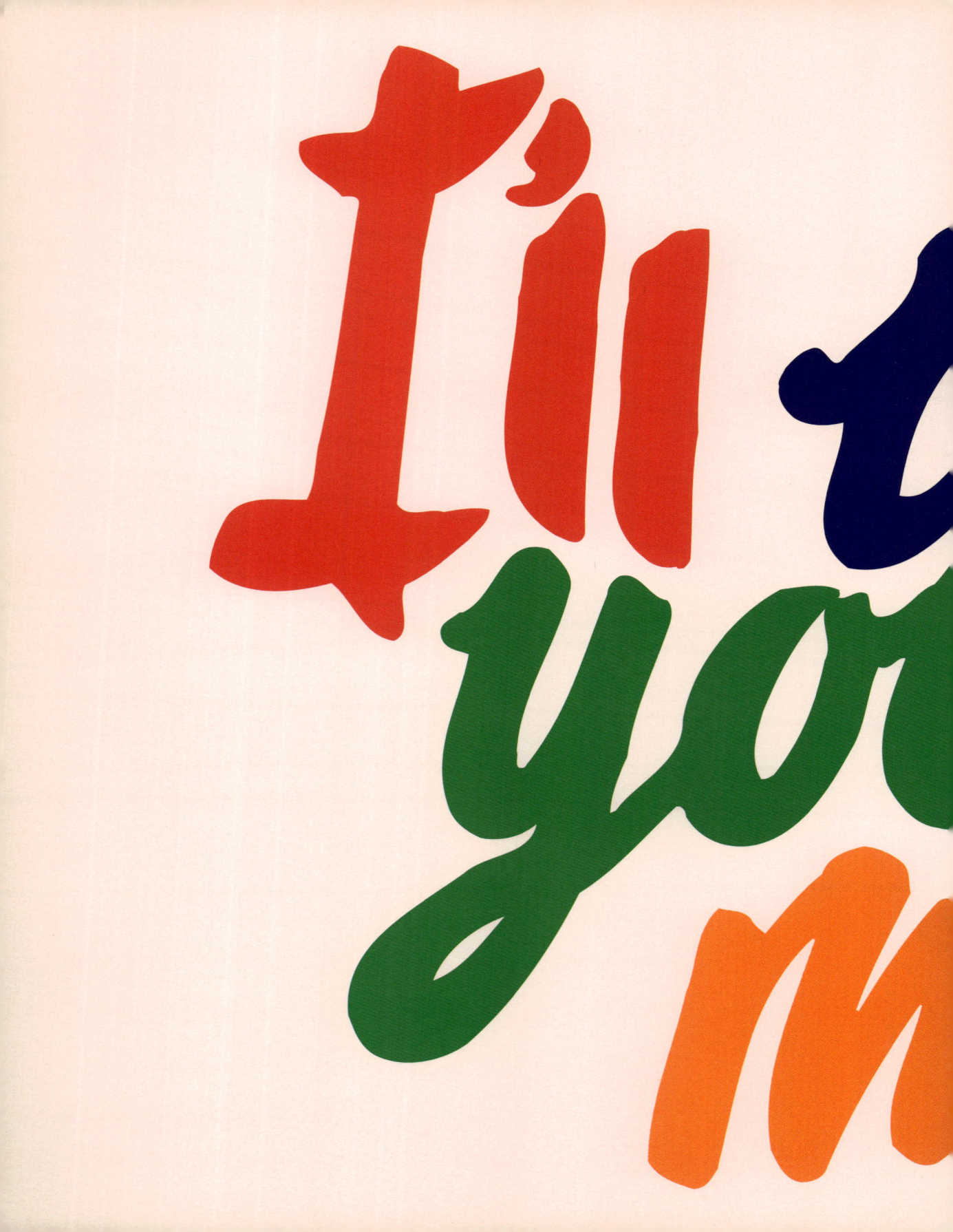

Creative companies often shy away from the important stuff and we were no exception.

During this year we entered a competition run by Shell to find the young entrepreneur of the year; the format was quite similar to Dragon's Den. This process bought real focus to our business – for the first time we had to write a business plan with financial projections and a working cash flow.

We were funding the brand through supplying graphic services to various clients and trying to build Rude at the same time. It was becoming a juggle and we made a decision to focus more on less by choosing to put all our energies into Rude and make it pay its own way.

2000

45.2000

Project
8 Hole Cherry Red

Discipline
Applied Graphics

Doc Martens have made a name for themselves by creating a punkish-rebel worker type boot that just about anyone can wear. So to celebrate the 50th anniversary of the 8 hole Cherry Red they invited ten designers to create their take on the classic boot.

Being known for applied graphics, we started with the leather panels that make up a the boot and screen printed 'Dr. Rude' all over so that the print would run into the seams when assembled. We sent the panels off with a pair of roller boots which were combined into one bootiful pair of rollers.

Dr. Martens

47.2000

Project
San Miguel and Café Del Mar Merchandise

Discipline
Advertising

As Rude's profile was gaining momentum, we were approached by San Miguel who commisioned us to design a bespoke range of merchandise for a promotion they were launching. They needed subtly branded illustrations to adorn tees, keyrings, beermats and bar towels. The result was an illustration of an American fridge bursting with San Miguels. The product was used as prizes for competition-based promotions which were held at pubs across the country.

As part of the project we agreed that San Miguel would pay for our next advertising campaign and in return we would place their product in our photographs. The collaboration worked quite well and allowed us to place the ads in more magazines.

San Miguel

2000.48

Café Del Mar

Volumen Siete: The only album you will need...

Contains exclusive tracks by Moby, Deep & Wide, Bedrock, A New Funky Generation and Slow Pulse. Plus the N.O.W. remix of 'Letting The Cables Sleep' by Bush

Available Now

San Miguel

San Miguel   San Miguel and Café Del Mar
              Merchandise

2000.50

Wierdy is 33, the SAME number AS HER
Bus Route to WORK. She is a little
KNoWn wonder IN
HER Home TOWN,
BarCeLoNa, Due
to HER OBSESSION
with collecting
Everyday objects,
Everyday FOR
19 YEARS.
Each item is
RecorDED BY DATE
In PLAStic
envelopes UNDER
HER BED, she
now Has
7 BEDS.
HOW WIERD
IS THAT?
San Miguel

THIS is CLAIRE age 21
(just) loves CRISPS AND
SALAD
CReAM
ROLLING
HER BUS
TICKET
INTO
TUBES
AND
LAUGHING
A
LOT
San Miguel

HE WON'T EAT TOMATOES
BECAUSE he BELIEVES
It's a FRUIT
TRYING TO
Be a
vegeTABLE
and Won't
EAT OFF
PATTERNED
PLATES
BECAUSE
THEY MESS
WITH HIS
MIND
San Miguel

51.2000

Rude

Project
Homeware

Discipline
Product Design

This was the year we decided to expand our product base and introduce a homeware element to our brand, to sit alongside our clothing collections.

Moving our prints onto larger surfaces was a natural progression and a duvet makes a great canvas. However, not being the best screen printers in the world, we had huge problems pulling a big screen evenly. It's a good job we had a reputation for a rough, handmade style.

The inspiration for these pool ball handles came from the snooker hall opposite my home in Battersea.

We embarked on the process of sourcing a small engineering firm in Coventry who manufactured the aluminium components and threaded them onto reclaimed balls. That meant each set had its own character, with the colours and numbers, randomly selected.

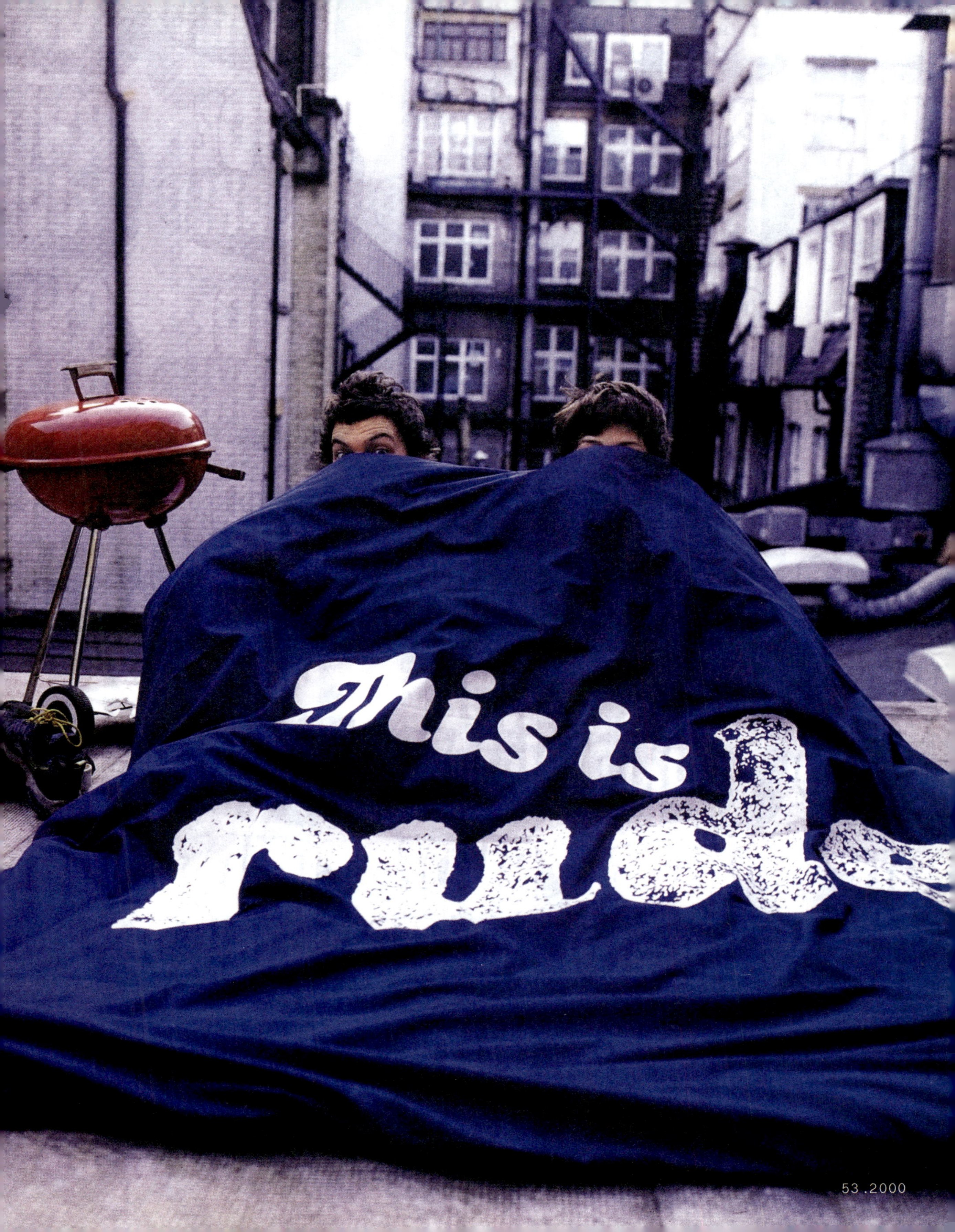
This is
rud

2000.54

Project
Family Clothing Collection

Discipline
Illustration

As a creative starting point, we often come up with a concept or a title to hang our ideas onto. In this instance the 'Rude Family' became an idea which could encompass clothing for all ages. This included our new baby range and once again we involved friends and family to feature in our ad campaigns, among them Rupert's dad and our friends' children.

Rude

MADE YOU LOOK MADE YOU STARE
rude

55.2000

Rude   Family Clothing Collection

2000.56

57.2000

CAFETERIA
RUDA
CAFETERIA
RUDA
CAFETERIA
RUDA
CAFETERIA
RUDA
CAFETERIA
RUDA
CAFETERIA
RUDA
CAFETERIA
RUDA

CAFETERIA
RUDA
CAFETERIA
RUDA
CAFETERIA
RUDA
CAFETERIA
RUDA
CAFETERIA
RUDA
CAFETERIA
RUDA
CAFETERIA
RUDA
CAFETERIA
RUDA

한

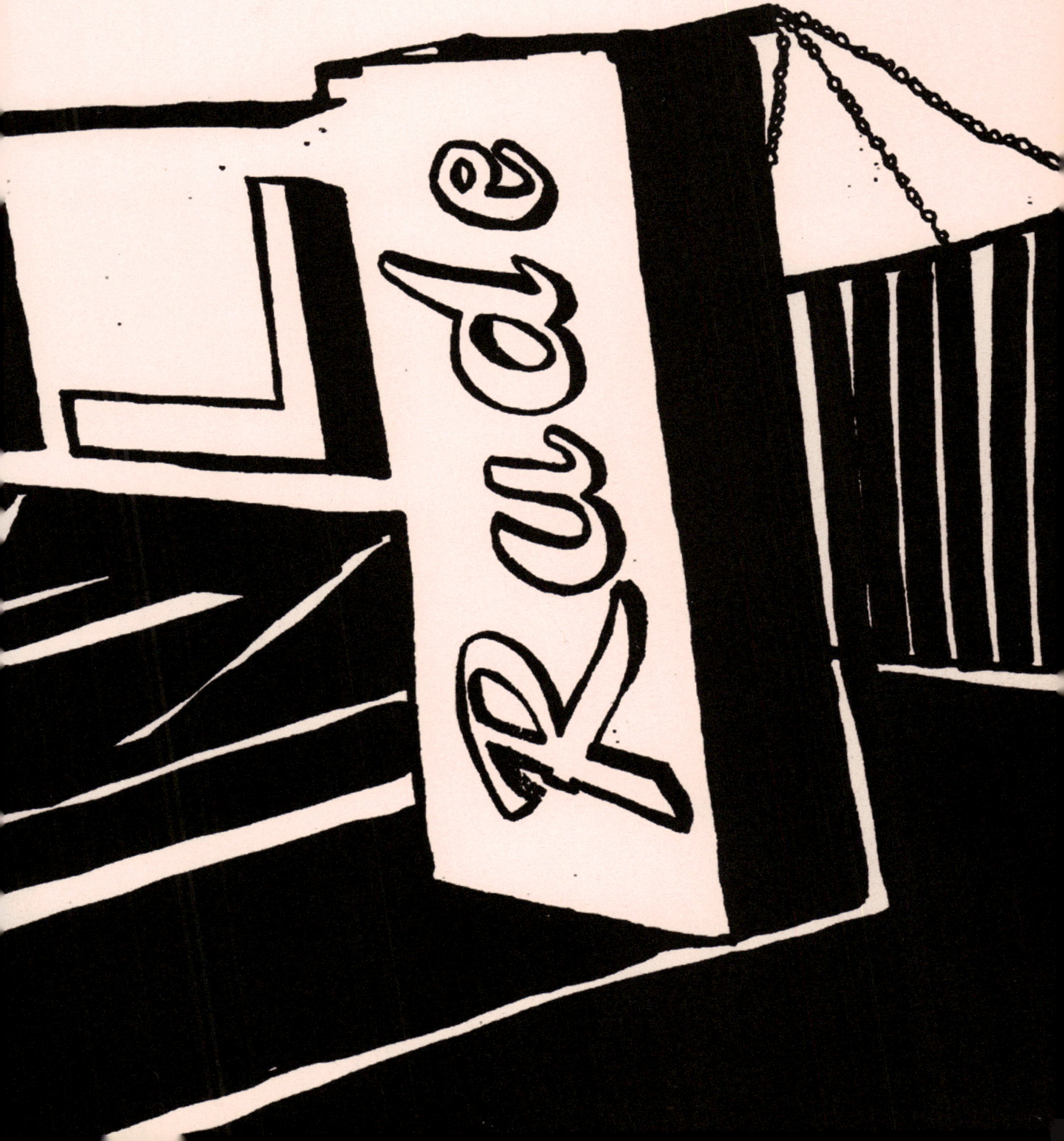
Rude

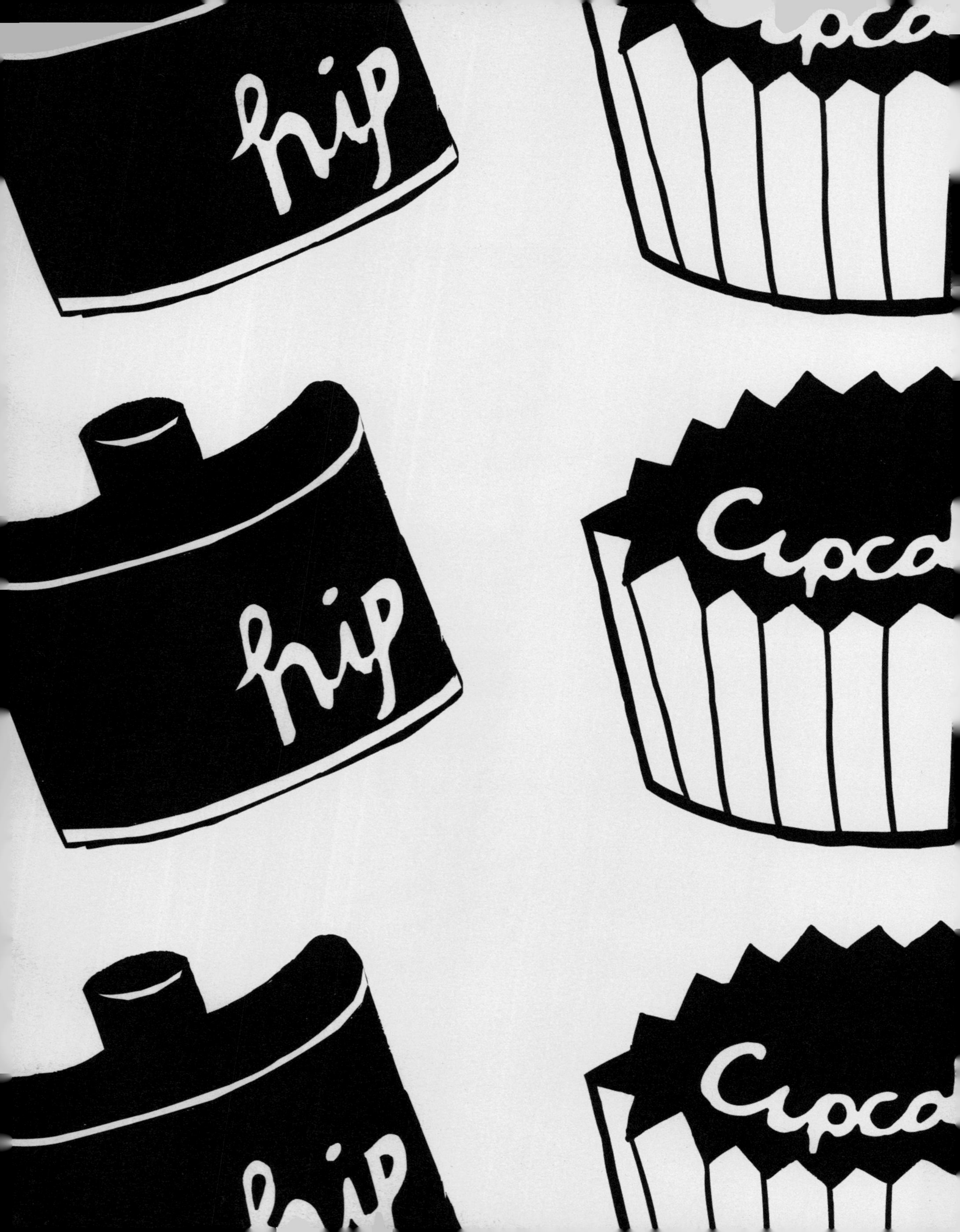
hip
hip
hip

big dog

big dog

As our company rapidly expanded, we moved our studio from Great Portland Street in Soho to the East End's Commercial Street. While this area is now fully established, back then the pubs shut at 9pm and very unsavoury characters hung around our new studio premises. Unperturbed by the grittiness of our new area, we moved our four staff, our stock and ourselves into Lana House.

This year would be one of international travel, introducing Rude to new countries and finding agents in multiple territories. We visited Japan for the first time, where we found a huge appetite for our label, and began looking for USA distribution. Taking on more staff to cover the expanding collections, we soon found ourselves with production, finance, sales and design departments. Our days were becoming more and more occupied with cashflow and overheads.

2001

65.2001

2001.66

67.2001

2001.68

Urban Outfitters

Project
Rude World

Discipline
Window Design

Rude are big fans of Urban Outfitters. One of the first stores in the UK to stock Rude, we have been collaborators ever since.

'Rude World' was a commission for a window display at their flagship store in High St. Kensington. The window was based around room sets to show off our interior products alongside the clothing. We utilised the 'Rude World' catalogue as wallpaper and made the models' heads, legs and arms spin round or go up and down.

The set was predominantly black and white, with the product providing a colourful contrast. In store the display continued, with Rude World floating clouds and hanging displays.

Style

Project
Rude go to Japan

Discipline
PR and Sales

When Style, our Japanese agent, invited us over for a PR and sales trip, we jumped at the chance. It was the first time we'd been to Tokyo and everything about the place was an eye opener. As the English speaking staff of Style guided us through their sparkling city, we visited stockists and were interviewed by magazines.

We were involved in photo shoots for various publications, where I was was made to look like Sheena Easton and Rupert looked like Ziggy Stardust.

Aside from discovering karaoke and sushi bars, we garnered lots of inspiration and gained a stronger understanding of the market we were selling to.

2001.70

Best Must Hit Shit

Project
Rude School

Discipline
Illustration

It started off with 'I'll tell your Mum' and 'Too cool for school' and before we knew it, we'd embarked on a Rude School themed route for our next collection.

Pairing icons with terms like 'hip' and 'cupcake', we carved out an easy route into the new campaign and lookbook concepts. The ad images featured naughty-looking models; these were shot as though for school portraits, then printed out and put into school photo frames. These were then captured in situ in a friends' mums' house, so they looked like the school photos your parents used to have.

The lookbook was an exercise book, with the whole collection shot and laid out as though a child had arranged the layout, complete with scribbles on the inside fronts and backs of the covers.

Strangely, we did this shoot on 9/11, making the whole experience quite surreal.

Rude

2001.72

73.2001

Rude   Rude School

2001.74

75.2001

Rude   Rude School

2001.76

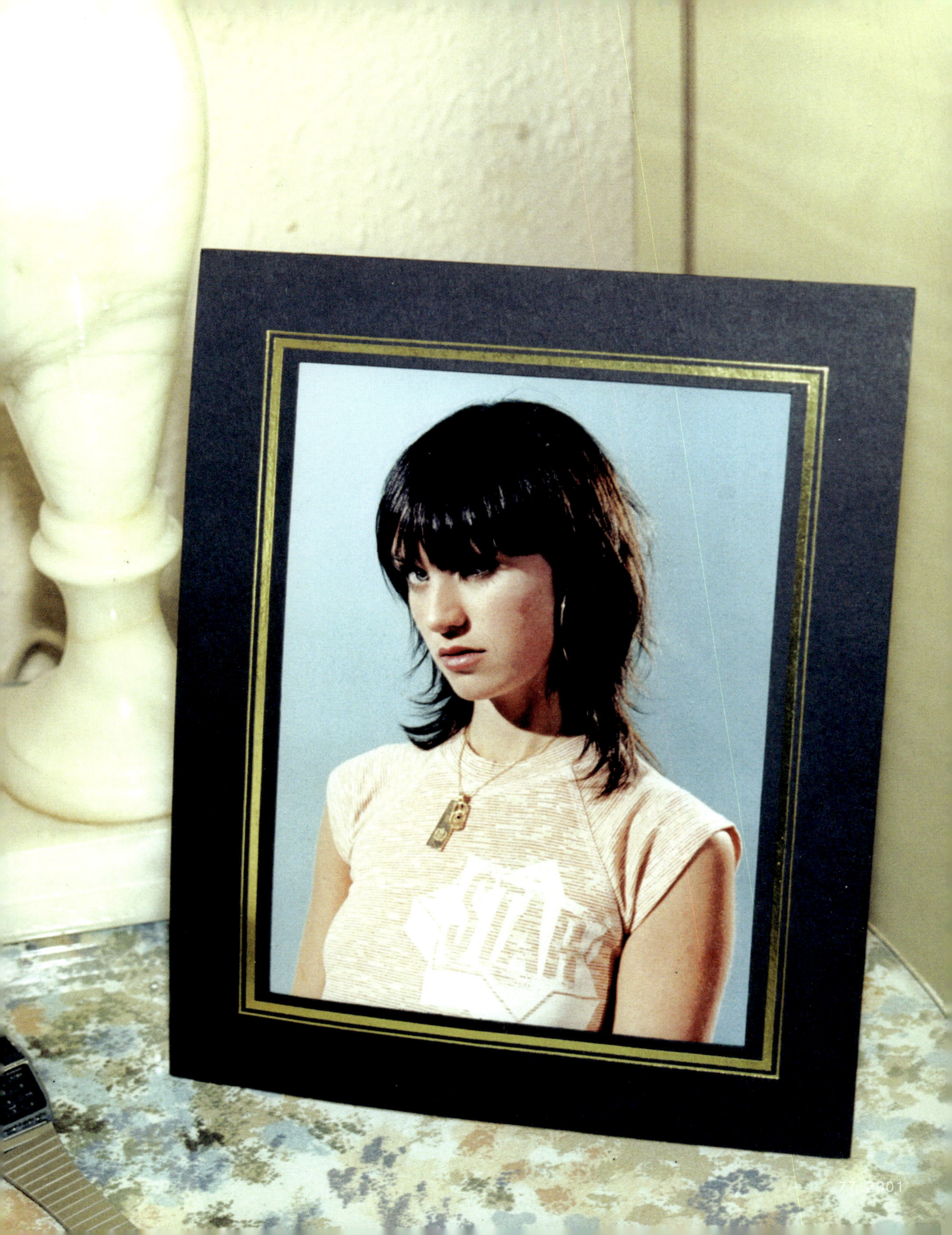

77 2001

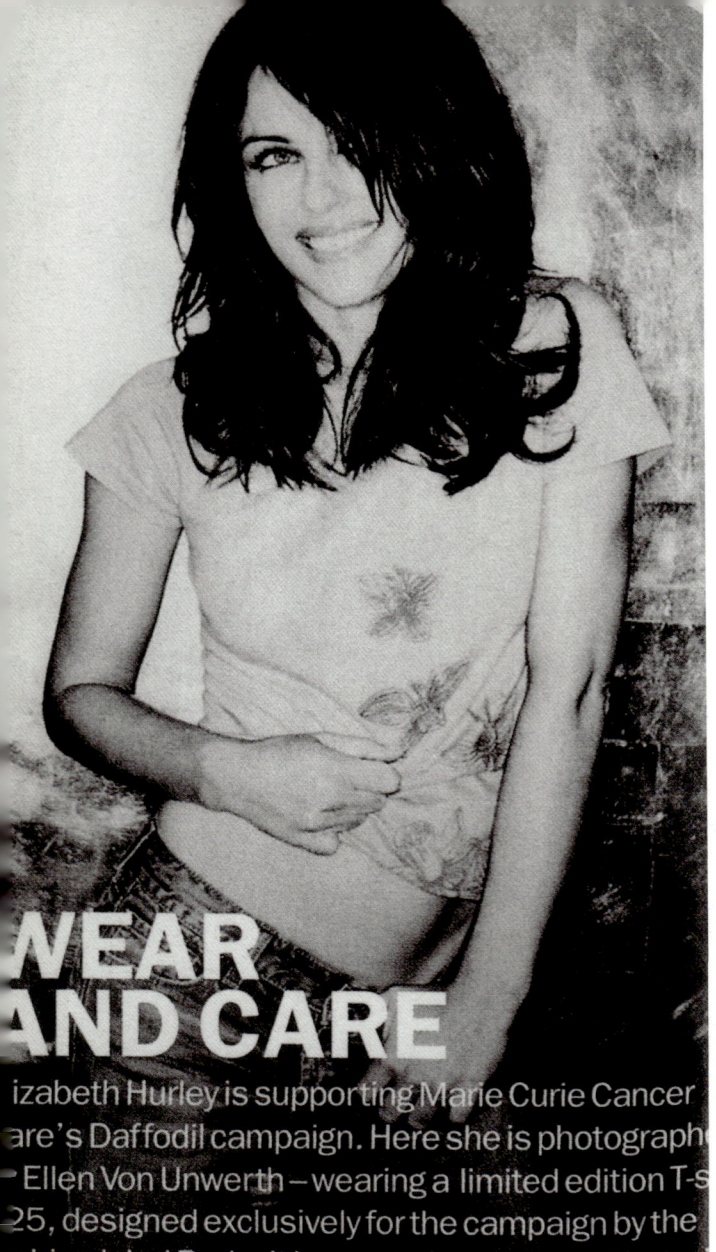

Project
Promotional T-shirts

Discipline
Illustration and Apparel

As part of Marie Curie Cancer Care's fundraising activities, Rude were invited to create an image and a range of charity T-shirts to help support their brilliant work and support for cancer patients. We liked the idea of creating an image of rejuvenation and life, so we went with an illustration of a daffodil metamorphosing into a butterfly.

These were printed two colour onto dusty pink T-shirts and were stocked nationwide, with even Liz Hurley treating herself to one.

Marie Curie Cancer Care

The Pet Shop Boys

Project
Closer to Heaven

Discipline
Illustration and Graphics

Closer to Heaven was a musical by Jonathan Harvey and the Pet Shop Boys. It premiered at the Arts Theatre in London and featured Francis Barber as retired rock icon Billie Trix.

The Pet Shop Boys provided a soundtrack to the show and Rude were asked to design the graphics for the CD cover and merchandise. We illustrated Billie Trix and many of her catchphrases, such as 'Mind the eyebrows darling'.

We also provided the cast with Rude clothes, which they customised and turned into crop tops. The result was very camp and great fun.

79.2001

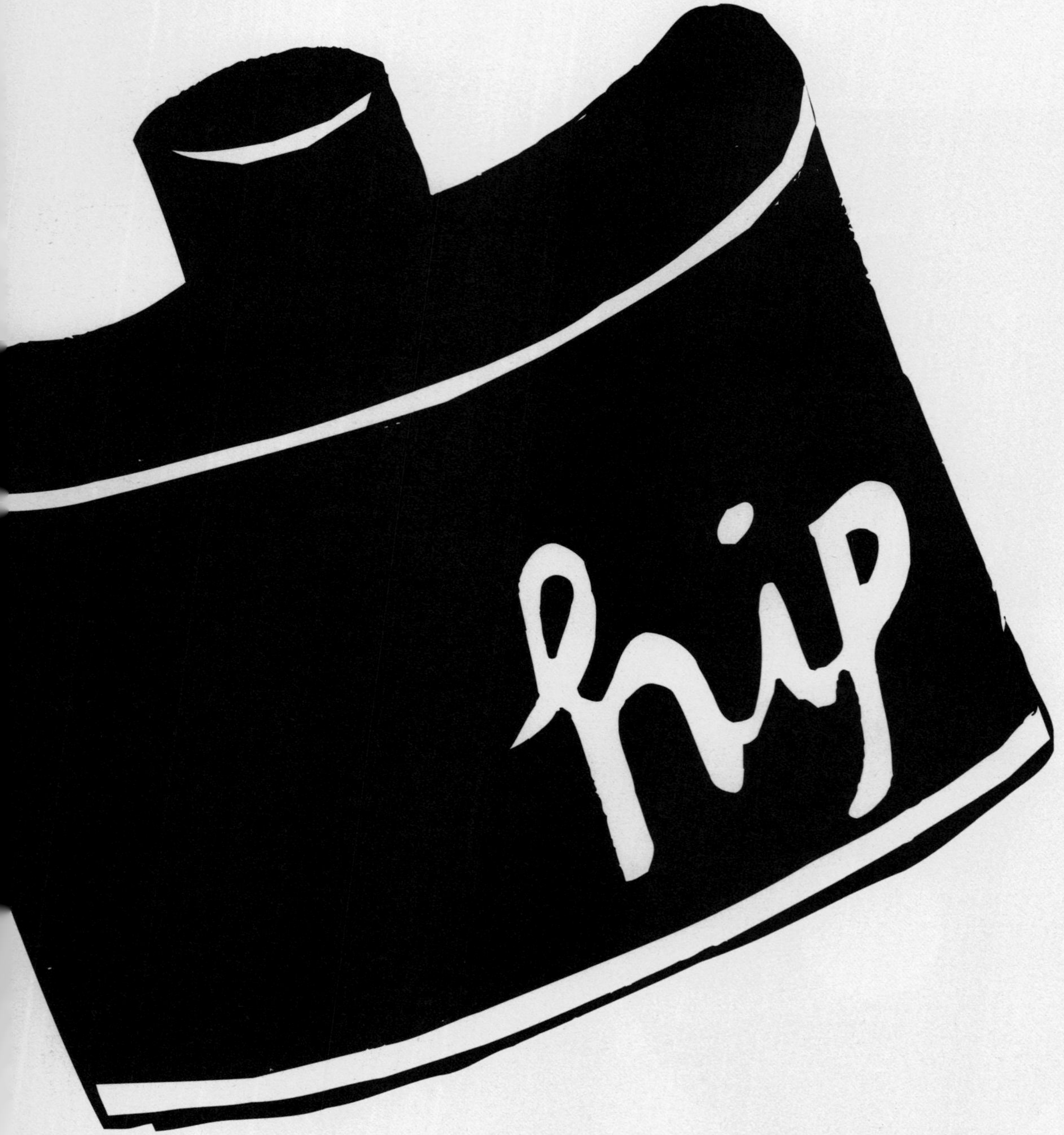
hip

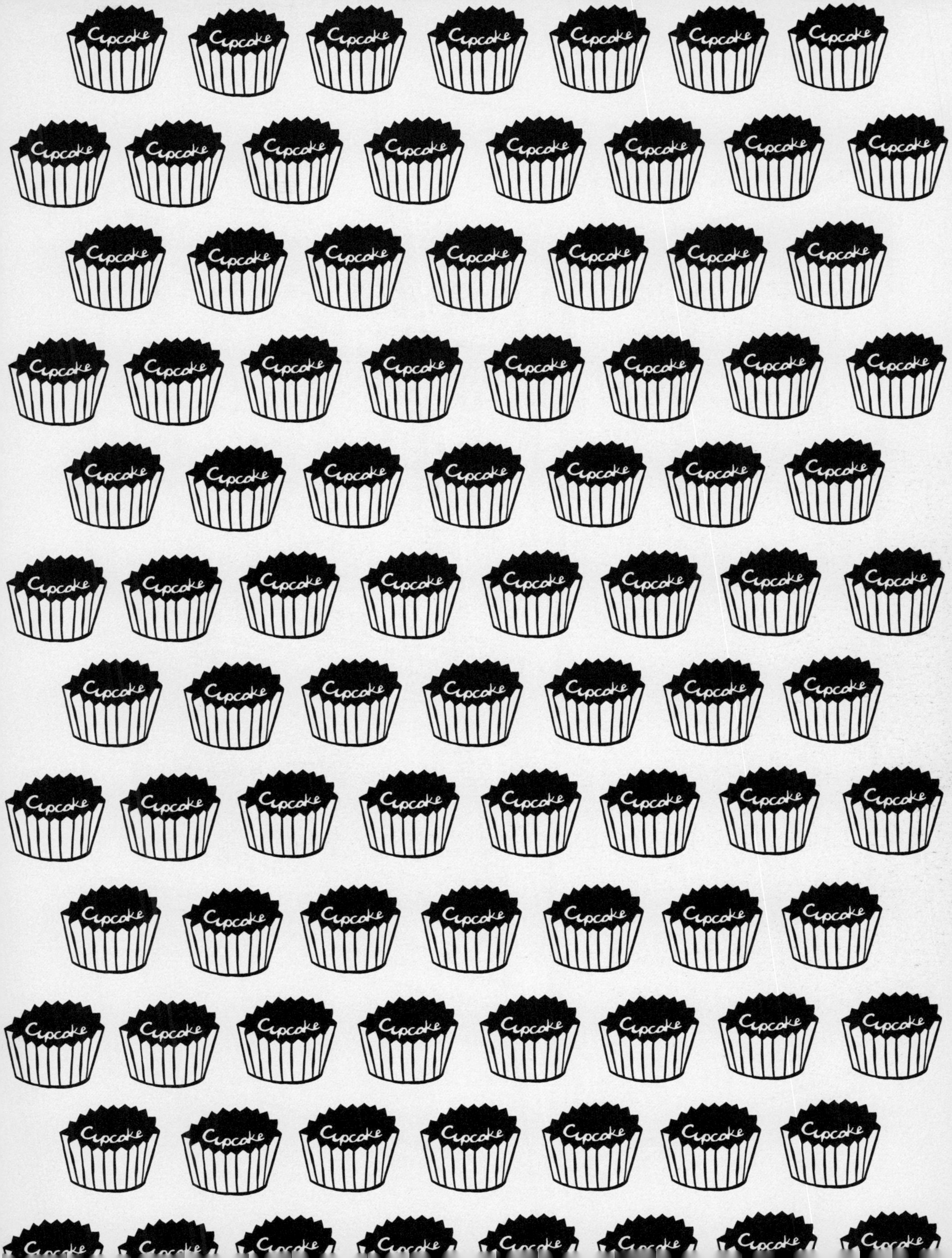
Cupcake

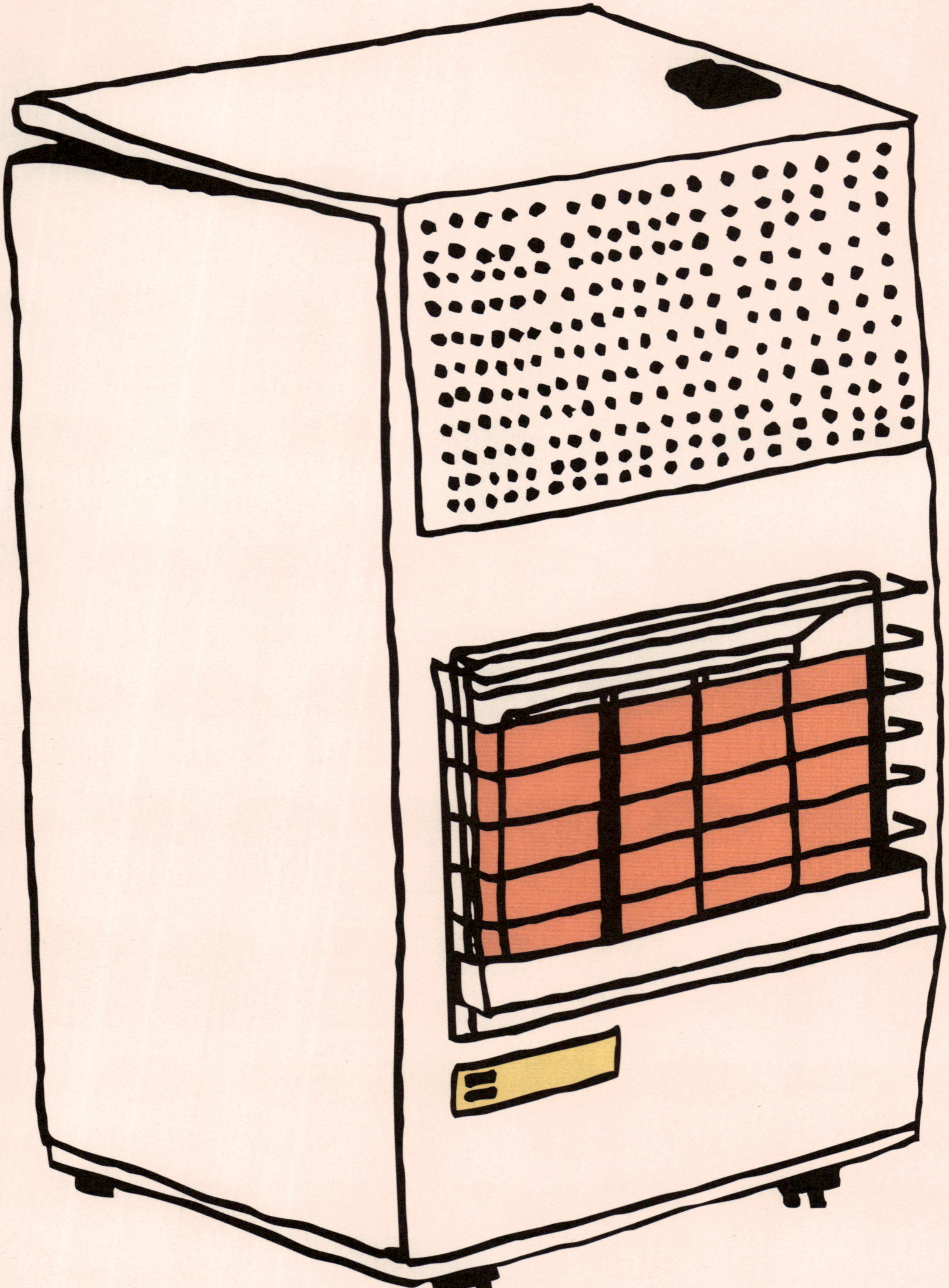

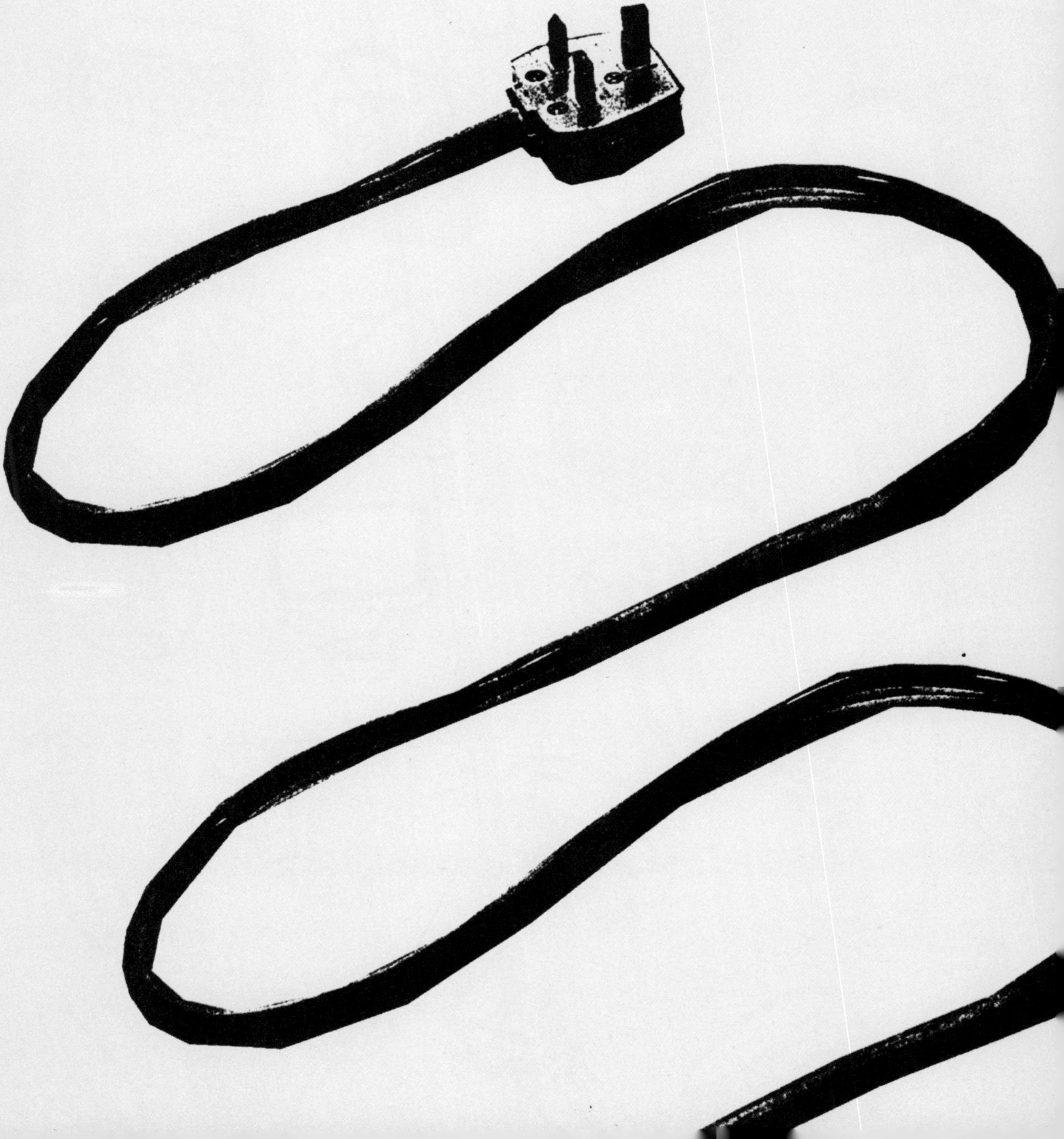

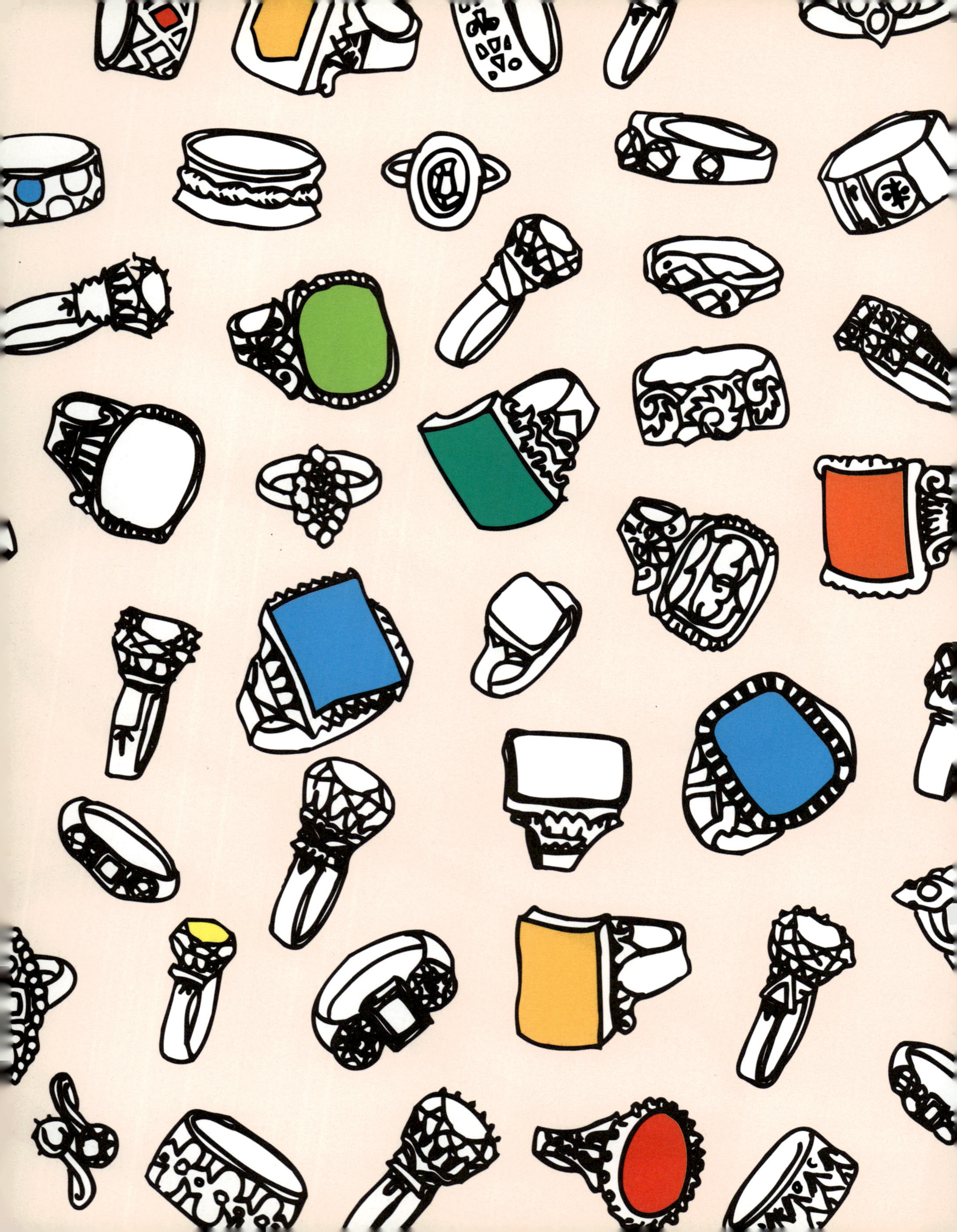

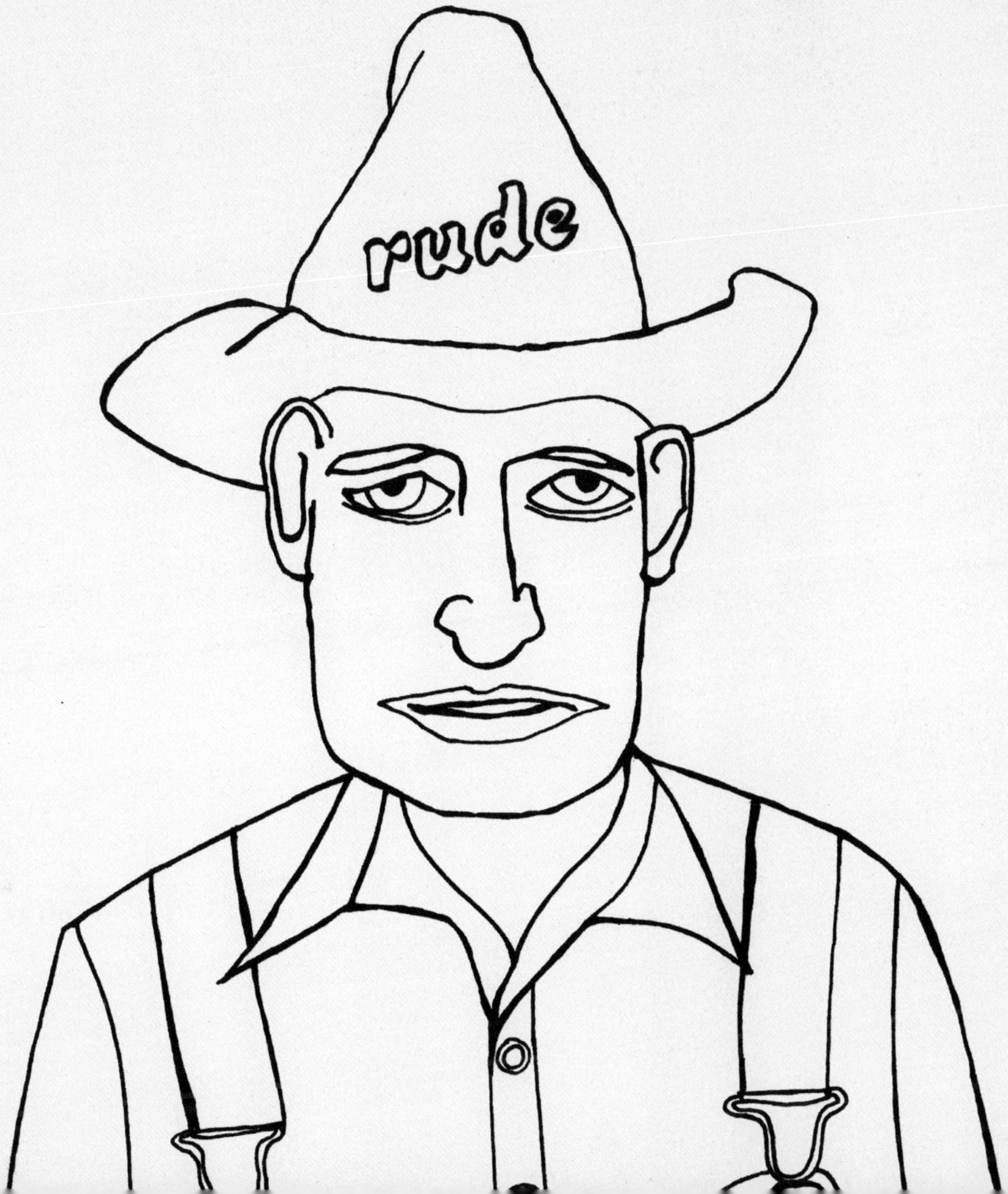
rude

After a few years of establishing the style and attitude of Rude, we embarked on our first full collections for men and women. To help us do this, we employed a fashion graduate from Saint Martins and a production manager. We split the collections into two brands, Rude T-shirts and Rude Clothing.

Up until now we had relied on simple starting blocks, like tees, A-Line skirts and basic shirt shapes. Now we were thinking more about trends, our customers and what they would expect of Rude. We replaced our logomania of the past with subtle bindings, discharge printing, embroidery and appliqué. We embraced silks, velor, denim and seersucker. In a nutshell, we were growing up, in a Rude sort of way.

2002

87.2002

Rude

Project
Things aren't always what they seem

Discipline
Menswear, Womenswear and Accessories Collection

This collection really started to define what we wanted Rude to be, kooky illustrations carried on contemporary garment shapes. This range was entitled 'Things aren't always what they seem' and one standout illustration was 'Aerial Animal', featuring a giraffe with a TV aerial for a head. 'Broken Leg Beetle' had a cast on his leg and 'Wheel Barrow Fly' was exactly that.

The menswear collection came complete with tailored trousers, jacket and shirts while the womenswear featured fitted skirts, dresses and knickers with ants printed on the bum.

The lookbook accompanying the collection utilised a set of photographs taken in Antigua. The images belonged to our graphic designer Sam and featured her family in the sixties. We dropped our graphics onto their outfits so it looked as though they were wearing Rude on the beach, adding to the surreal feel of the collection.

2002.88

89.2002

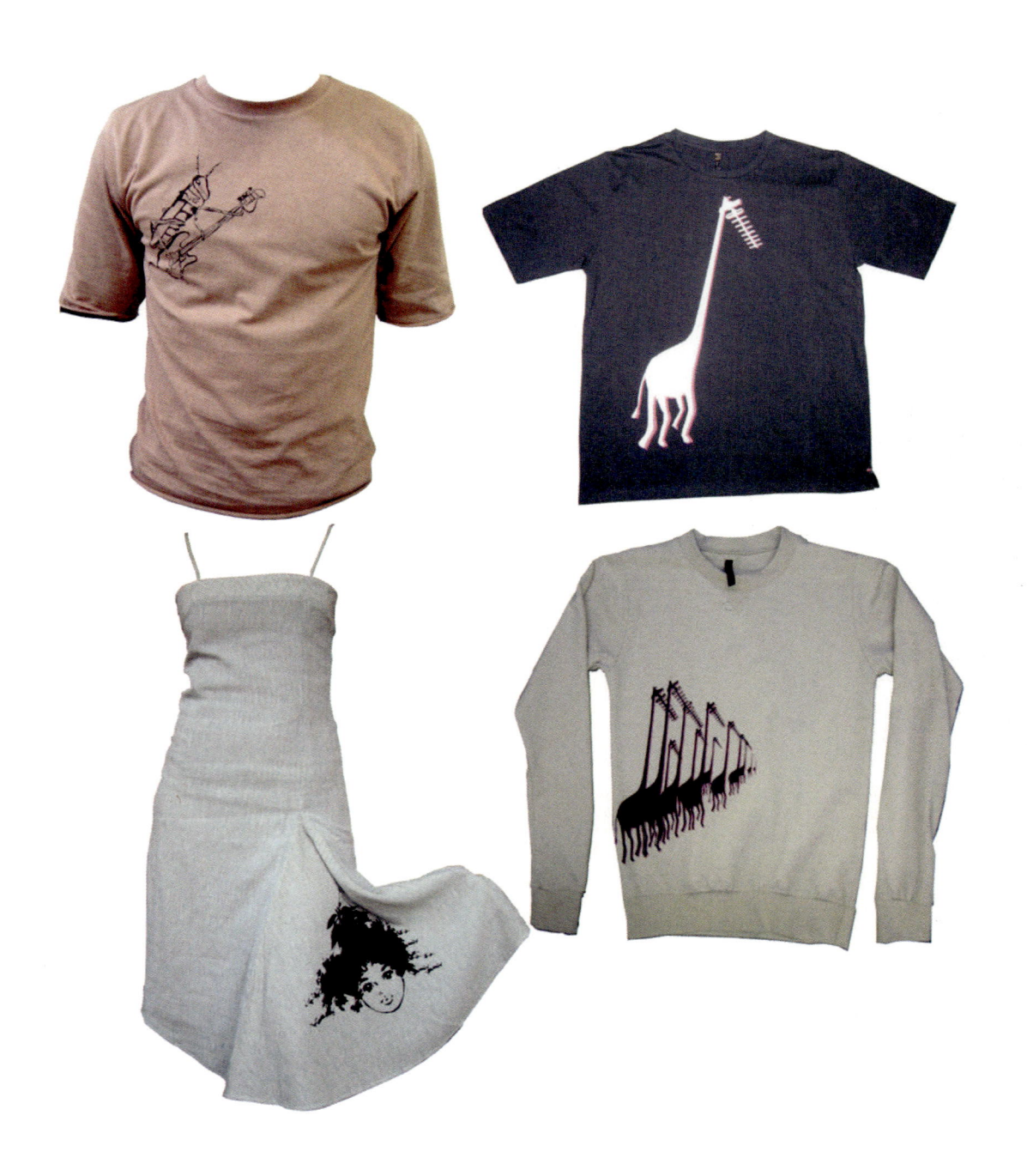

Rude   Things aren't always
        what they seem

2002.90

'things aren't always what they seem'
issue 7, SPRING/SUMMER 2003 T-SHIRT CATALOGUE

Rude, Studio 101, Lana House, 118 Commercial Street, London E1 6NF
Tel +44 (0) 20 7247 3000 Fax +44 (0) 20 7247 3131 www.thisisrude.com
Registered in England and Wales Company no. 3824709 VAT no. 743 5622 33

rude
t-shirts

Rude

Project
Keep Smiling with
Dwayne and Eileen

Discipline
Menswear, Womenswear and
Accessories Collection

For this collection, our design team came up with a story called 'Keep Smiling'. It was a rousing tale involving two ginger haired leaders Dwayne and Eileen, who struggled to avoid capture by two humourless monsters and become the leaders of the Rude revolution. This became the overriding theme of the collection and we illustrated the story in a comic strip, picking out graphics to create the prints for the range.

The ad campaign followed suit and we booked two ginger models, who were shot against simple props and backdrops.

Our knitwear range featured a knitted sash lambswool jumper for women and a men's sweater with a jaquarded image of Dwayne. To launch the collection, we held our first catwalk show in the middle of Spitalfields Market.

93.2002

Rude   Keep Smiling with
         Dwayne and Eileen

2002.94

95.2002

Rude   Keep Smiling with
        Dwayne and Eileen

2002.96

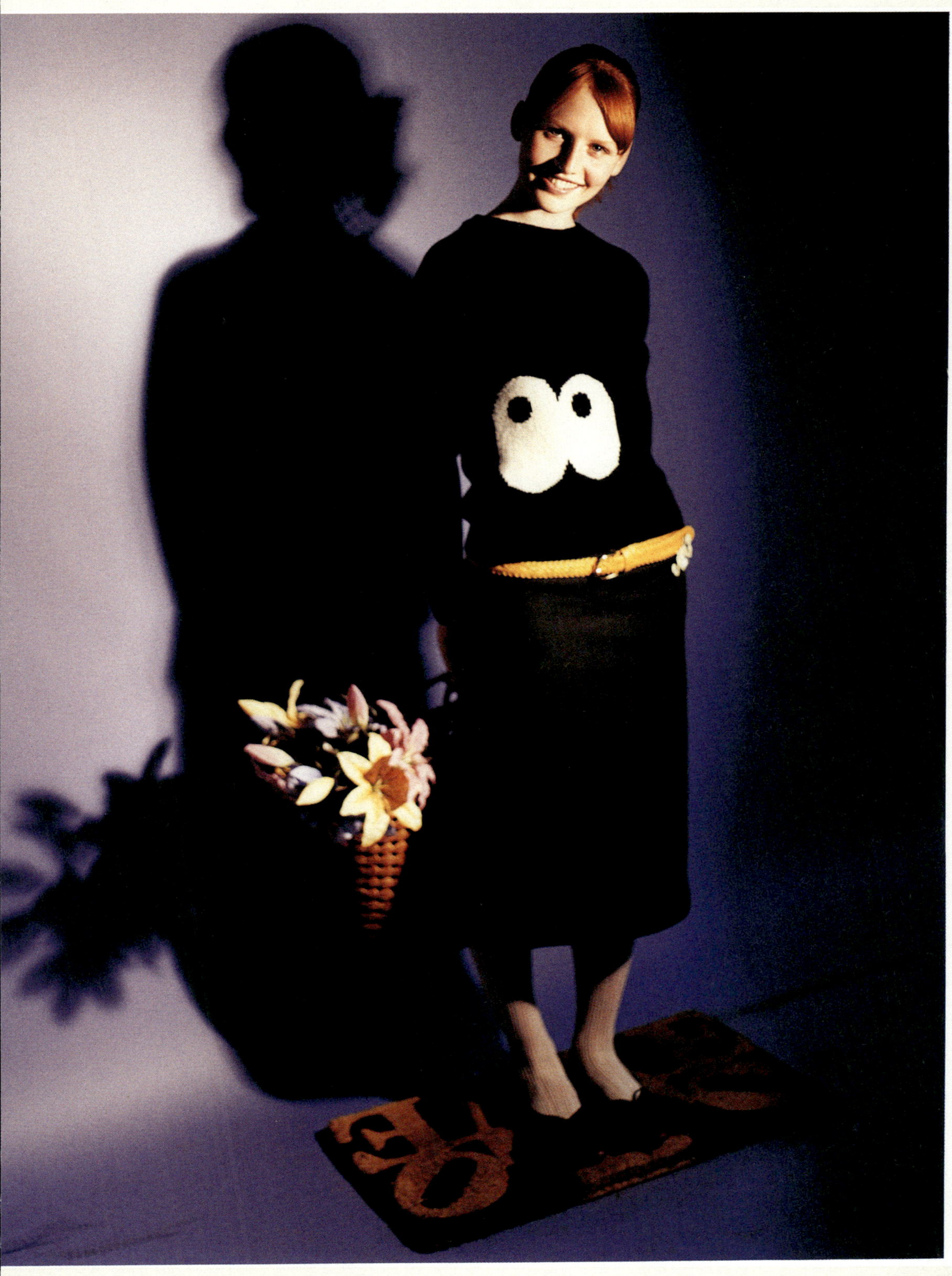

DAISY MARLENE
Betty pearl
Doris Alice
Tot Annie
deloris EVA
mAy GRACE
BUNTY eilleen

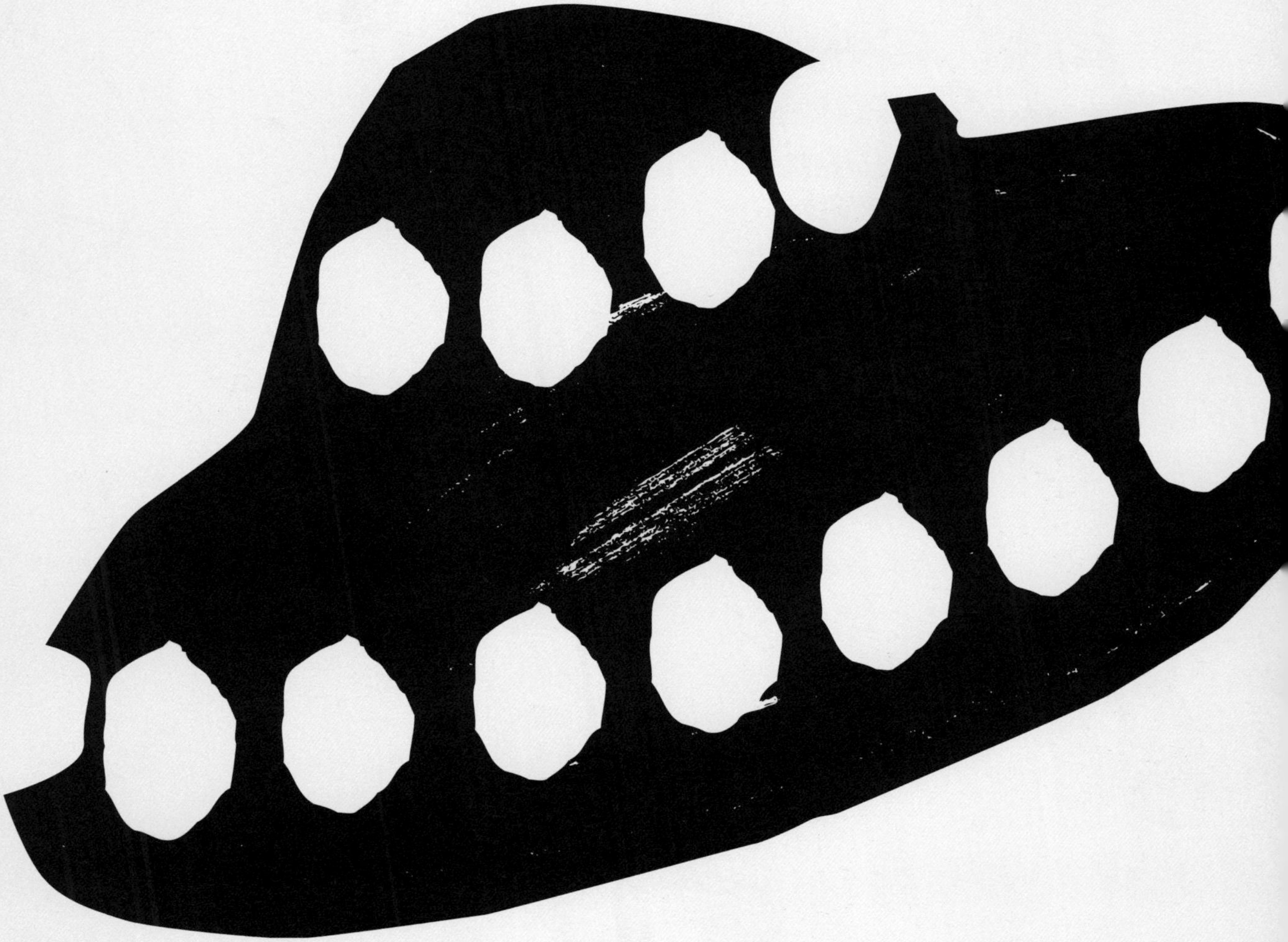

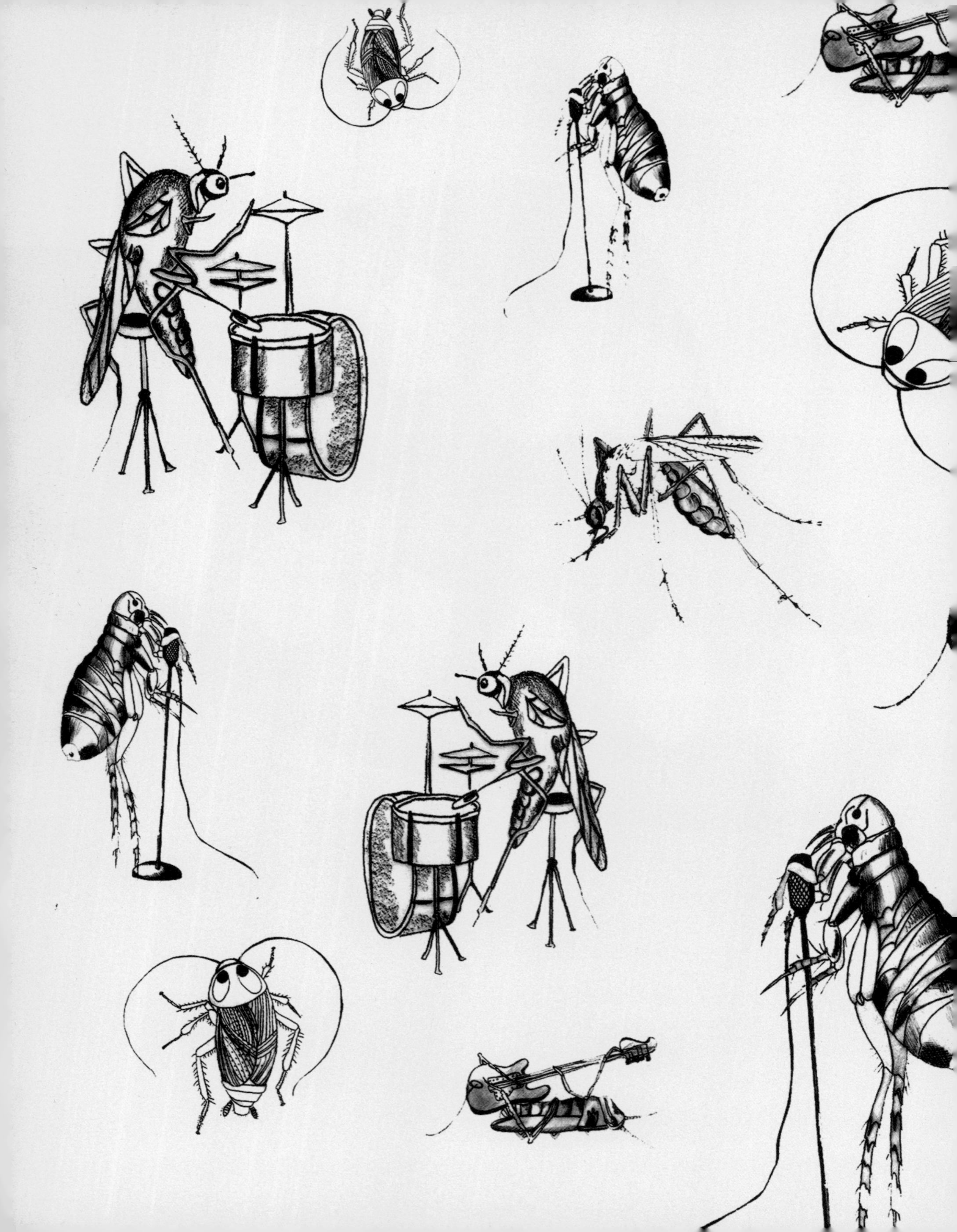

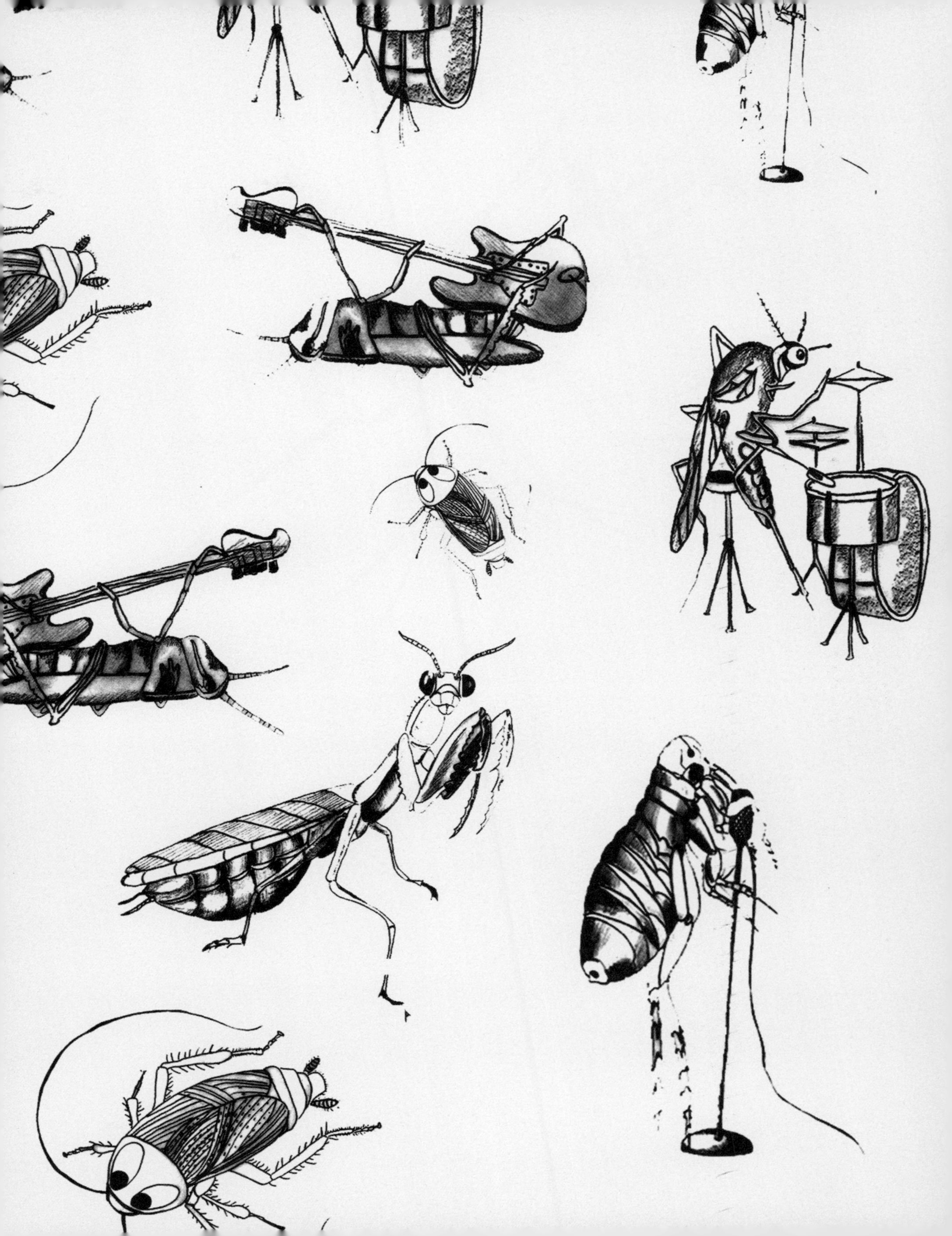

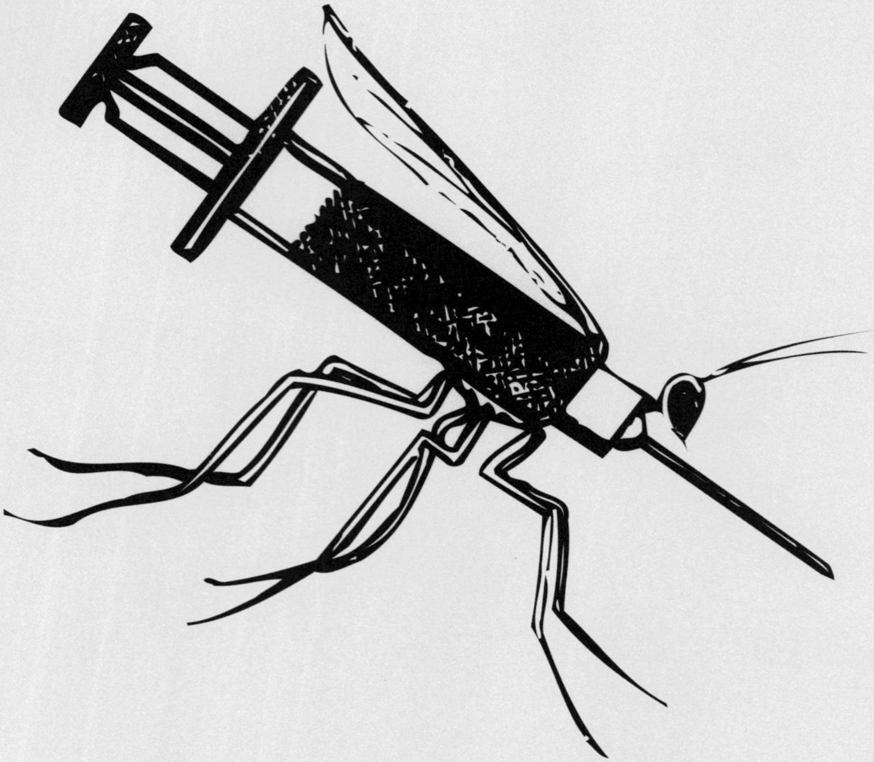

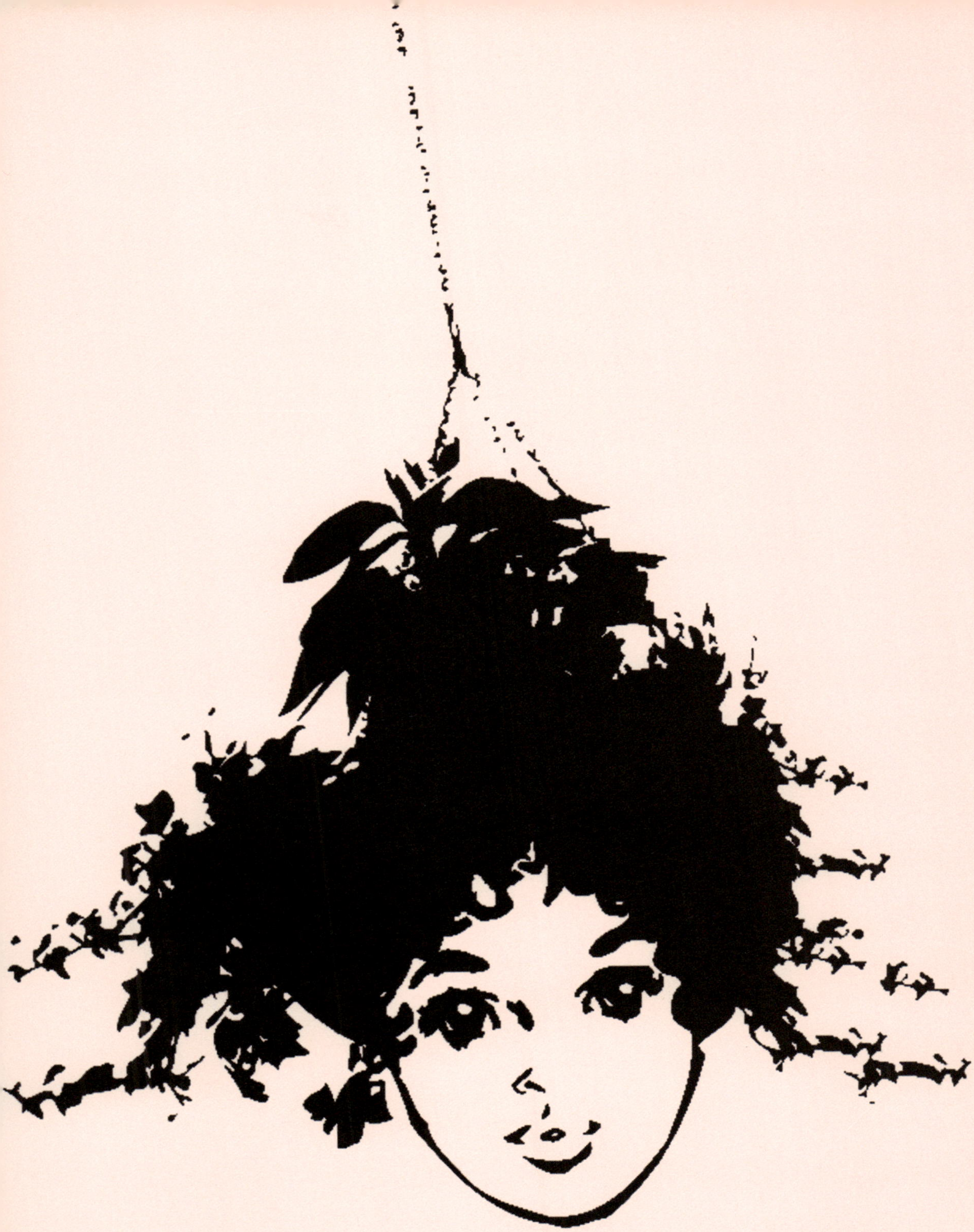

This was both a very exciting and taxing year for Rude. At the beginning of the year we opened a concept store called Let's Make T-shirts (LMTS) in Hanbury Street, just off Brick Lane, London E1.

The rear of the shop featured a screen printing workshop, where we printed bespoke T-shirts for customers while they waited. The tees were then folded into pizza boxes, ready for collection. This idea inspired our clients so we replicated the printing experience at various venues, including Earls Court for Sony Playstation.

Aside from the shop Rude also launched two new collections this year, as well as working on some very creative collaborations.

2003

105.2003

Rude

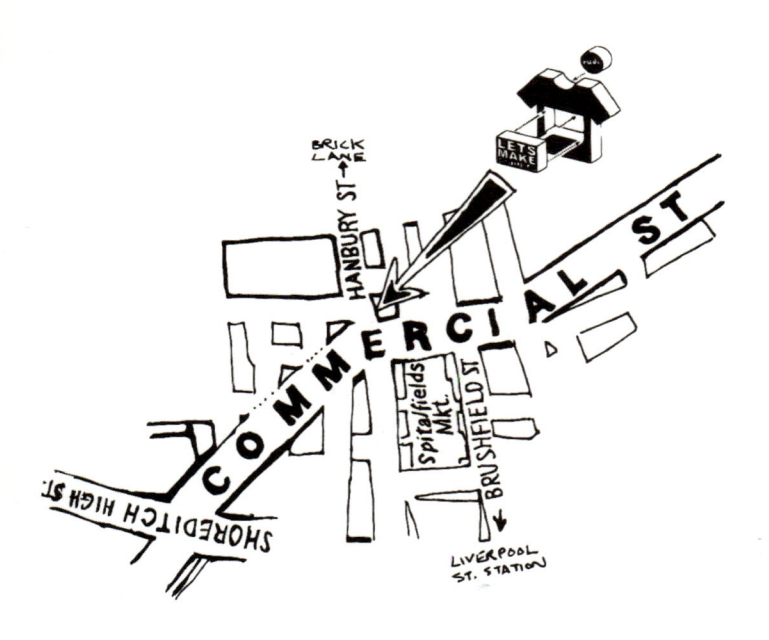

Project
Let's Make T-shirts

Discipline
Shopfit and Retail

Our ultimate goal was to create a home for the Rude brand. It was important for us to offer more than just a retail space – we liked the idea of the shop being multi-functional and offering a theatrical experience.

With this in mind we turned the back half of the shop into a visible screen printing workshop where we could create our collections while also printing T-shirts for our customers.

The site we chose was on Hanbury Street, between Spitalfields Market and Brick Lane. The area was undergoing a real transformation at the time and we felt our shop would be a good fit.

Inside the store we created a print menu, from which the customers could pick an illustration. This would then be screen printed onto a T-shirt and boxed, ready for collection within the hour.

At times the workshop would become overrun with orders and the whole shop would turn into a printing frenzy. Let's Make T-shirts became a real hub for friends and like-minded creatives.

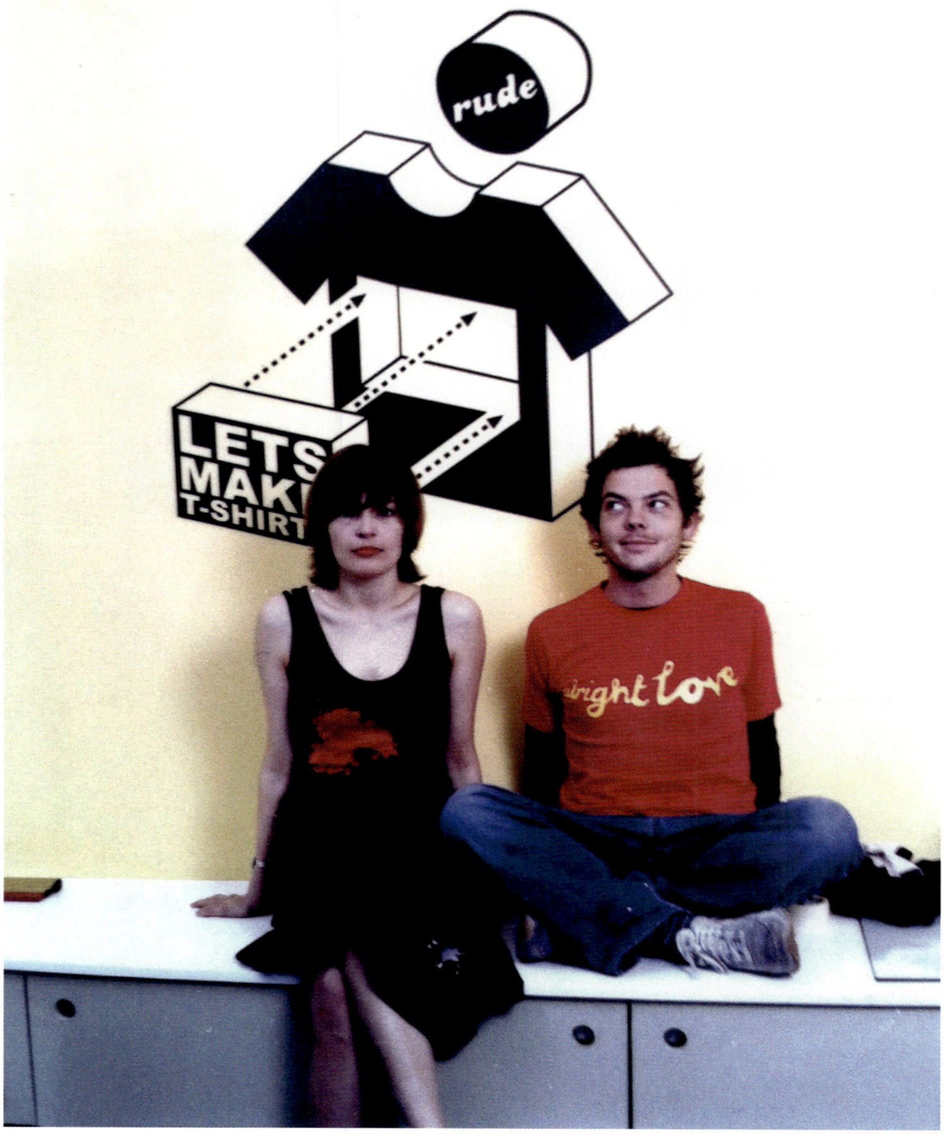
rude
LETS
MAK
T-SHIRT
alright love

Rude   Let's Make T-shirts

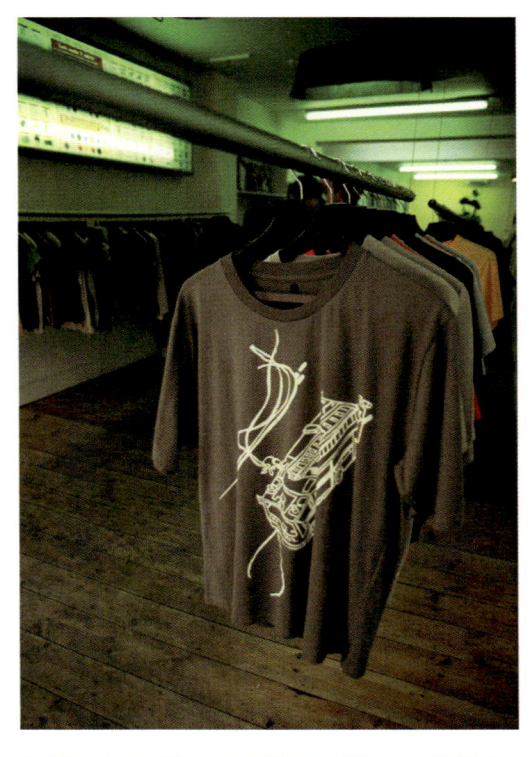

From left, Rupert Meats, Abi Williams, and Anthony McEwan

GRAPHIC DESIGNS

Rupert Meats and Abi Williams, the duo behind Rude, which puts groovy graphics onto affordable clothing, have opened **Let's Make T-shirts** in Spitalfields. Ready-printed T-shirts, separates and accessories are on sale at the front; while Anthony McEwan works at the back, custom-printing designs – such as the "ants in your pants" knickers, *right* – before packing them in pizza boxes. *14 Hanbury Street, E1 (020 7247 2929). KO'D*

Rude   Let's Make T-shirts

111.2003

Project
Kruel Summer Collection

Discipline
Fashion, Textiles
and Graphics

The theme for our Spring/
Summer collection this
year was called 'A Kruel
Summer'. To launch the
range and create a special
catalogue, we collaborated
with paper supplier GF
Smith. Design agency George
and Vera designed the
book and co-ordinated the
project. Photographers and
illustrators were invited
to contribute a piece of
work under the same theme.

The entries included images
of exotic roadkill and
glamorous lady boys from
Brazil, displayed next
to lighting designer
Claire Norcross' fabulous
product designs.

To accompany the lookbook,
we held a huge party and
invited all the buyers,
clients and fans of Rude
along to celebrate.

Rude

2003.112

113 .2003

GF Smith   Kruel Summer Collection

2003.114

115.2003

GF Smith   Kruel Summer Collection

2003.116

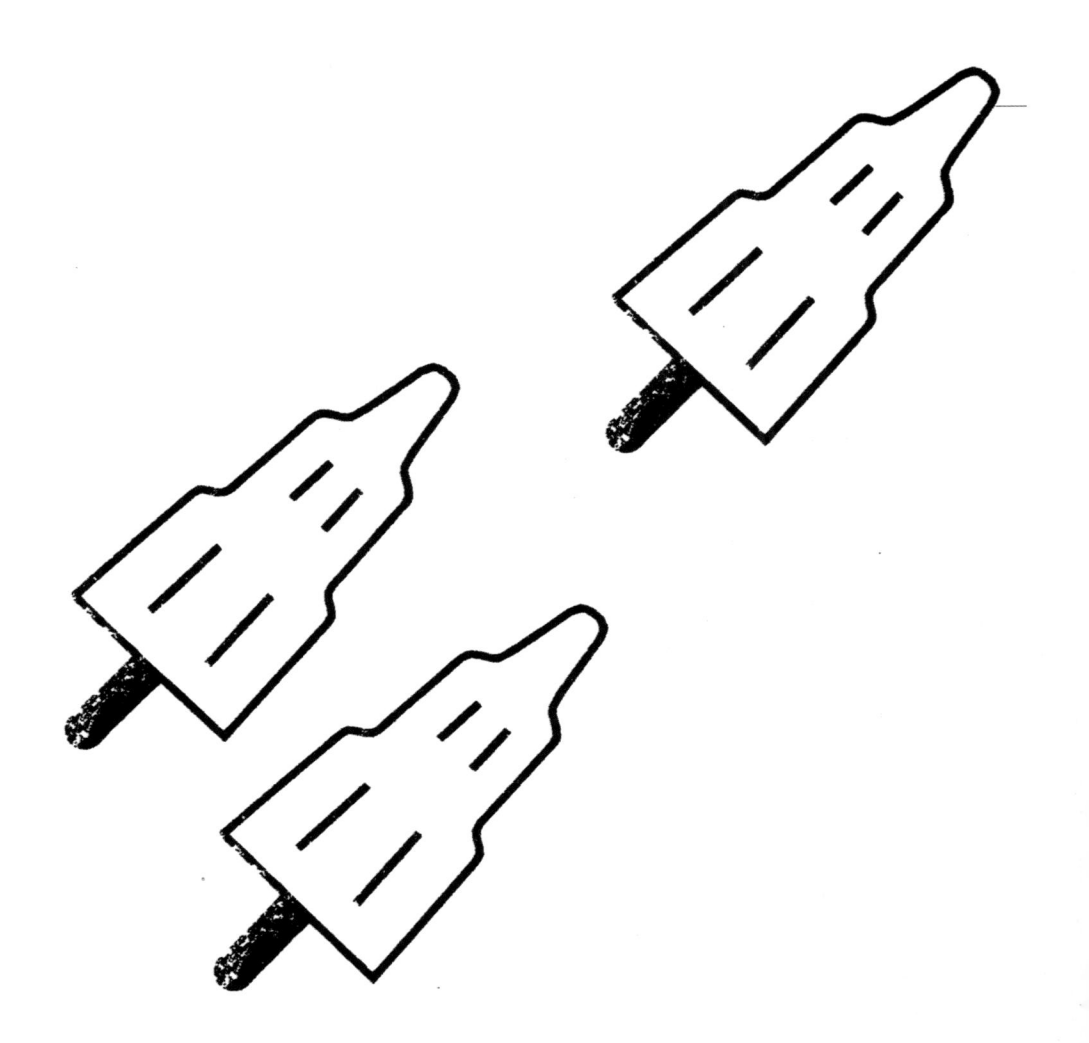

Sony Playstation

Project
Playstation Experience

Discipline
Fashion Graphics and
Screen Printing

It was around this time that we began working with Sony on creating bespoke merchandise for the launches of their new games. When we invited them to the shop for a meeting, they fell in love with the idea of re-creating our screen printing space for their Playstation Experience, which was to be held at Earls Court, West London.

Our brilliant graphics protégé Matt designed a set of graphics with prints like 'Chess is Crap' and 'Thumb Envy', which were to feature on the print menu in the exhibition.

The system worked in the same way as the shop, where the customer would choose a print and have their T-shirt created while they waited. The whole project was brilliant fun and would go on to inspire similar projects in the future.

119.2003

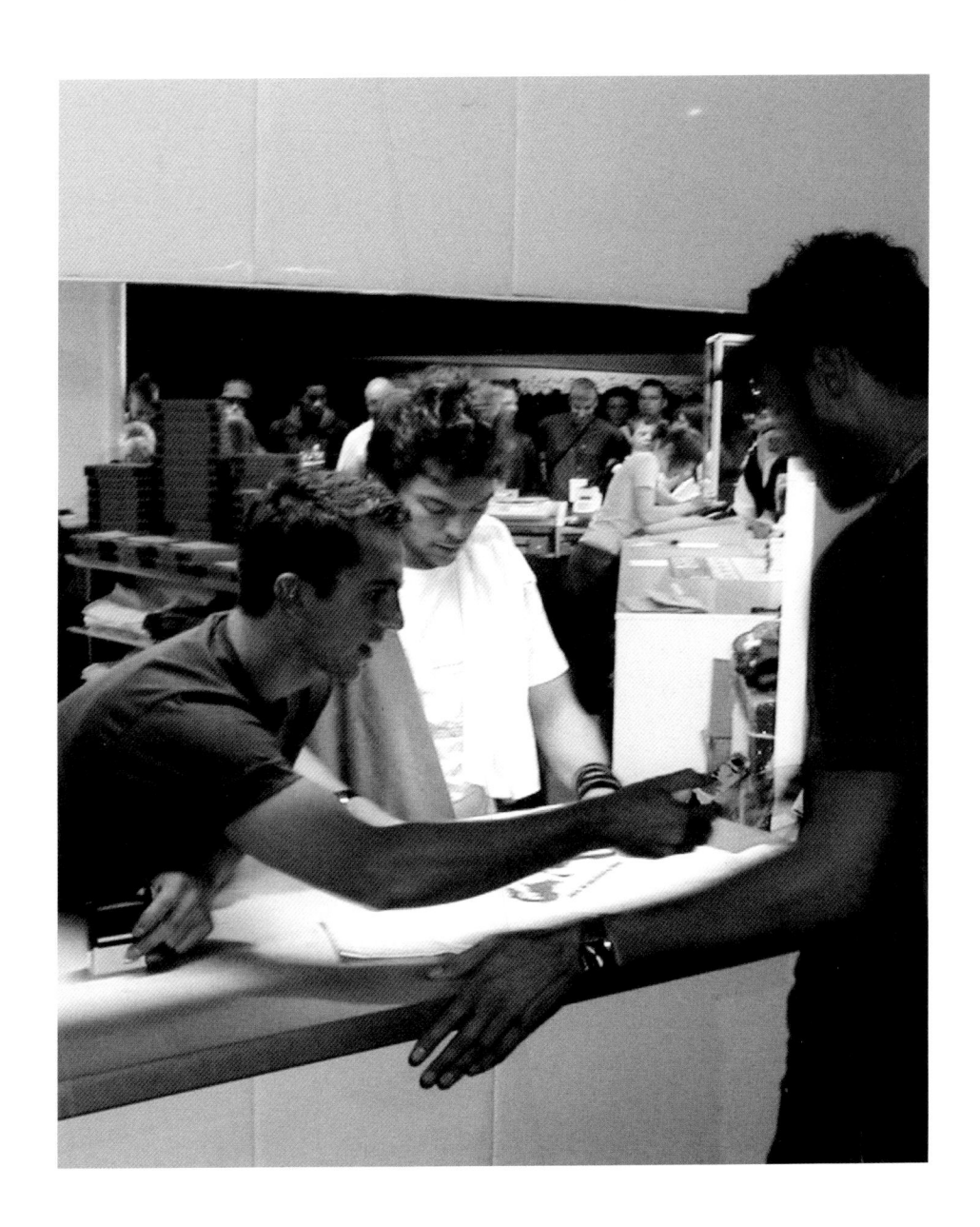

Sony   Playstation Experience

winner stays on.

CHESS IS

THUMB ENVY

2003.120

YOUR PLAYSTATION OR MINE?

CRAP
PlayStation 2

Geek
PlayStation 2

121.2003

GeoffWears'BudgieWithEar'
AvailableFromAllGoodStockists
thisisrude.com

GeoffCapesPhotographedByLarryDunstan(PCP)
ArtDirectionByGeorge&Vera

rude®

2003.122

Project
Geoff Capes
Advertising Campaign

Discipline
Photography, Art Direction
and Illustration

Geoff Capes

Who would have thought that 1970s strong man Geoff Capes would be the UK's biggest breeder of budgerigars? We found out after we'd made a T-shirt image called 'Budgie with human ear'. Our designer James Groves from George and Vera came up with the idea that Geoff Capes would make the perfect model for our next advertising campaign. We approached him and remarkably he responded with a yes.

We had to use an 8XL size t-shirt, which we bought from Harrods, to print our massive budgie image onto. T-shirts and photographers on hand, we trouped down to meet Geoff at his house, where he served us afternoon tea and showed us his Clarice Cliff teapot collection.

Geoff was a fantastic sport and we placed some great ads with the images.

Geoff Cappes   Geoff Capes
               Advertising Campaign

2003.124

125.2003

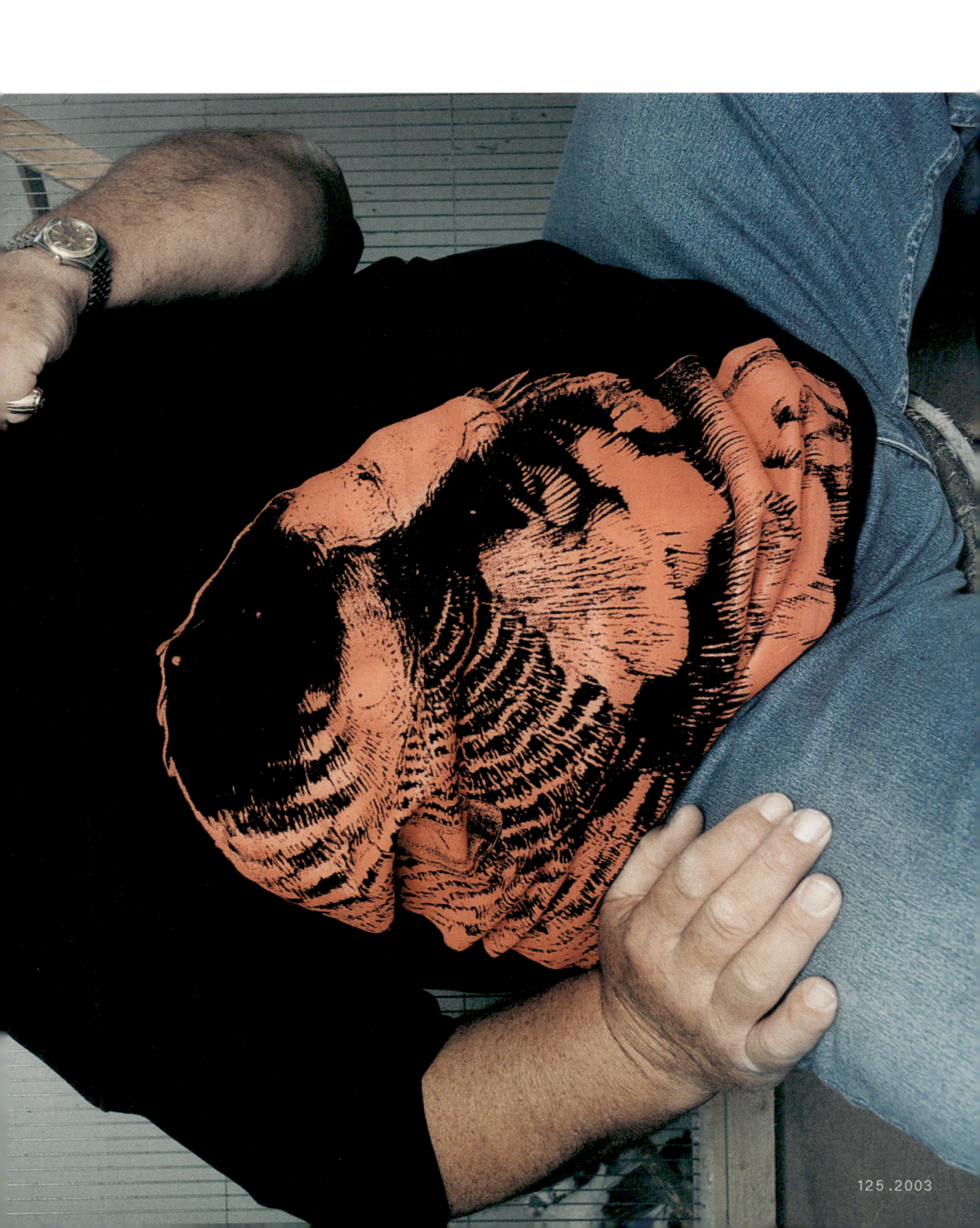

DELUXE

DIET KING

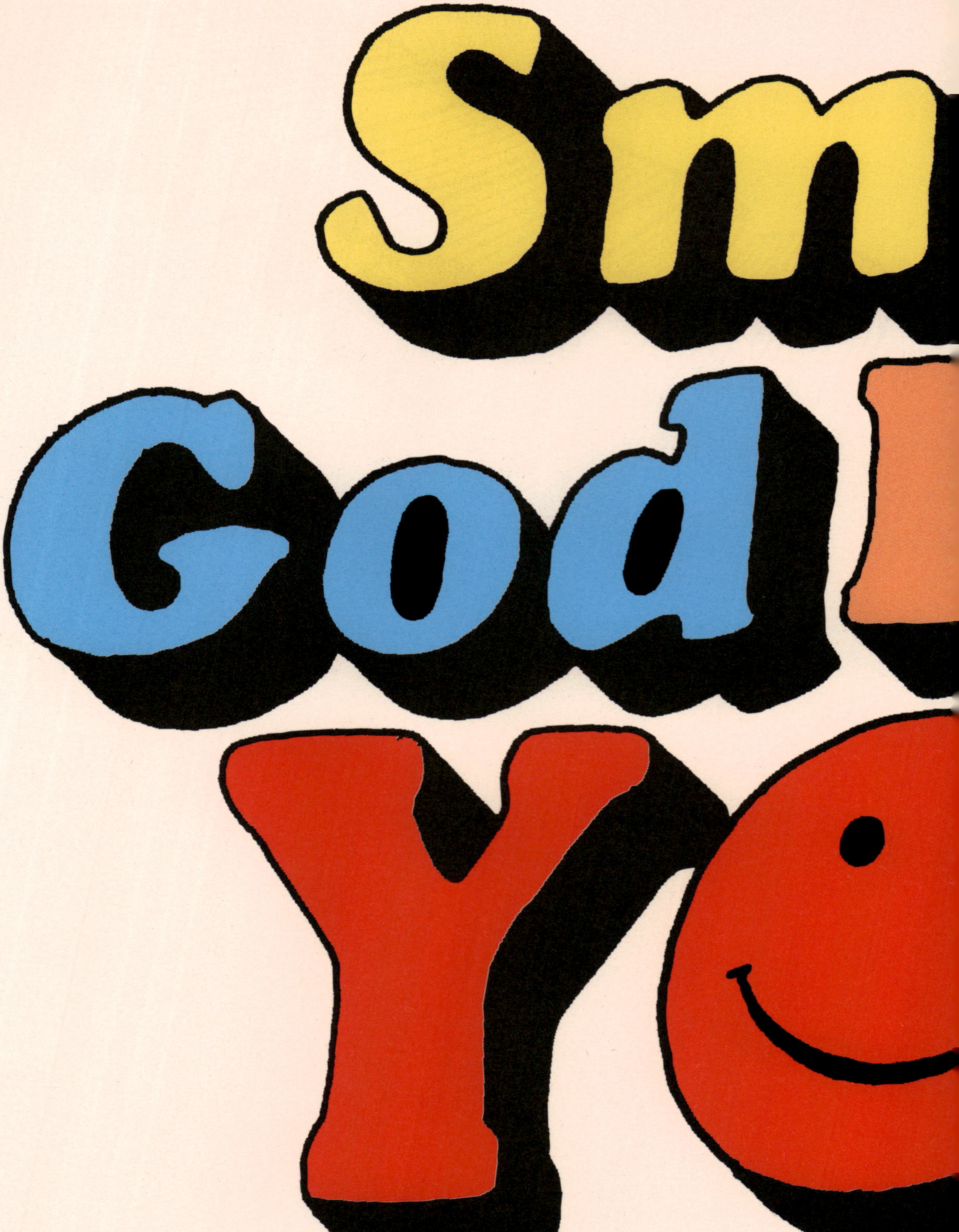
Sm
God
Y

ile,
oves
U

Our year started with the birth of our first son Billy Meats. His arrival was a surprise, one that pulled our craziness into sharp perspective and got everyone envolved. Our shop staff Helen and Kim became Billy's carers as well as our PAs, shopkeepers and wholesale account handlers and mail order department. The parcel courier would walk Billy round the block for parcels and the landlady from our local pub bought him a playpen, so he became the centre of attention on the shop floor.

The following year was a really difficult one as cash flow hit an all time low. Shops were closing and retail seemed to slow right down, clients were taking longer to pay while suppliers were demanding money up front. We were looking desperately for a financial backer and fire fighting at the same time. By the end of this year, we would release the final Rude collection and be forced to make our staff redundant.

2004

131.2004

Project
Rude Portrait

Discipline
Hoarding Campaign

Spitalfields Regeneration

As part of the Spitalfields regeneration scheme, an advertising agency commissioned portrait photographer John Spinks to take pictures of the residents and workers in the vicinity. We were chosen alongside our friends from local businesses to represent the area.

Spitalfields was undergoing a huge transformation at the time and a shopping centre was replacing half of the market area. Our images were used in large format to provide the hoarding around the boundaries of the new development.

133.2004

Sony Playstation

2004. 134

Project
Eyetoy Merchandise

Discipline
T-shirt Graphics

Our continuing work with Sony led us to create some more graphics for their latest game releases. Eyetoy and Eyetoy Groove were great games that allowed the player to put themselves on the screen and become part of the game.

We designed images such as 'Caught in a Box', 'Mono Crowd' and 'Controllers Eyes', which depicted the player as the hero of the game. Eyetoy Groove was more about the experience of participation and playing with team mates; these featured 'Your Next Shirl' and 'Groovy Girl'.

2004.136

Tate Enterprises

Project
Edward Hopper Merchandise

Discipline
Applied Graphics

This would be our first foray into working with museums, many of which had started to work in very innovative ways to produce bespoke product for their shops and exhibitions. In order to tailor-make collections, they would collaborate with an artist or designer/maker who suited the project; this resulted in some diverse merchandise.

A buyer from the Tate asked us to come up with a collection to support the Edward Hopper exhibition at the Tate Modern. Without lifting any original artwork, which we weren't allowed to do, we re-drew parts of his paintings, such as the fire hydrant, the clocks, and the hat of the lady sitting in the corner bar.

'Rude loves Edward Hopper' became the brand mark for the collection and we used the icons as repeat and placement prints onto tees, mugs, pin badges and tea towels. We used a muted palette to reflect his work and placed the graphics big and bold onto product.

Although not technically one of Hopper's icons, we couldn't resist doing a 'Space Hopper' print for kids' t-shirts.

Rude

Project
Health, Wealth and
Happiness Menswear and
Womenswear Collection

Discipline
Illustration and
Graphic Design

This turned out to be our last clothing collection for Rude, but our uplifting title of Health, Wealth and Happiness was a buoyant note on which to finish.

Our brilliant designers Matt and Sophie designed a humorous set of prints, from 'King Cock' to 'God Loves You'.

As money was tight, we decided that we would model the collection ourselves and rather than employ a photographer, we'd pop down to the Trocadero in Piccadilly and get one of those hilarious Victoriana pictures taken.

I love this image; it's a contemporary take on Victorian times but with 'Pills' and 'Lucky Dice' repeat prints used across skirts and shirts. Our son Billy was asleep in his car seat just out of shot of this image.

139.2004

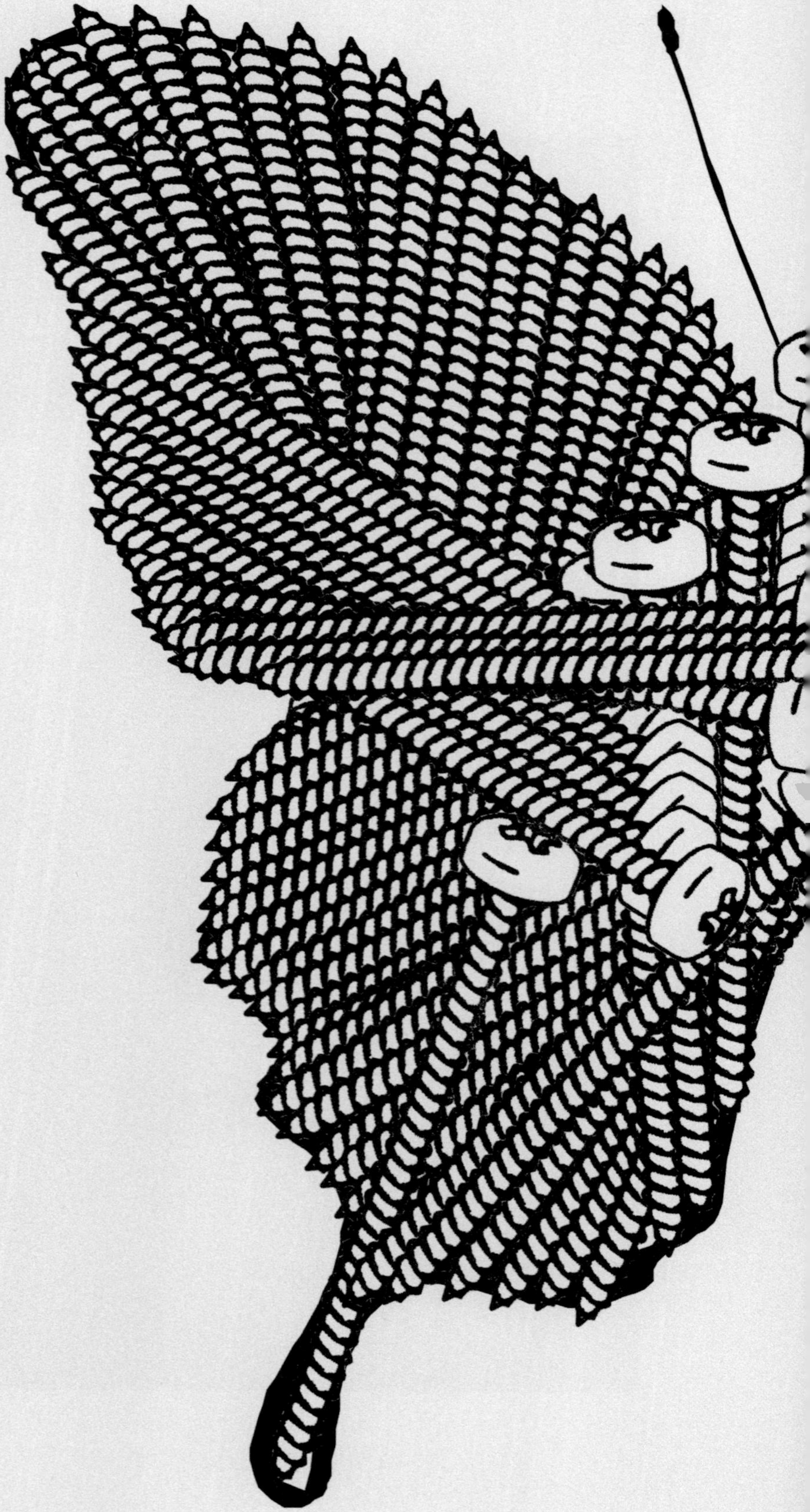

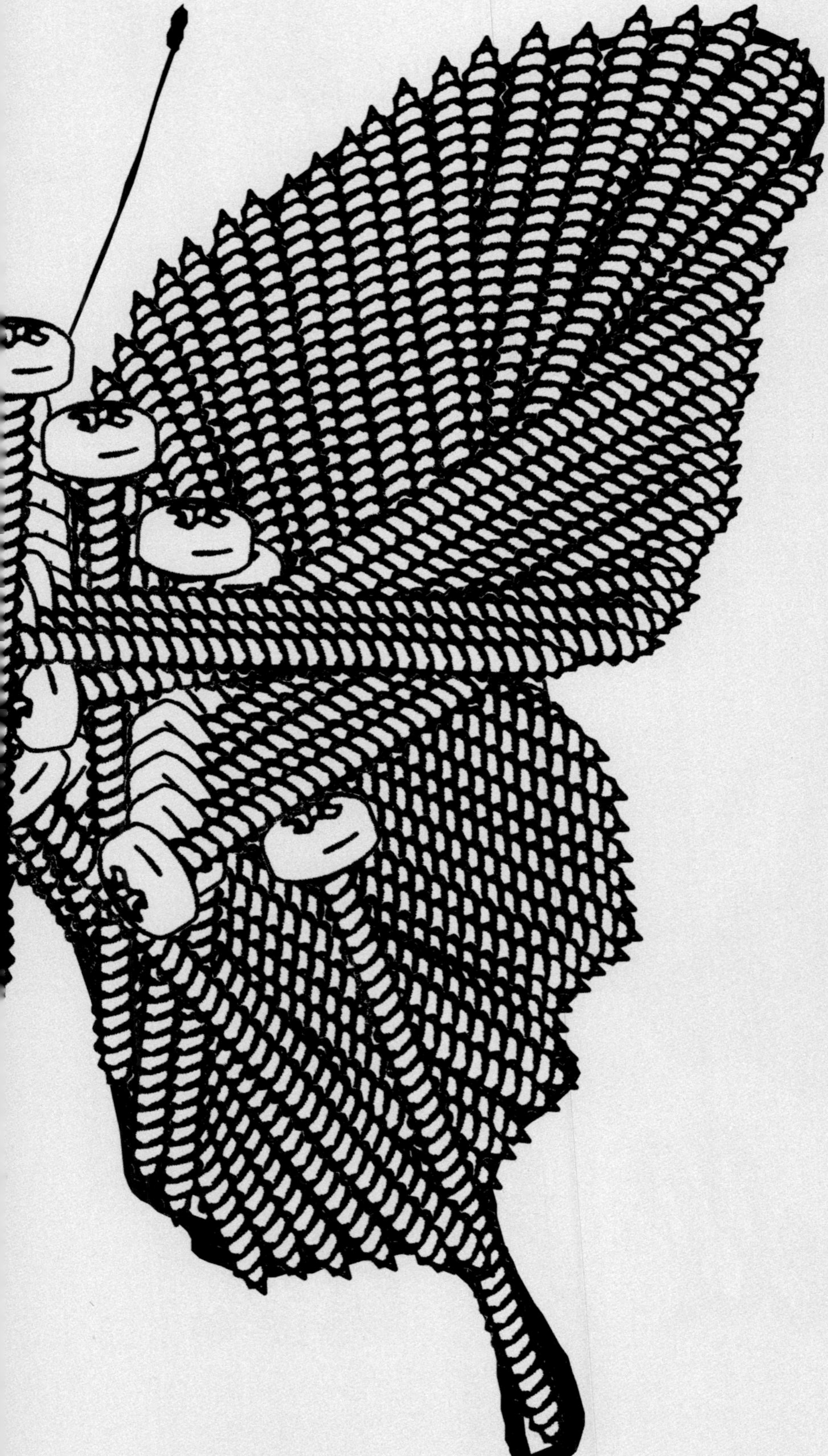

Dull Fruit

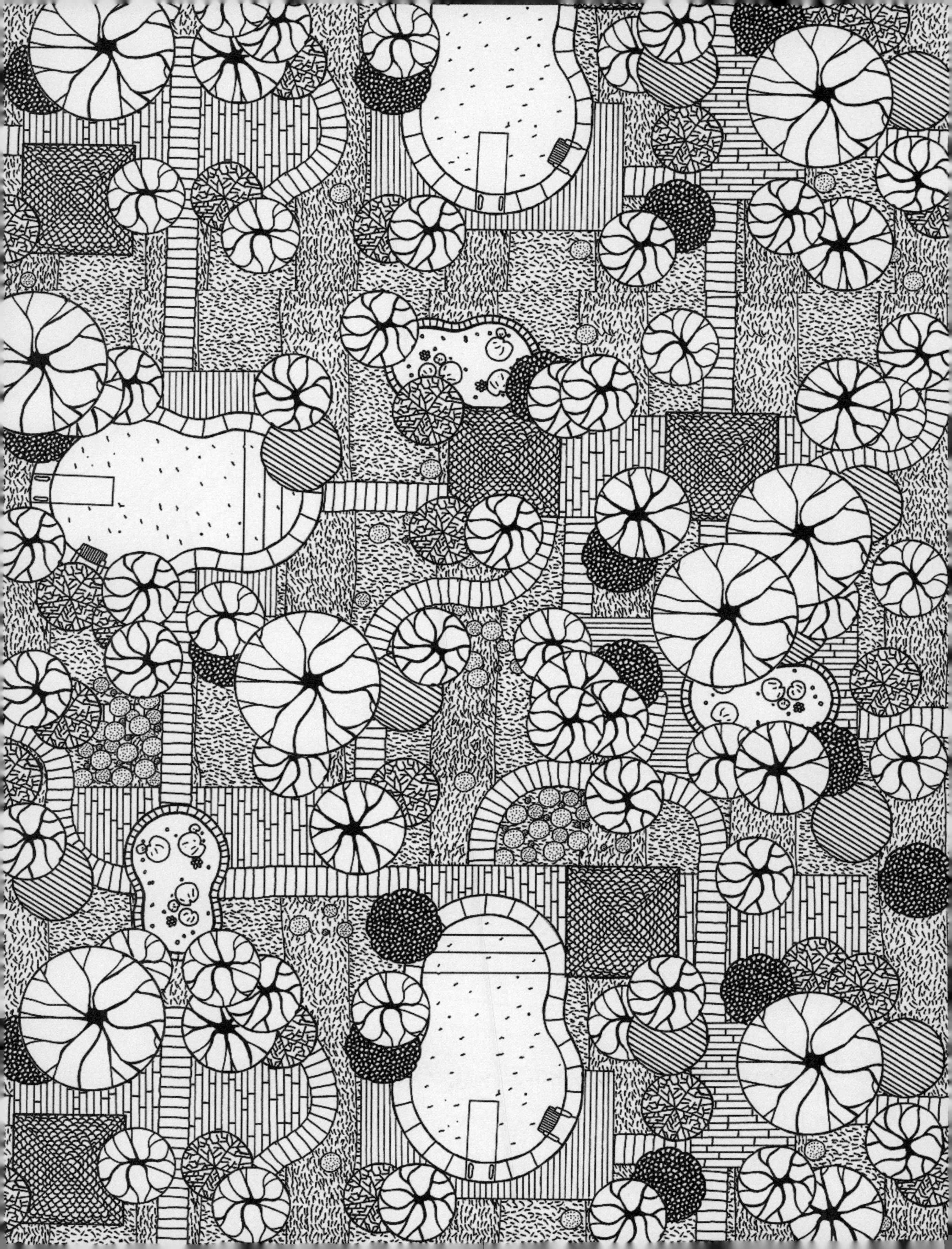

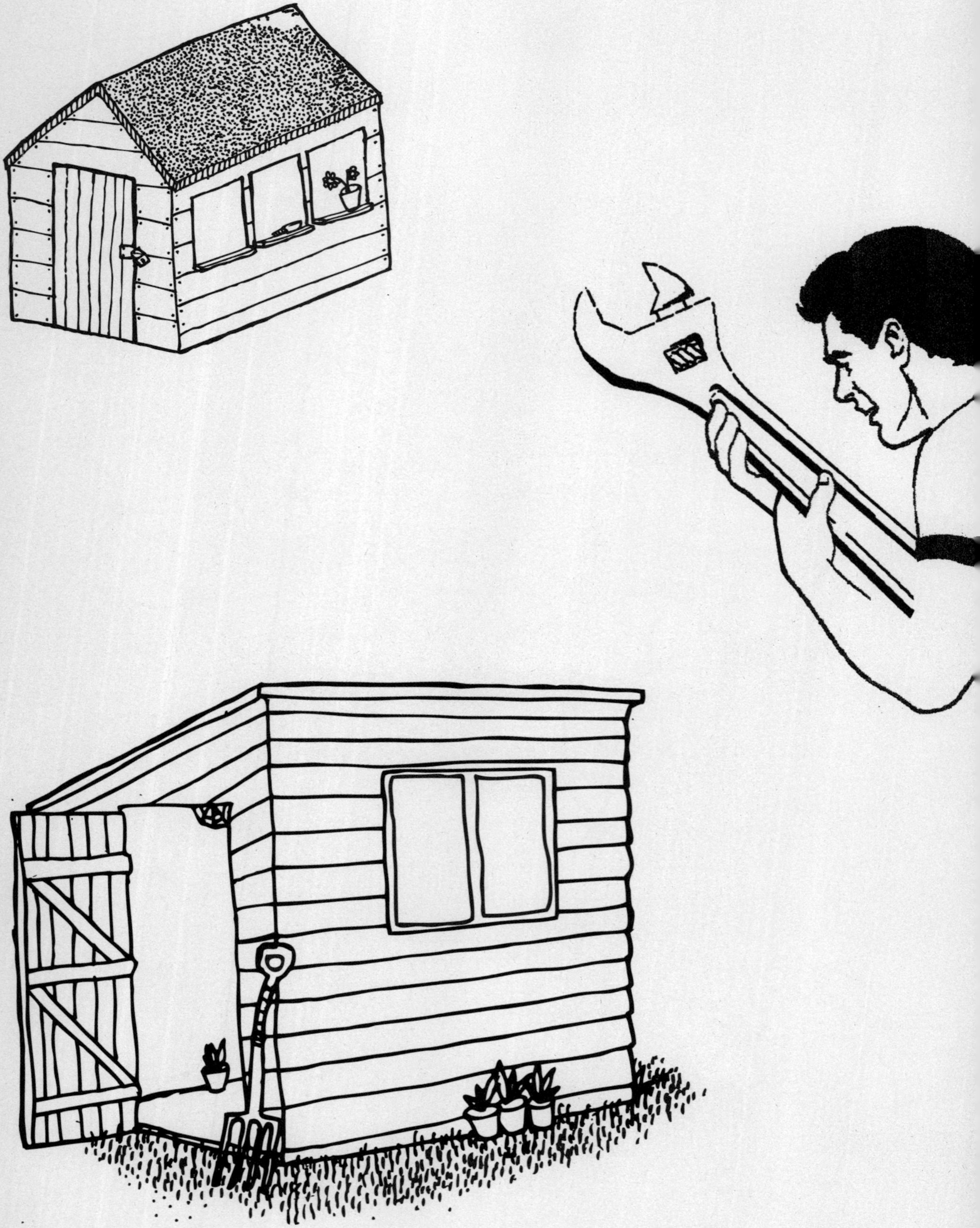

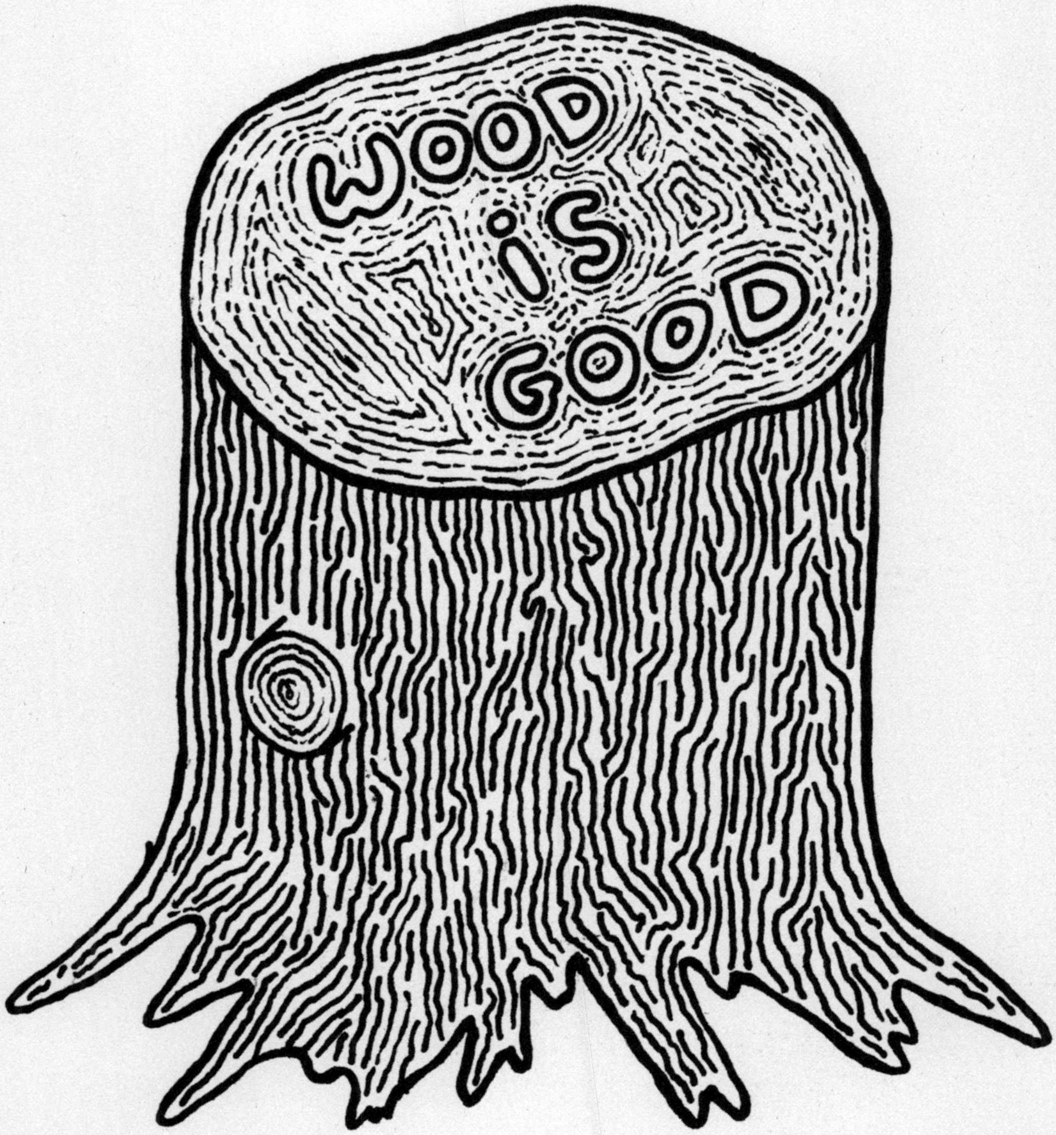
WOOD IS GOOD

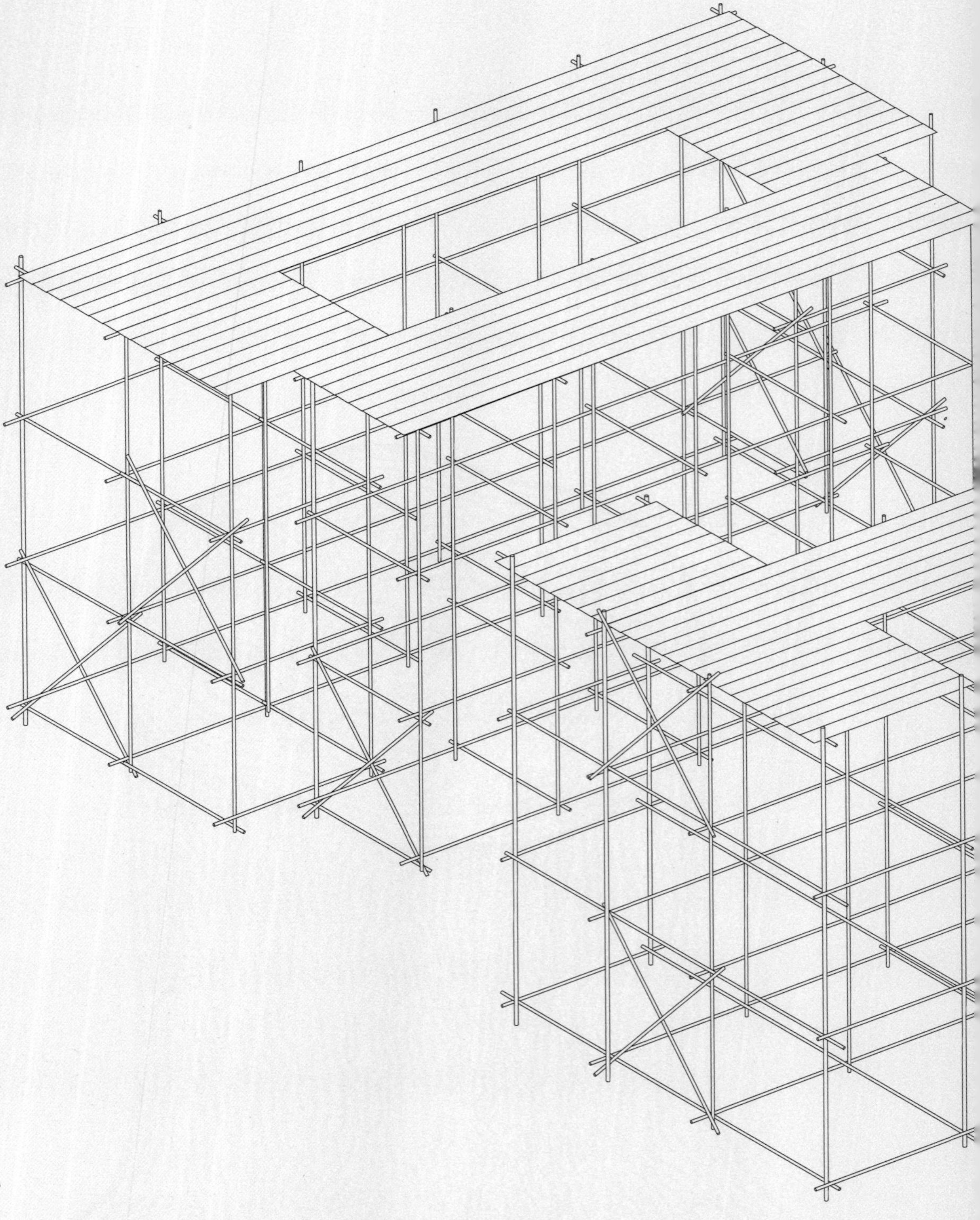

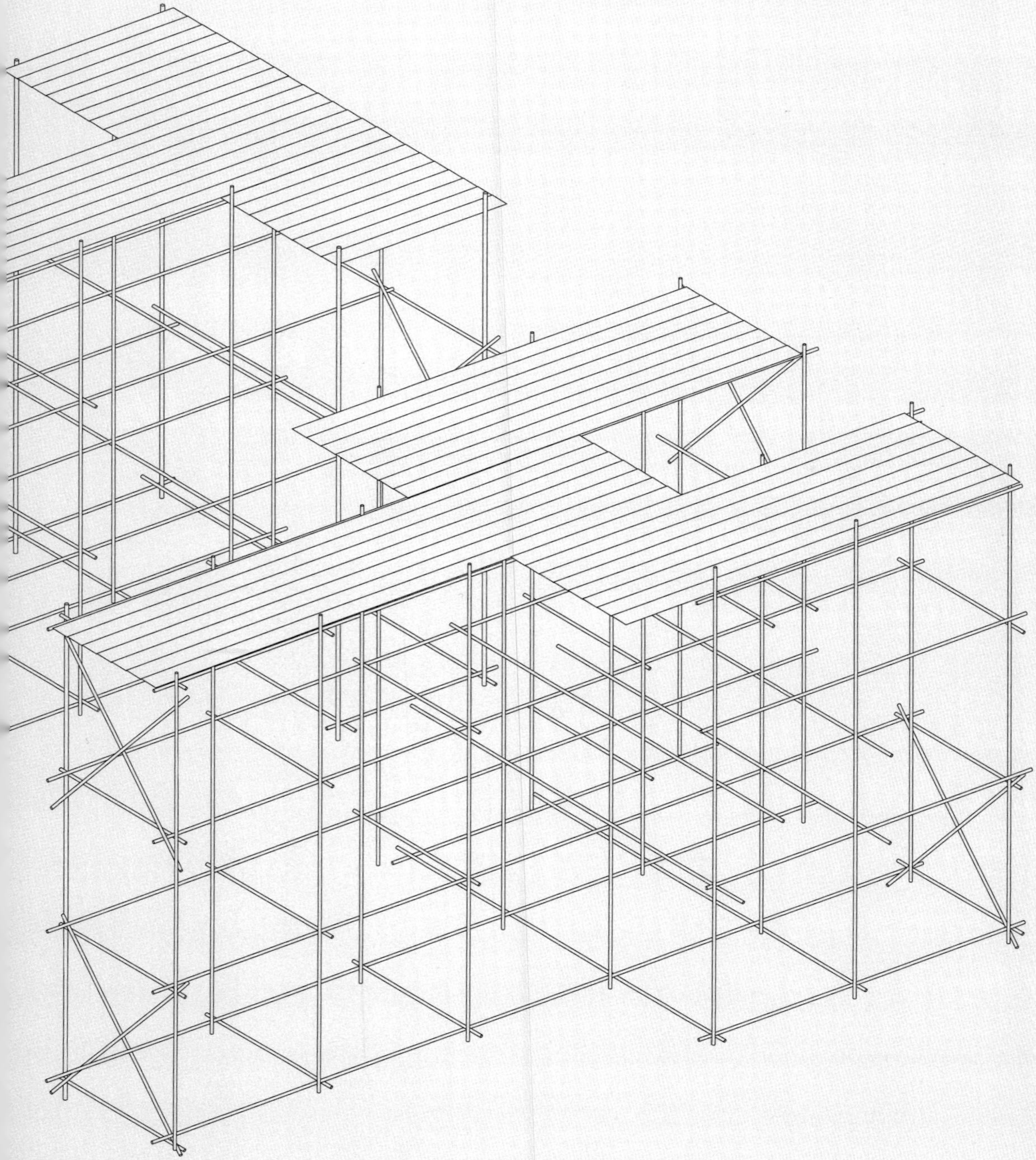

After a difficult trading year in 2004, along with a baby to care for, we decided to scale back our company and take stock of our situation. Rather than compromise the brand we took another tack. We weren't in a position to take financial risks so decided to play it safe and look for fee paying work rather than buying and selling in an unstable market.

Over the previous years, we had built up a good client base and illustration portfolio, which we decided to turn into our core business. We joined forces with illustration agent Blunt, whose endless enthusiasm propelled Rude into the advertising sector.

We kept the brand alive through collaborative projects that kept Rude in the public eye, and although it was a marked change to the business we had previously run, it felt like a huge relief.

2005

149.2005

BMI

2005.150

Project
More Legroom to Moscow

Discipline
Illustration

Ha, a moustached man with an extra long leg? Yep, we'll draw that, thanks. This project was commissioned by the BMI airline, who were promoting their More Legroom to Moscow campaign, with hand-selected hoardings to display the 48 sheet posters. We drove past one near Heathrow and it looked really effective, especially with his foot shooting off the end of the hoarding. I loved the mainly monochrome man with the accent colours on his socks and tie.

Ace Magazine

Project
Just Ask Jamie

Discipline
Illustration

Ace is a specialist tennis publication who commissioned Rude to illustrate some double page spreads. The subject matter was tennis star Jamie Murray and his on-court antics. Ace required a brightly coloured typographic approach, the result of which is bouncy and fun.

DDB Advertising

Project
Montag

Discipline
Illustration

Sometimes we create test illustrations to help the clients envisage the final piece, especially if it's in a previously uncommissioned style and they need to get client sign off. In that case, we work mainly with the art buyers and creatives to get the most from the test. This was the case with 'Montag', a piece for a German client designed with ad agency DDB.

Weiden Kennedy

Project
Coca Cola Campaign

Discipline
Illustration

Advertising agency Weiden Kennedy commissioned Rude to illustrate Coca Cola's next major advertising campaign 'Open Happiness'. The theme was traffic and the ads were to be placed on motorways and dual carriageway hoardings. Unfortunately the project was dropped at the last minute, however we loved it so much, we thought it was worth featuring.

155.2005

Project
Dumb Menswear Collection

Discipline
Fashion Design

'Dumb' was an idea generated from the licensing department at Nickelodeon. One of their properties, SpongeBob SquarePants, was a huge commercial success for kids and they noticed uptake with a young male market of 18-25 year olds. As a result, Nickelodeon required a more subversive approach to licensing.

The characters and scripts are so funny and surreal that we decided to design a menswear collection called Dumb. The concept is based around fashion/garment mistakes and subtle details such as upside down pockets, and grandad shirts with wonky button plackets.

The label was sold into Urban Outfitters and to accompany the launch we designed the windows and in store displays with large, sponge Christmas Trees. However I had a slight accident and dropped an 8ft tree from the balcony onto a customer's head - thank goodness it was only sponge.

Nickelodeon

2005.156

157.2005

Nickledeon   Dumb Magazine   Adoption

159.2005

Travelocity

Project
Hello World Merchandise

Discipline
Apparel Graphics

Alan Wicker is an iconic
travel journalist and TV
reporter, so naturally he was
selected to become the face
of travel agency Travelocity.
To launch the company they
required a set of imagery
to use across merchandise
and ad campaigns with the
strapline 'Hello World'. We
loved drawing him, you can't
go wrong with moustache
and glasses.

The tees had a camera print
drawn to look as though it
is hanging from around the
wearer's neck - the result
was quite funny actually.

161.2005

QUEENS PARK
I LOVE LONDON
BEAUTIFUL PARKS LINKING UGLY STREETS AT NIGHT TIME
KENSAL ROAD

Rude

Project
I Love London

Discipline
Screen Printing

As an introduction to the world of advertising agencies, we instigated a set of limited edition screen prints called 'I Love London'. There were six in the set, and each one was based around an area of our great city. The text was positioned so that it spelt out the name of a specific ad agency; for instance, 'Brilliant Boozers for Happy times' became the acronym for well-known agency BBH.

Rude took these posters on tour around the agencies and exhibited them in their offices. It turned out to be a good introduction and we managed to sell most of them.

I LOVE LONDON

TANTALISING BUILDINGS & WICKED ARCHITECTURE

SOHO THIS WAY
I LOVE LONDON
THE THREE KINGS
THE GOLDEN HEART
THE RED LION
BRILLIANT BOOZERS FOR HAPPY TIMES

DANCING DAY TIME BRIDGES

I LOVE LONDON

RIVER THAMES

ART
CAFE
CITY
PUB THIS WAY
HEAVEN
IN THE
AFTERNOON
BAR THE BAR THE
I LOVE
LONDON
THE PARK LIFE

In retrospect this year was a real mix of our core strengths: designing product and illustrating for both clients and ourselves. The great thing about this approach is having the creative freedom to push yourself to new directions but also getting commissioned for doing the work you love. It felt as though we had reached a happy medium – one where we were regaining our confidence with producing our own product again, but on a much smaller scale.

The year started with an unusual commission by kitchen product design company Joseph Joseph. We had worked with them since the launch of their brand, designing various prints for them over the years. This time they wanted something more unusual, so we came up with iconic portraits made from fruit and vegetables. The first one was Elvis who had aubergines for hair.

2006

169.2006

Joseph Joseph

Project
Icons Homeware Collection

Discipline
Image Making

When contemporary kitchenware brand Joseph Joseph commissioned Rude to come up with a collection of images for their glass chopping board collection Icons, we wanted to do something different. We decided to make them from fruit and veg, hence our Elvis Presley made from aubergines, lentils and liquorice.

Shortly afterwards we received a call from Paul McCartney's PA, inviting us in to meet Sir Paul, who loved the images we'd made. Aside from being completely starstruck (us, not him) we had a lengthy conversation about his first encounter with Elvis and Linda McCartney's sausages.

It transpired that he wanted us to make a similar image of him and suggested that we use green beans to make his hair. The meeting concluded with Paul putting Elvis's song 'Hound Dog' on his jukebox and the three of us dancing around to it.

171.2006

Joseph Joseph   Icons Homeware Collection

2006.172

173.2006

Joseph
Joseph   Joseph Joseph

2006.174

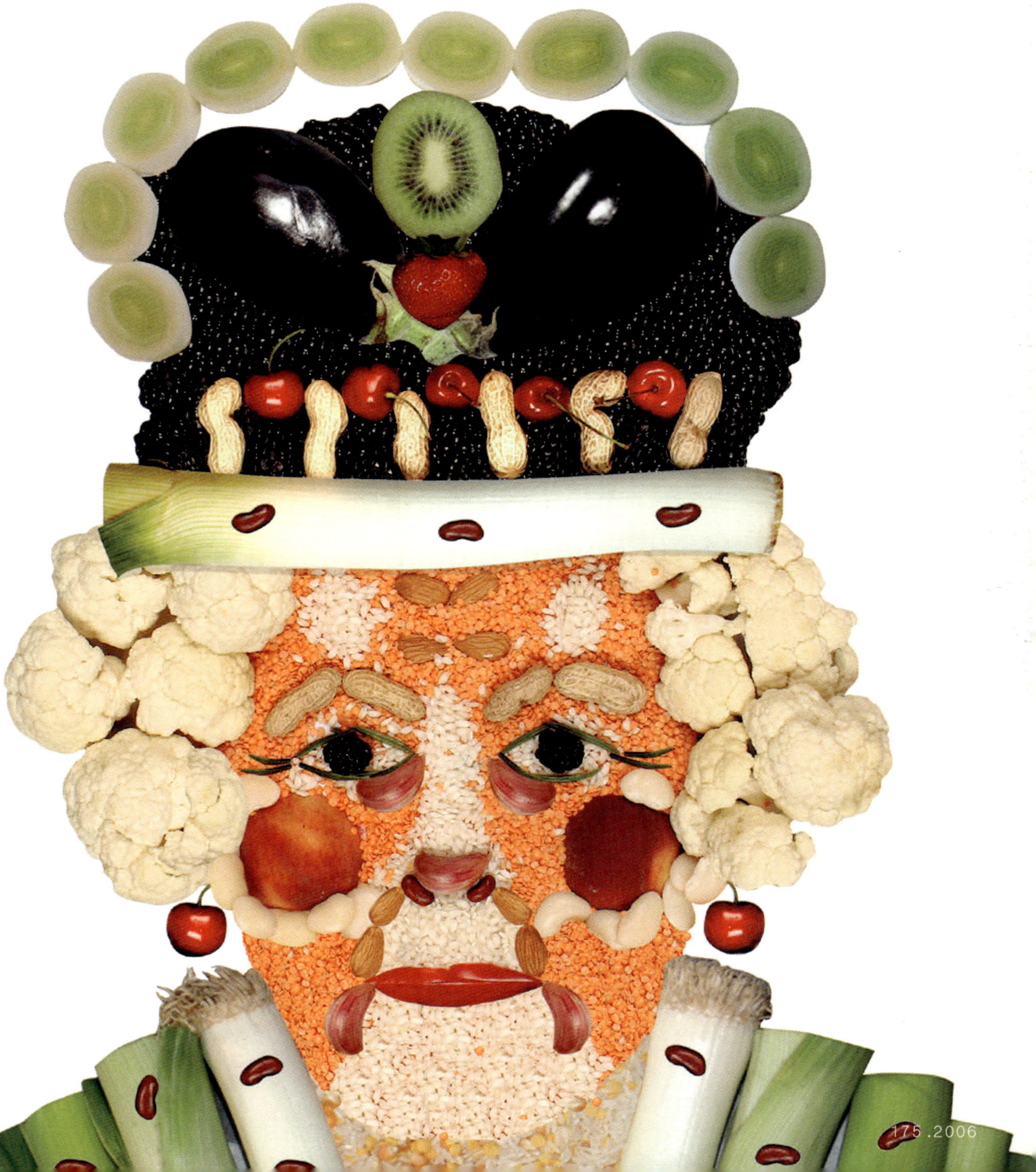
175 .2006

Love is Blind

Project
Window Blinds Collection

Discipline
Printed Textiles

Product design company Adapt and React partnered up with Rude this year to create a collection of roller blinds. The inspiration for the brand came from the idea of placing shadow based images onto blinds, creating the impression that something is casting a shadow from outside the window. We made our own shadow images and sourced a manufacturer in China, before producing and importing the blinds into the UK.

After designing a few collections and building up stockists, we were approached by an online curtain and blind business who were keen to buy them. We made the decision to sell as we didn't want to specialise in window coverings. We realised that it had been great to work on this as a special project and not something that had to become a permanent part of the business.

177.2006

Topshop

Project
Rude for Topshop
Womenswear Collection

Discipline
Fashion

As a way of continuing our label but with more control, we sold into the womenswear concession in Topshop. We worked with great suppliers of apparel in Portugal who could produce short runs of garments with quick turnaround. The printers allowed us to use some of their archive roller-prints from the fifties, sixties and seventies, which helped create a different feel for Rude.

The capsule collection was jersey based and featured limited shapes of over sized T-shirts, hoodies and drop waist dresses.

As part of their in-store advertising, we asked photographer Colin Lane to shoot some key images for us. They featured a lively group of 15-year old girls who came round to our house and dressed up in the clothes. We wanted a youthful, bright and fun approach, which stylist Rachel Zilli and Colin managed to capture for us.

2006.178

179.2006

Project
T-shirt Graphics

Discipline
Illustration

No Added Sugar is a fantastic kidswear label set up by husband and wife founders Rick Ramswell and Deborah Medhurst. Their rock and roll attitude sees edgy prints combined with classic tailoring. Initially a graphic-led brand, they have evolved into a progressive kids' label, selling internationally.

When I happened to see that they were advertising for a graphic designer, I suggested that they use us instead. Since then we have continually illustrated slogans and come up with iconic prints for them. It's always fast and fun.

No Added Sugar

181.2006

No Added Sugar   T-shirt Graphics

LAUGH out LOUD

2006.182

WHY DON'T YOU TURN OFF THE TELEVISION AND DO SOMETHING EXCITING INSTEAD

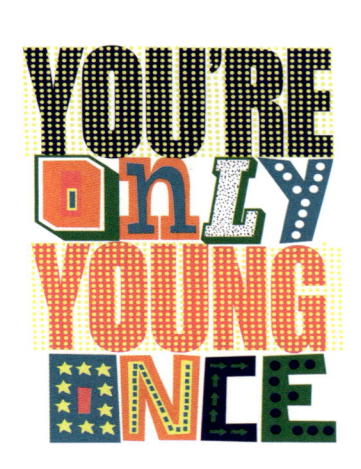

No Added Sugar   T-shirt Graphics

185 . 1999

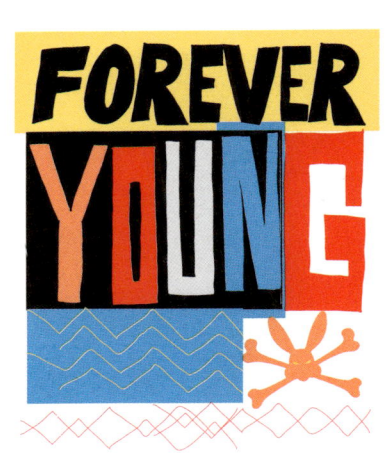

No Added Sugar · T-shirt Graphics

187.2006

Rude

Project
Wonderful Collection

Discipline
Bags and Accessories

Throughout the life span of Rude we have worked closely with a manufacturing agent in Portugal. Luisa, the owner of the company, has become a great friend and together we have weathered the ups and downs of business and life. This was a year that saw us placing some decent orders through her company and Luisa agreed to help us put a small collection of bags and accessories together. We launched the line at a trade show in London and began to build our label again.

The range was called 'Wonderful' and featured vector based illustrations of repeat prints, with simple optical illusions. An image of umbrellas turned into a row of smiling faces for example, and likewise, a sea of boats became a landscape of swiss chalets when turned the other way.

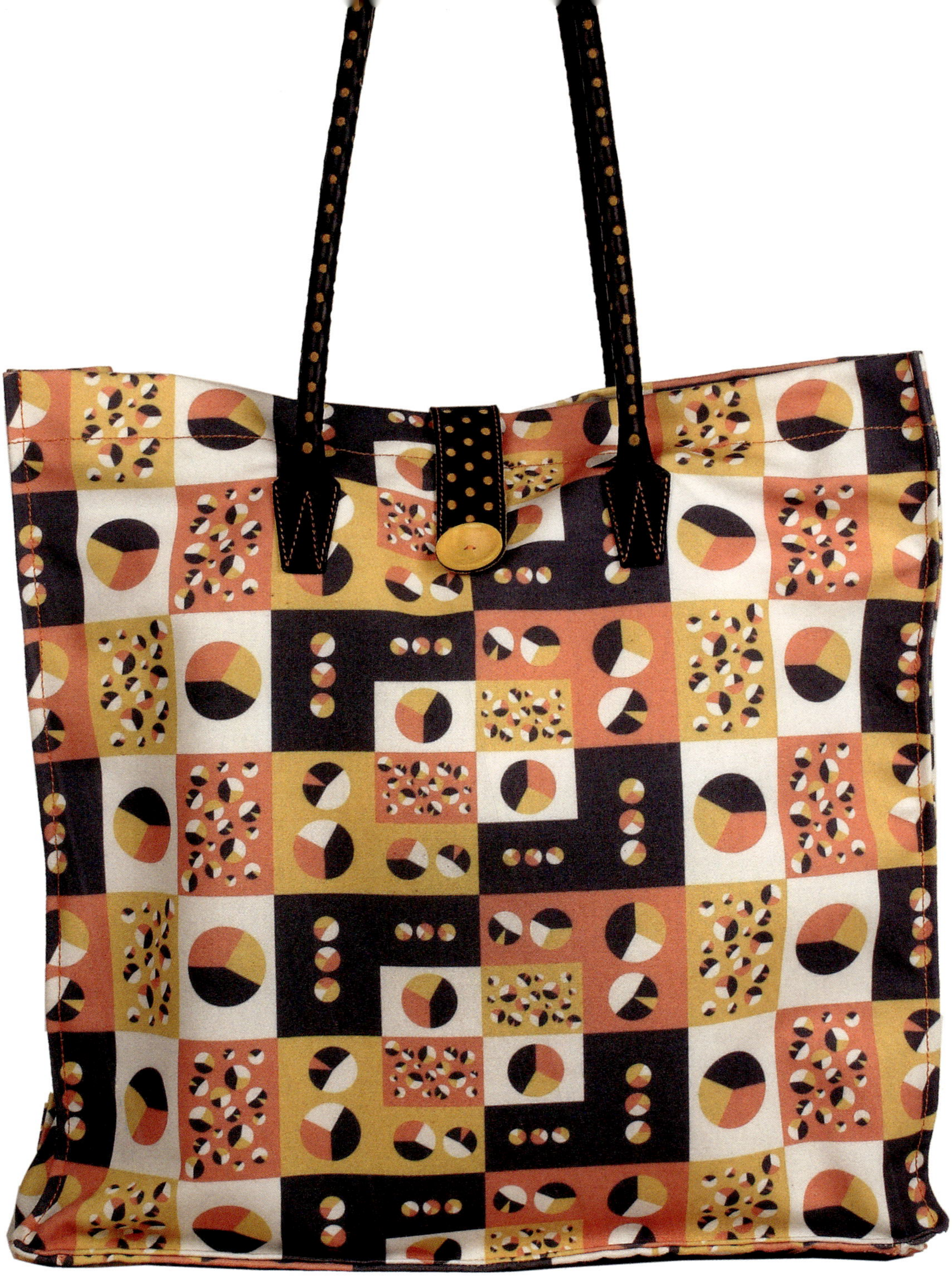

189 .2006

POLYDOR

THANK YOU FOR 2006

5 M
THE UNDISCOVERED
GIRLS
CHASING CARS
+ MANY MORE

OLYMPIA

Polydor

Project
Christmas Poster

Discipline
Illustration

As an internal thank you to its staff, Polydor commissioned Rude to illustrate an image depicting some of the highlights of the year for the company. They ordered five hundred of these screen printed and individually framed illustrations as Christmas gifts for their employees.

They gave us free reign to do as we liked and we decided to make it look like a large neon sign, similar to the kind you'd find outside a cinema. We worked the names, icons, bands and events into the image. They were printed in four colours and framed with handmade black wooden frames. They looked really quite smart.

made
in
JAPAN
ade
JAPAN
LOVELY
made
in
JAPAN
made
in
JAPAN
amazing
TRAINERS
made
IN
JAPAN
made
in
JAPAN
LOVELY

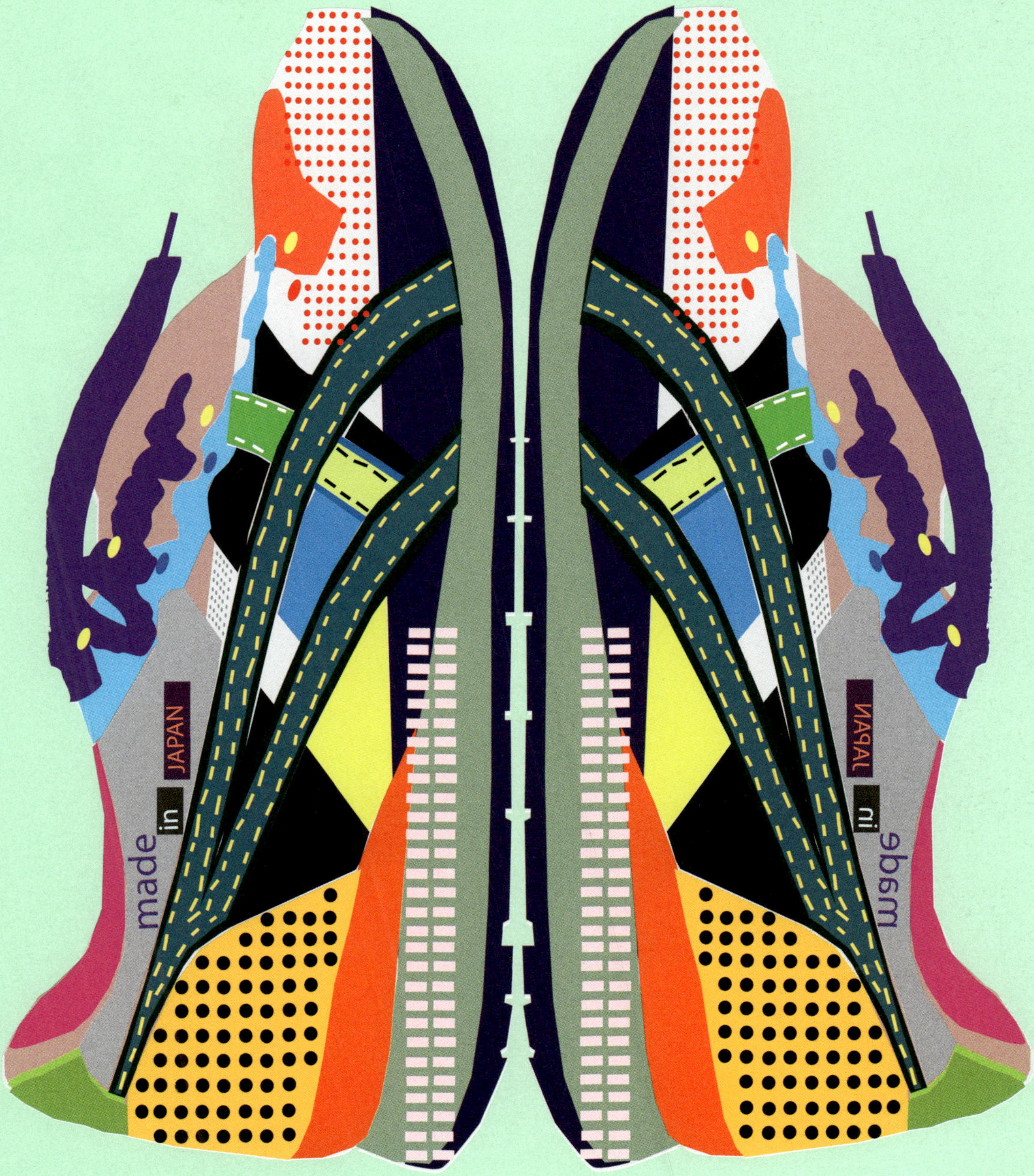
made in JAPAN

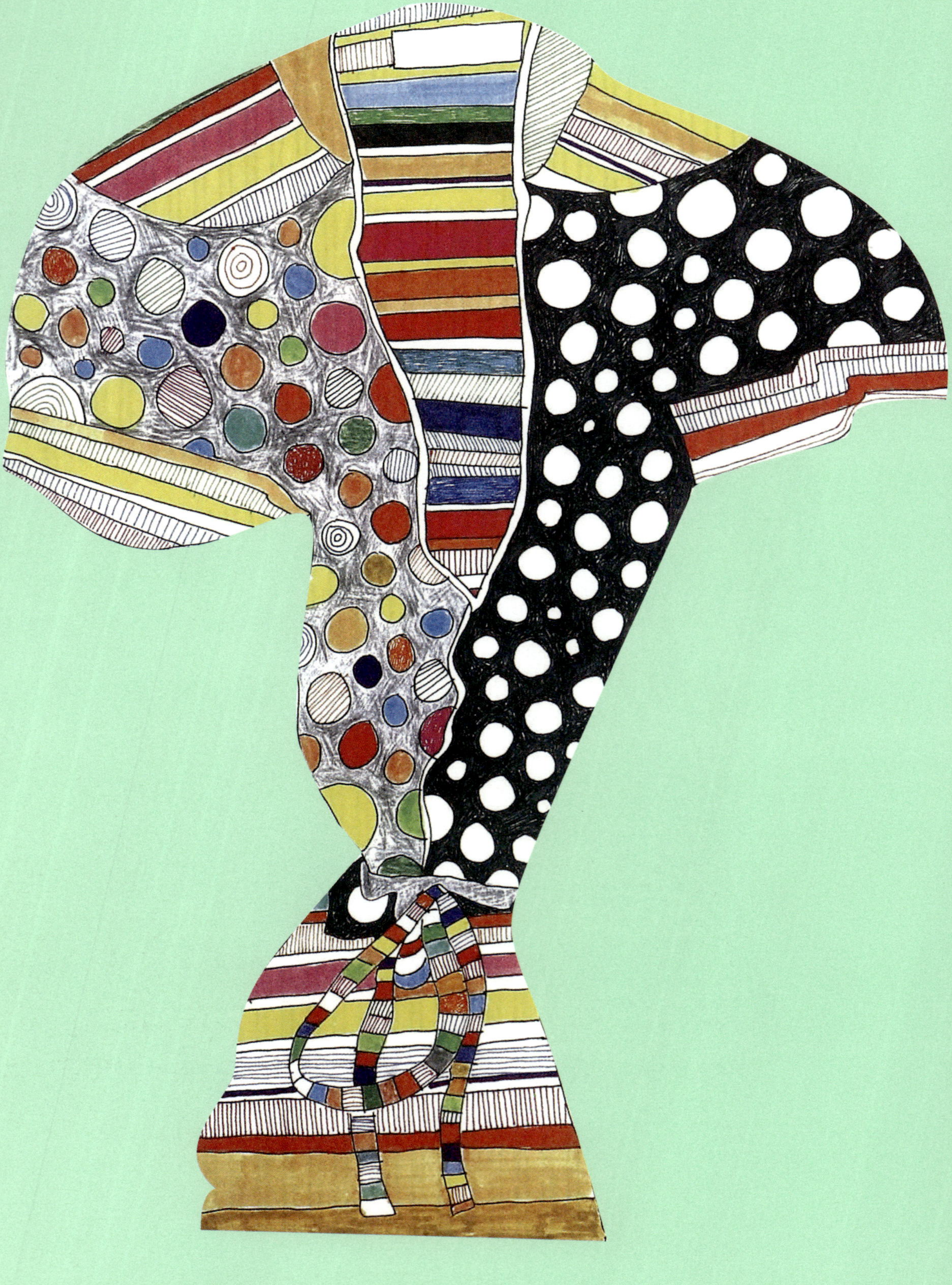

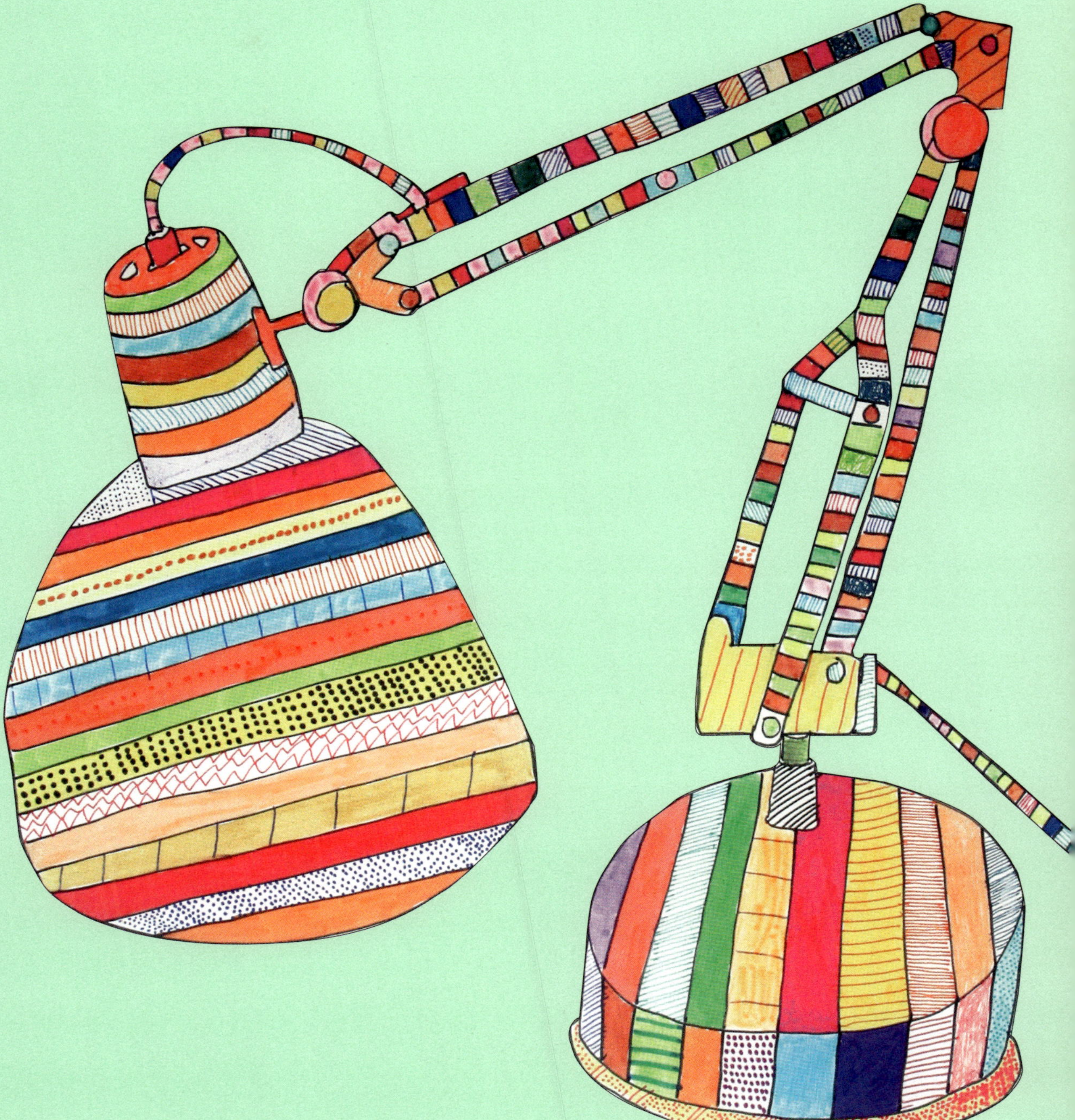

Over the previous two years, our advertising work had begun to grow and our illustration had started to follow a typographic route. This was amusing, especially as dyslexia plays a big part in our lives and our illustrations are created organically. Needless to say, there have been a few typos and re-draws over the years.

Rupert's hand drawn style had begun to treat type in an illustrational way, blending images and letterforms together to create integrated artworks. This was when we started to draw experimentally, filling sketchbooks with alphabets, sayings and images of everyday type.

This creative period of image making and sketching would take us back into screen printing and we started to produce sets of limited edition prints and push our art style.

2007

197.2007

Project
TV Advert

Discipline
Colour and Print Design

Ben White and Chris Rule are the founders of a company called Conkerco and the creators of brilliant adverts and film. They were commissioned by Homebase to direct an ad showcasing their vast palette of paints. The concept revolved around the decoration of a mundane and normally colourless space, like a car park.

The 30 second ad shows an army of decorators roller painting the ramps, walls, floors and ceilings of this grey monolith. Rude were drafted in for our use of colour and pattern. We started off by looking at their swatches and then picking a warm selection, one that would create the biggest transformation. We played with pattern and then dropped it onto location pics of the car park to check that it would work.

We kept the patterns and shapes simple but made the best use of the dimensions of the split levels and reveals you find in a car park.

Homebase

2007.198

199.2007

2007.200

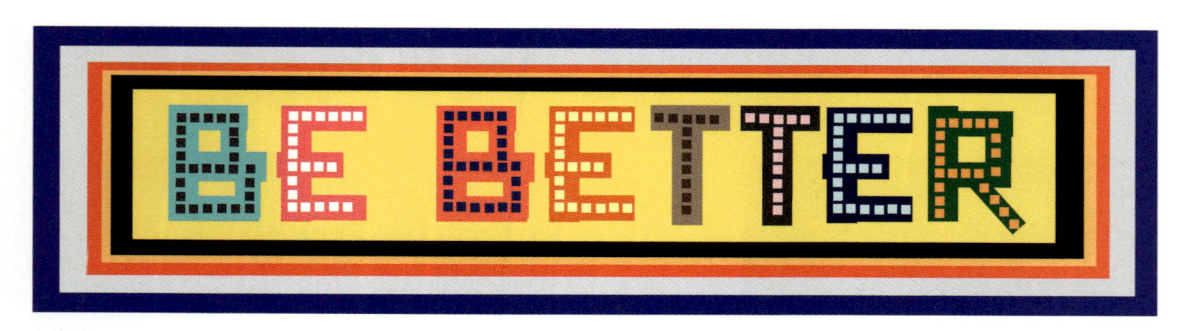

Project
Exhibition

Discipline
Screen Printing and
Illustration

We were kindly invited to exhibit a new body of work, offering both one-off and limited edition pieces.

As typography began to play a bigger role in our portfolio, we realised that a collection of handmade signs could be an interesting direction to take.

We also illustrated a set of posters around the theme of life. One of these was 'Exciting Life', which depicted the words wrapped around a roller coaster, while another was 'Sea of Life' based on a photograph we'd recently taken on holiday near Brighton.

Both of these images would be used in various animations further down the line. I love the intricacy of the line work and its 3D quality. Strangely we did end up selling quite a few prints to psychotherapists.

Rude

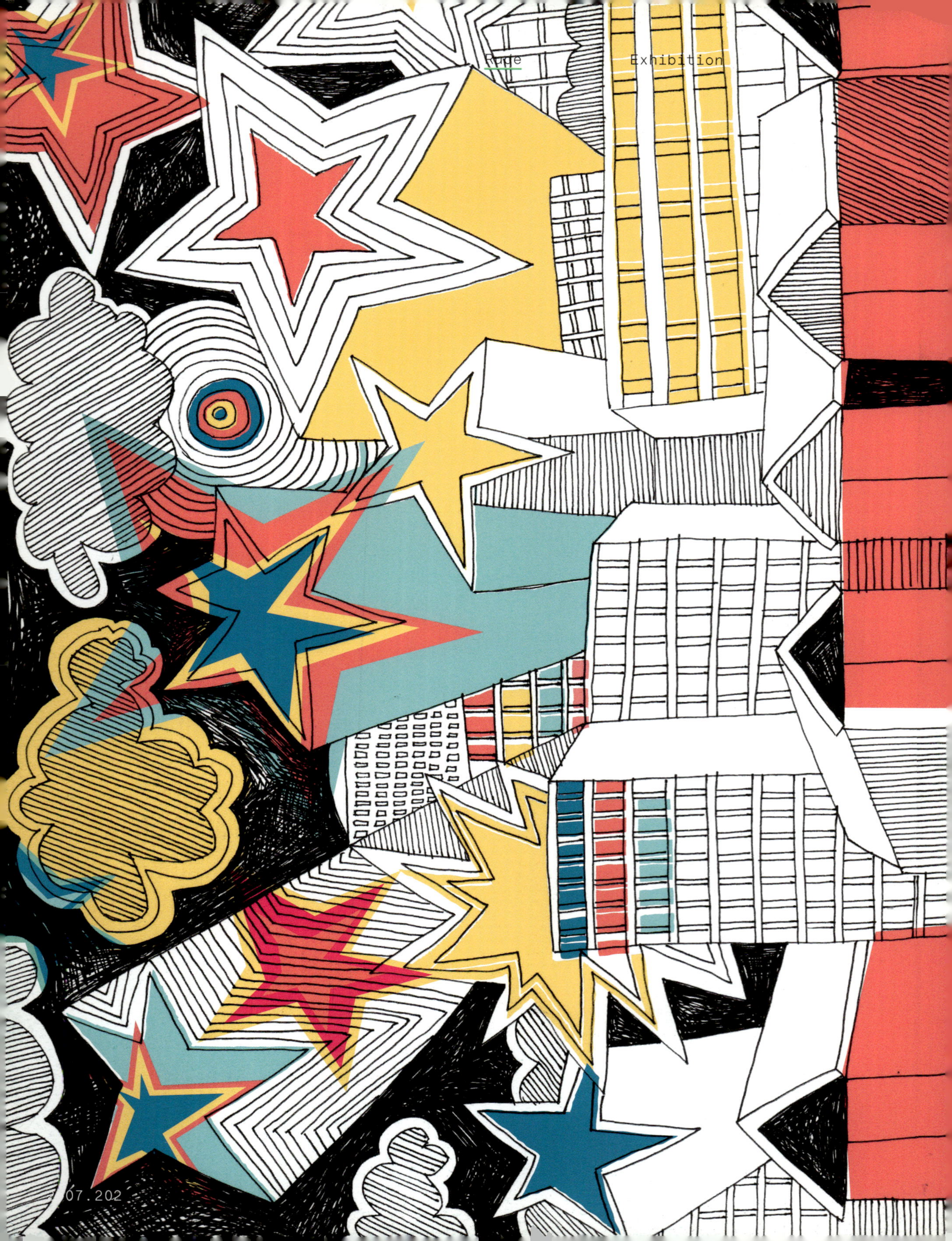

SEA of LIFE

203.2007

Rude   Exhibition

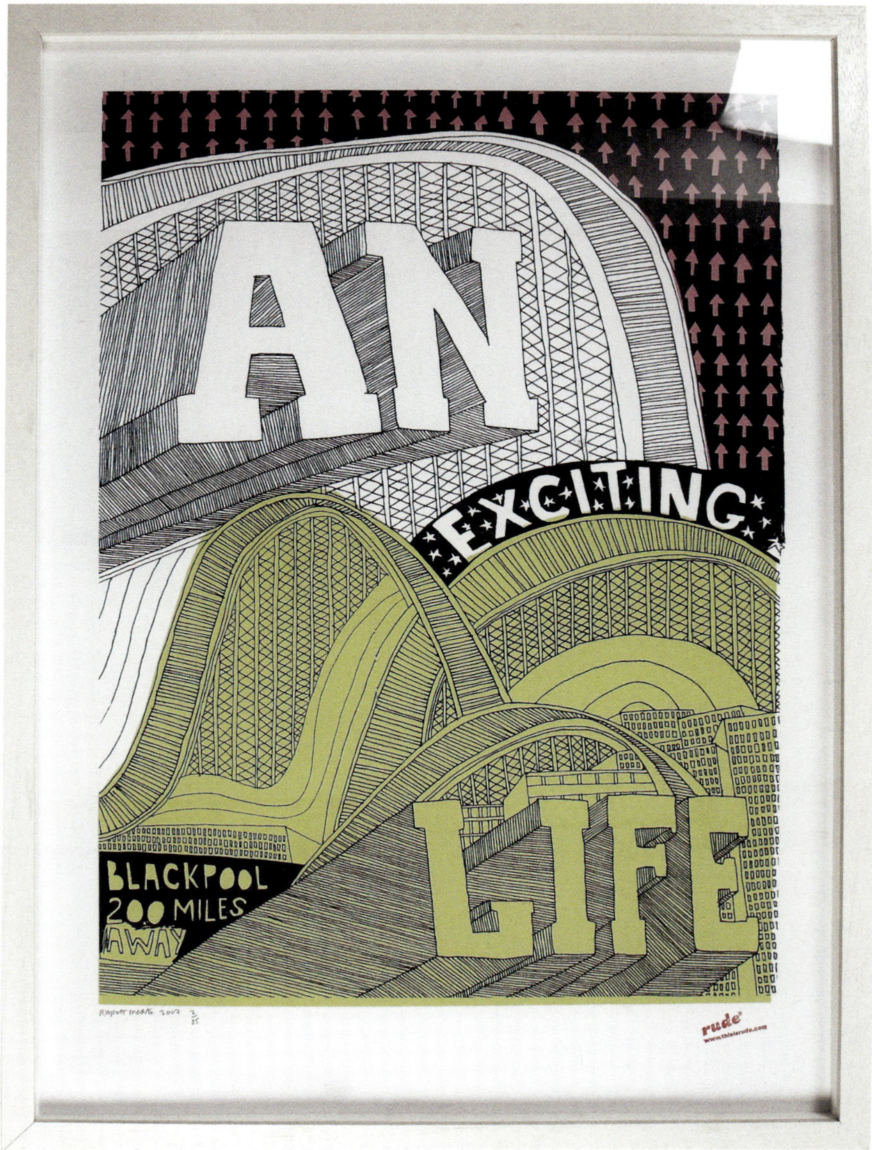

205 .2007

Transport for London

Project
Below the Line
Advertising Campaign

Discipline
Image Making

'Cut your carbon emissions and save money' was the message of this advert. The brief was as simple as the resulting image – it had to get straight to the point and state the obvious. Predominantly typographic, the text is seen through the vast amount of smoke emitting from the exhaust of the car. TFL's campaign aimed to get people to reduce the amount of time they spent in their vehicles and to explore alternative ways to travel that are lighter on the environment and the pocket too.

FUEL EFFICIENT CARS DON'T JUST REDUCE CO_2 EMISSIONS, THEY REDUCE YOUR FUEL BILLS TOO.

Rude

Project
Do You Want to Escape

Discipline
Illustration

An ever evolving part of what we do is illustration. It has been integral to our company from the very beginning. One of the reasons for setting up Rude initially was simply to be able to apply illustrations onto varied mediums, whether it be a canvas, wall, car or egg cup. The challenge is how to make that image work and get the best out of it. This image was created for our portfolio but we also used it as a large mural, which looked great.

The Chocolate Factory N16

Project
Invites and Promotional Artwork

Discipline
Illustration and Graphics

We have a lovely studio based in Stoke Newington in north London, at a site called The Chocolate Factory. It's home to about thirty artists, ceramicists, designers and bookbinders. It's been our spiritual home for many years, with the mix of talents and mediums around us providing a constant source of inspiration.

Bi-annually, the studios open their doors and invite the public in to look around and buy the artists' creations. Rude design the graphics and illustrations for the invites and promotional literature to support the events.

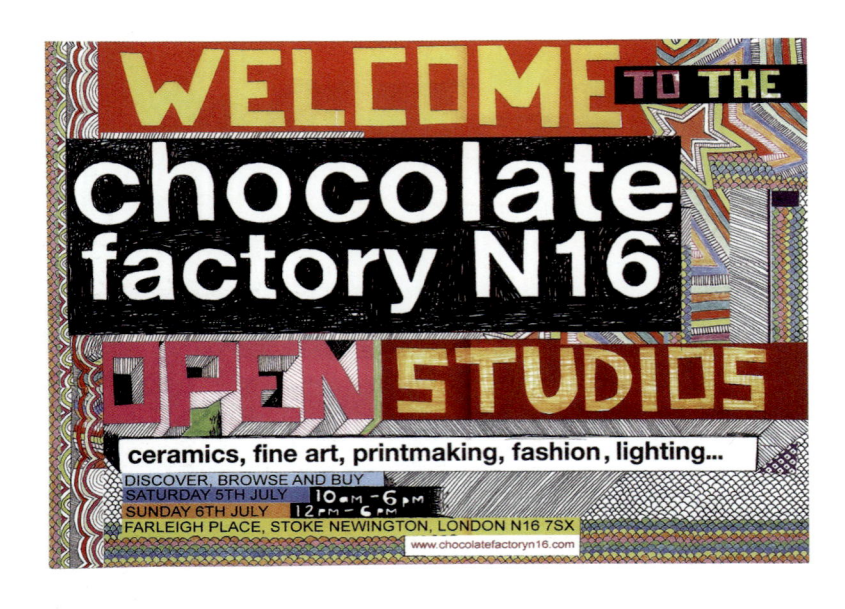

THE CHOCOLATE FACTORY N16 OPEN STUDIOS

FARLEIGH PLACE

STOKE NEWINGTON

Saturday 24 November 10am - 6pm
Sunday 25 November 12noon - 5pm
Saturday 1 December 10am - 6pm
Sunday 2 December 12noon - 5pm

The Chocolate Factory N16 — Invites and Promotional Artwork

THE CHOCOLATE FACTORY N16 ARTISTS SUMMER OPEN

2007.210

STUDIOS SAT 18TH & SUN 19TH JUNE 2011

11:00am – 6:00pm
http://www.chocolatefactoryn16.com

211.2007

GOOD LIFE

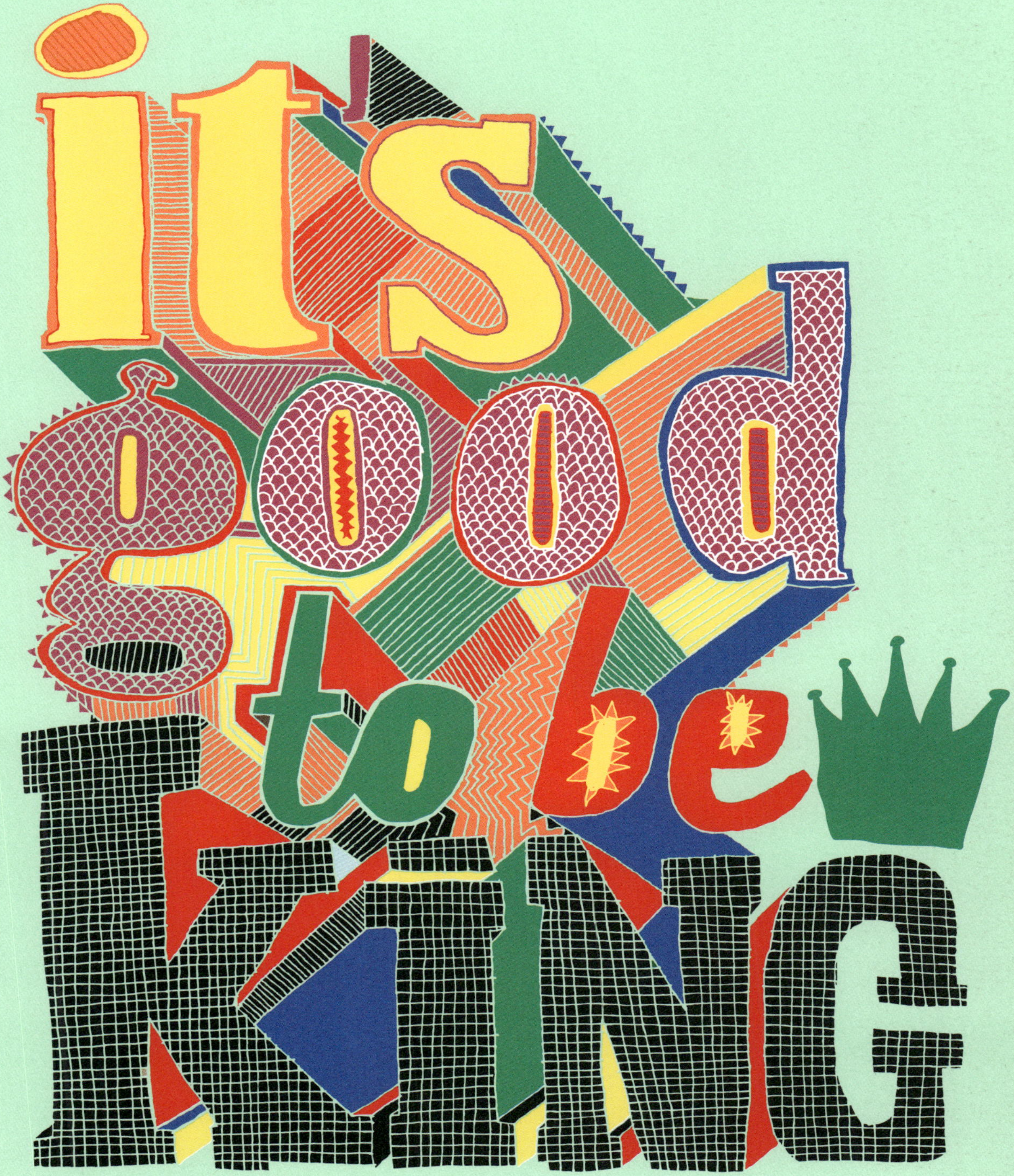
its good to be KING

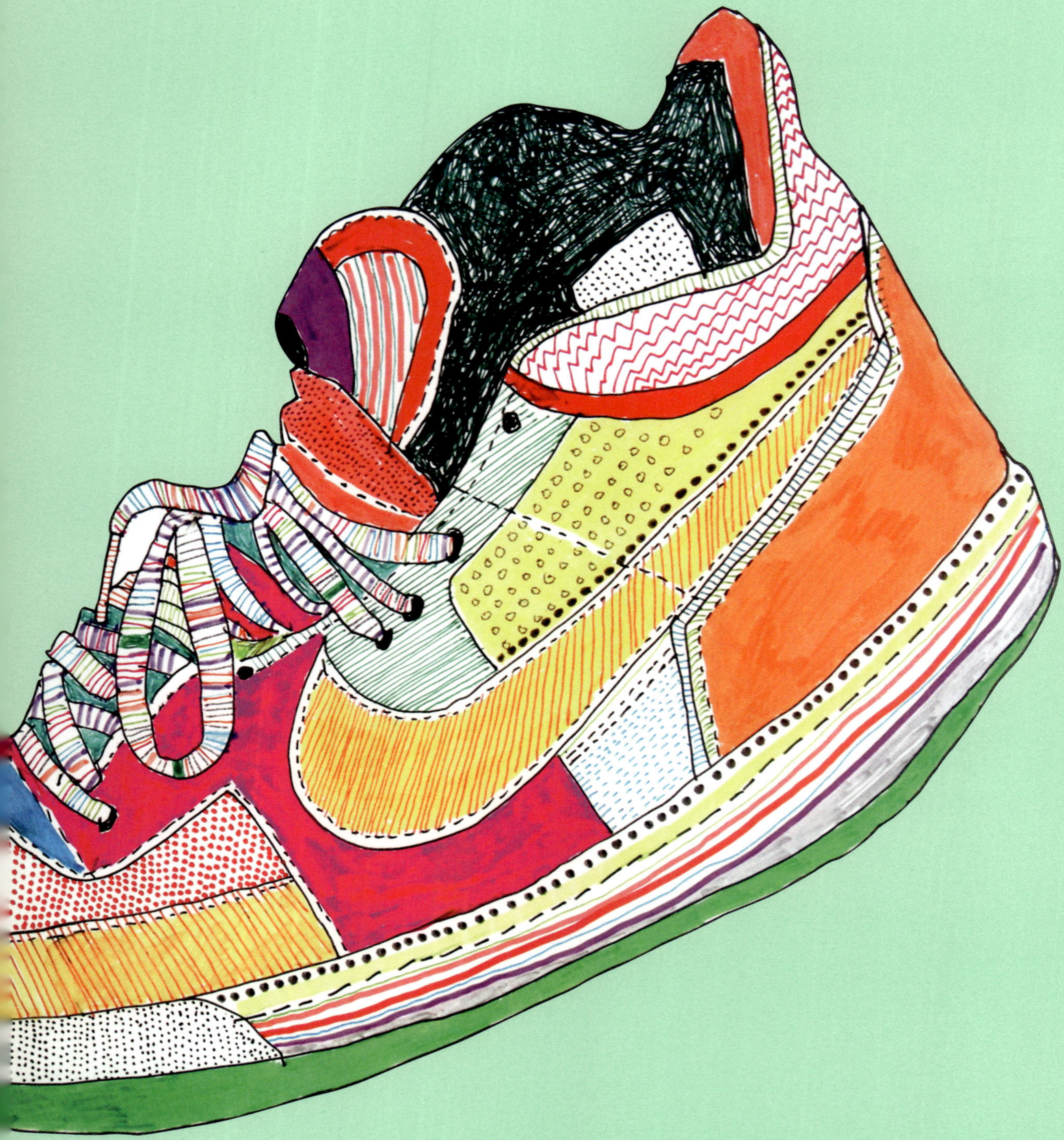

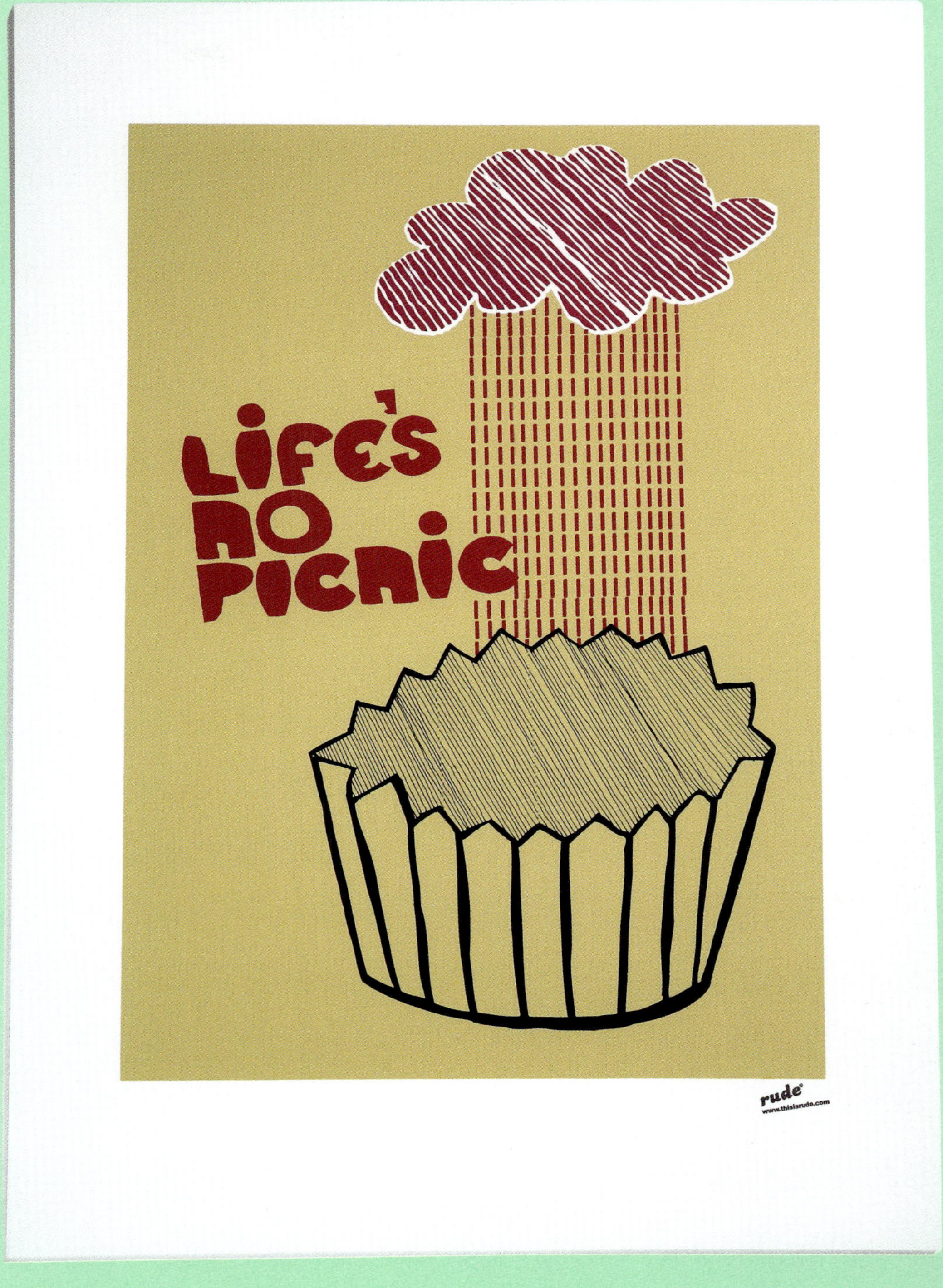
Life's
no
picnic
rude®
www.thisisrude.com

Rude's next step was always going to be towards animation and moving image. In particular, we wanted to see our illustrations in action, what they would look like if they weren't still.

I set to work learning animation and editing software and took on some small jobs that I could learn from. Enrolling in a film making night course gave me some basic camera skills and I read the software manuals from front to back.

I was also pregnant with our second son Herbie, so it seemed like a good time to sit down and concentrate. It set me onto a path I really enjoyed and it would ultimately become a part of what Rude had to offer.

We had Herbie in August of 2008, an amazing non-sleeping addition to the family.

2008

217.2008

CRANBERRY SAUCE WITH CHEAP BITS

BUDGET TURKEY NOT MUCH MEAT

2008.218

Rude

Project
Credit Crunch Collection

Discipline
Graphics

In a year when the recession began and austerity measures ruled, we designed a collection called Credit Crunch. This was a set of back to basics greeting cards, tees, lampshades and bags. The production quality was rough and ready and the price point was low.

We kept to reduced colour prints and used basic stock. The Christmas collection featured 'No Bang' crackers and 'Basic Brandy Butter with No Brandy'. They went down a storm.

Project
Eat Me Now Tour
Poster Campaign

Discipline
Illustration

Cadbury's ad agency Publicis threw a fantastic eggs-hibition of artists' interpretations of the classic Creme Egg. The event was used as a launch for their press campaign, with the A1 limited edition prints auctioned off for charity, no yolk.

Cadbury Creme Egg

2008.220

creme egg towers

EAT ME NOW

22.1.2008

Weiden Kennedy

Project
Nokia TV Ad

Discipline
Illustration

Celebrated advertising agency Weiden Kennedy were tasked with creating an ambitious TV ad for the Nokia 6220, their latest phone with new mapping techniques. The concept was to film illustrators drawing parts of the world, parks, cities and whales in the sea with felt tips, paints and marker pens. We see close-ups of the artists at work and when the camera pans back it reveals a huge illustration of the globe being drawn in Central Park in New York.

It was a massive production and Rude played a small but significant part. Rupert features in the closing scene, where he illustrates a bright cityscape wrapping around the phone itself.

It was an eye-opening and interesting job to be part of.

2008.222

Project
Ear to the Underground
Poster Campaign

Discipline
Illustration

In 2008 we were commissioned by advertising agency DKLW Lowe to illustrate a humorous set of images featuring large ears. The campaign was used to promote a competition for buskers and raise support for live music on the underground.

Capital Radio and the London Paper were behind the campaign and produced 48 sheet posters, bus shelter, underground and bus side advertising. It was an exciting time to travel around on public transport.

Capital Radio
London Paper

GIRL WE'RE GONNA REAP JUST WHAT WE SOW

John Power

Project
Pop Promo

Discipline
Animation

Being a huge John Power fan (formerly of The La's), we were thrilled to film John's three piece band playing some dirty rootsy blues. We styled the band in relaxed fifties attire and provided the drummer with a huge quiff. The film was shot on a blue screen and later we added an animated backdrop of type and stop frame photography.

The type was inspired by letterpress printing from the early 20th century, giving it a Nashville sort of vibe.

Print Club

Project
Print Exhibition

Discipline
Illustration

Print Club is based in Dalston, east London and is the brain child of Fred Higginson and Rose Stallard. Rose had worked with us as a screen printer in our Let's Make T-shirts shop and came up with the bright idea of starting a screen printing club with great facilities and a workshop mentality.

Print Club has a talented extended family of artists that not only use the facilities but also collaboratively exhibit together at Print Club.

This year we were invited to exhibit and came up with a print each. Mine was called 'Beauty is in the Eye of the Beerholder' while Rupert's was a list of uplifting expressions printed in orange neon. All the prints were limited editions of 25 and it worked on a first-come, first-serve basis, with guests buying the prints on the night.

2008.226

ACE
GREAT
BRILLIANT
FANTASTIC
WONDERFUL
LOVELY
PERFECT
AMAZING

Project
Poster Campaign

Discipline
Illustration

Rakish Heels

Rakish Heels is a highly innovative footwear brand that launched their first collections in 2007.

All their shoes have an emphasis on the heel, which usually have printed designs or detachable heel covers that turn plain shoes into fancy pieces of footwork.

Since their conception, we have provided all the support graphics and imagery, including two viral campaigns, lookbooks and web design.

2008.228

Spring Summer 09

Time flies when you're being Rude

2009 – 2014

RUDE®

Rude Ups and Downs

4–5	**2009**
6–7	The Guardian Guide Glastonbury The Guardian Guide
8–9	Pop Promo Cornershop
10–13	Art Exhibition House of Propellers
14–15	Blunt Mural Blunt
16–17	Lamp Design Habitat
18–19	Music Matters Island Records
20	Video Promo Vespa
21	T-shirt Designs Graniph
22–25	Christmas, Home & Kidswear Tate
30–31	**2010**
32–35	Advertising Rude
36–37	Editorial Oh Comely
38–39	The Great Indoors Manchester Int. Festival

40–41	This is Now Mural Root	82–85	Thunderbirds Menswear Collection ITV	126–129	Anniversary Poster National Theatre
42–43	Viral Book Promo Picador	86–87	Plan Charity Booklet AMV	130–131	Taste Magazine ico Design
48–49	**2011**	88–91	Children's Merchandise Range Science Museum	132–133	In-store Merchandise Cass Art
50–51	Book Cover Hodder Publishing	92–95	Window Mural AMV	134–145	Homeware Urban Outfitters
52–53	Wedding Invite Kay & Dave Buchan	96–97	Heritage Collection Tetley Tea	146–147	Veolia Havas Worldwide
54–55	Music Boxes Poster Manchester Int. Festival	104–105	**2013**	148–149	I Love Manchester Museum of Science and Industry
56–57	What Did the Hippie Have in His Bag? Manchester International Festival	106–107	Homeware Collection Rude	150–151	T-shirts and Merchandise Education First
58–61	In-store Merchandise National Theatre	108–111	Furniture Rude	152–153	Building our house in Kyverdale Road Rude
62–63	One Man, Two Guvnors National Theatre	112–113	Soutbank Collection Southbank Centre		
64–67	Print Exhibition Printa	114–115	Eliza Doolittle Tapes Parlophone		
68	House of Cards Poster Shelter	116–117	Magazine Cover French Elle		
69	Advertising Campaign Rimmel	118–121	Flying Scotsman The National Rail Museum		
78–79	**2012**	122–123	Spy Packaging Imperial War Museum		
80–81	Doctor Who Homeware Collection BBC	124–125	Teenage Cancer Trust Poster Boxfresh		

In 2008, we got the ball rolling on producing animations and music promos and this year would see the process continue. We started to take on more ambitious projects and I began to draw up full characters, looking at body movement and lip-syncing to make them more realistic – though truth be told, we were always fans of the clunky Monty Python style.

That same year, we held our first proper art exhibition and began working on larger multimedia pieces. The expression of animation and large art fed into each other, with some surprising results.

2009

5.2009

The Guardian Guide

Project
The Guardian Guide to Glastonbury

Discipline
Illustration

As avid attendees of Glastonbury we jumped at the opportunity to illustrate The Guardian Guide's Glastonbury cover.

The result was a highly coloured typographic treatment, featuring cut out images of Bruce Springsteen waiting for a bus and Dizzee Rascall hanging out at the traffic lights.

If memory serves me well, we raided the paper stand at Glastonbury and showed off our artwork to anyone that would listen.

2009.6

guide

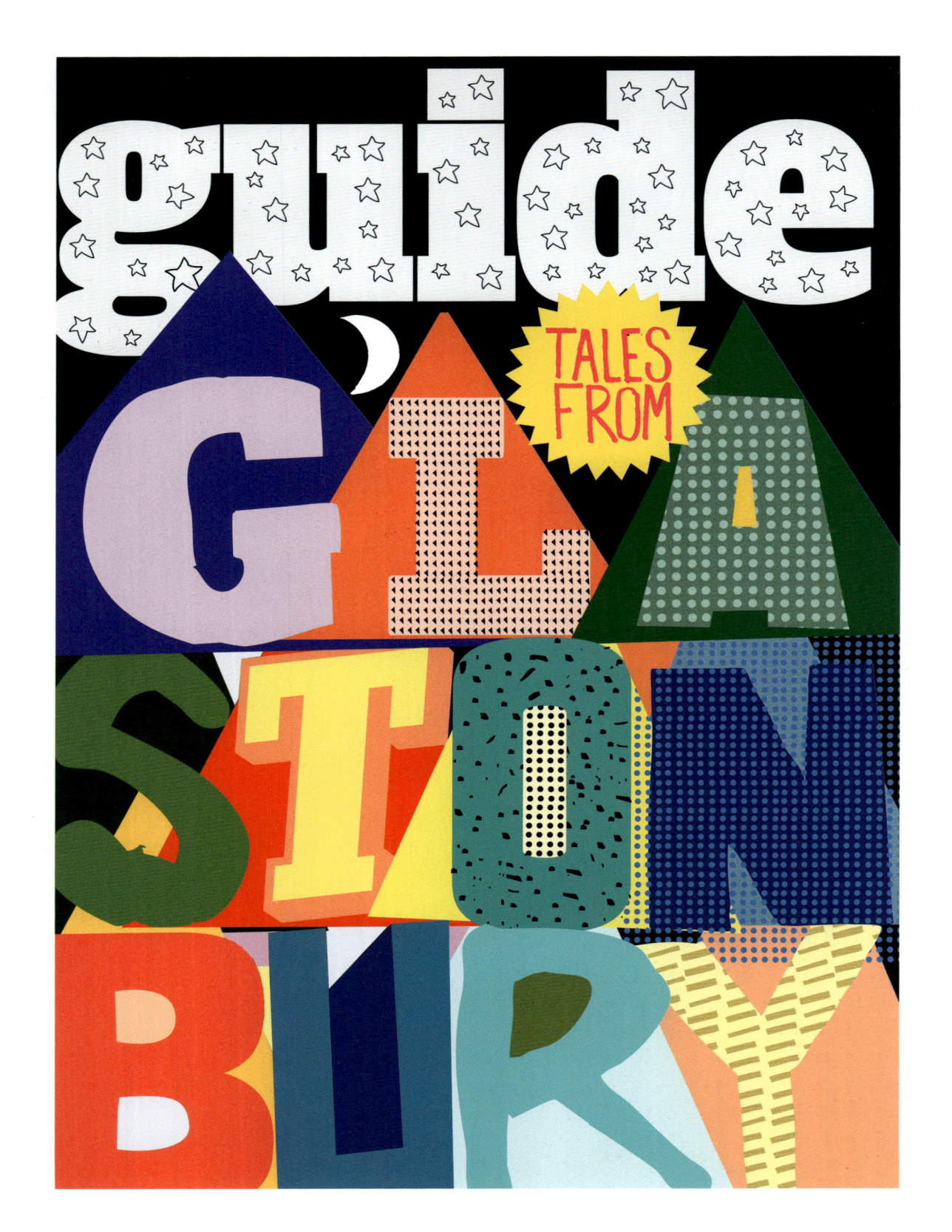

TALES FROM GLASTONBURY

7.2009

Cornershop

2009.8

Project
Pop Promo

Discipline
Illustration and Animation

In 2009, prolific band Cornershop released a fabulous album called Judy Sucks a Lemon for Breakfast. I met the singer of the band, Tjinder Singh, at our son's nursery and after some pestering, he let us animate a pop promo for their catchy song Soul School.

As we were new to animation, this was a real testing ground for us, with not just the software to conquer but also the art of storytelling.

The story describes a journey across the world that reunites the seven band members. We chose to go with illustration and montage to create this piece and utilised some great travel photos. The characters were animated over the moving collage to create a vibrant energy to match the song. It's had thousands of hits on YouTube, so we're pleased.

9.2009

2009.10

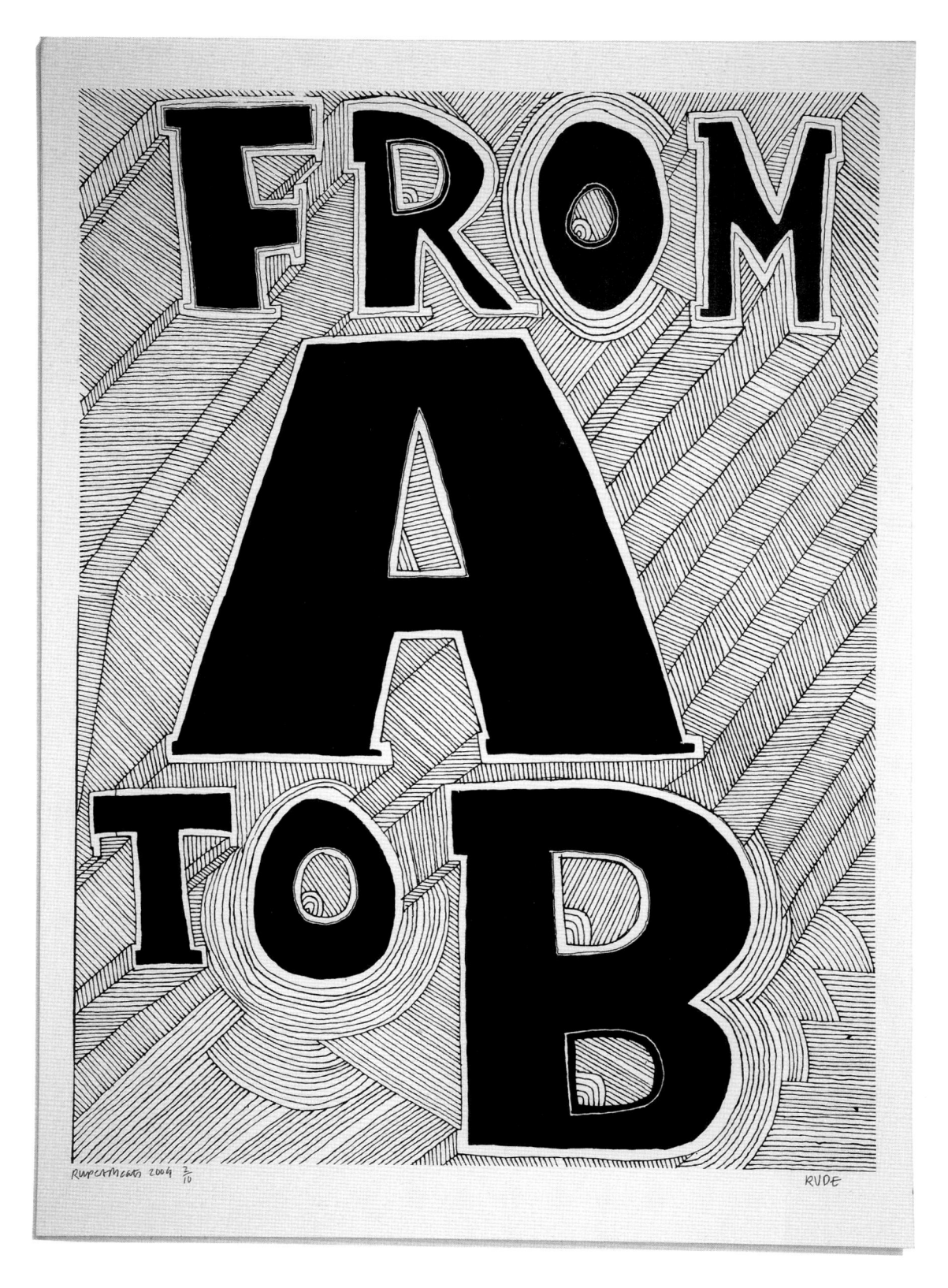

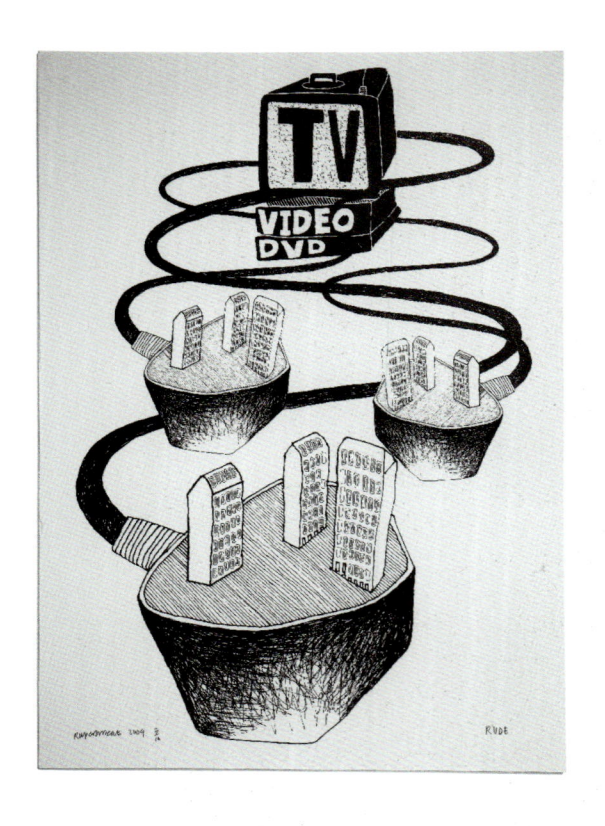

Project
Art Exhibition

Discipline
Illustration, Painting
and Montage

Putting on an art exhibition
was a real chance to get the
paints out and work in large
formats, in stark contrast to
the computer-based animation
we had been doing for so long.

We showed the work in a gallery
space in Clerkenwell called
the House of Propellers, where
we exhibited a new range of
screen prints and ten large
fine art pieces.

House of Propellers

11.2009

House of Propellers   Art Exhibition

2009.12

13.2009

2009.14

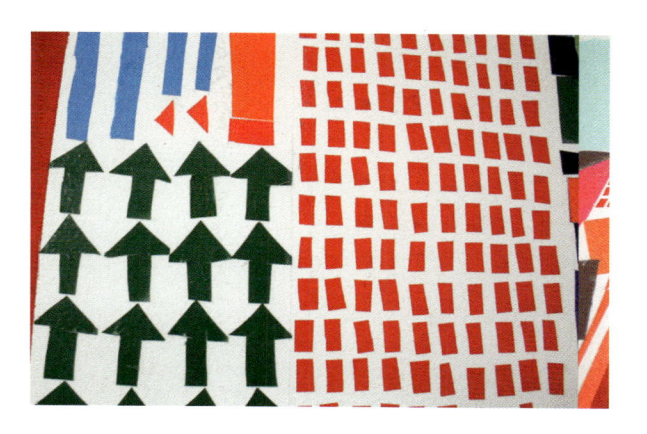

Project
Blunt Mural

Discipline
Paint and Montage

The project begun when the fabulous gang at Blunt London kindly let us experiment on their wall with our paints and tapes. A big bold Rude city would eventually burst into life behind their studio sofa.

Mural work had been a long-time ambition of ours, and this was where it began.

Blunt

15.2009

Project
Lamp Design

Discipline
Illustration

Rude are diehard fans of
Habitat, so we were delighted
when we were asked to design
a range of metal die cut lamp
shades for them.

We supplied an illustration
of a beach scene, the negative
parts of which were punched
out of sheet metal, leaving
an interconnecting image. The
metal was then dip dyed black
and formed into a lamp shade.
The light casts fantastic
shadows on the wall.

Habitat

17.2009

Island Records

Project
Music Matters

Discipline
Animation

Music Matters was a campaign created by Island Records to rail against illegal music downloads. Part of the series was a moving image piece in which Tinchy Strider sings the praises of Jay-Z. We followed his musical journey through New York and the building of Jay-Z's huge empire.

Likewise, Florence Welch talks about the inspirational Janis Joplin and the part she played in her career. Aesthetically, it was gritty in style and used rough photocopied textures set against bright spot colours.

19.2009

Vespa

Project
Video Promo

Discipline
Animation and Film

We're never ones for turning down a job riddled with innuendos, so agreed to take on this moving image piece through Canadian ad agency Denstu. Their client, Vespa were in need of some quirky content to enhance online awareness.

The agency provided us with blue screen footage of a guy on a Vespa singing 'I don't like sex anymore', as he proceeds to be chased by girls throughout. The result was funny and full on.

Graniph

Project
T-shirt Designs

Discipline
Illustration and Textiles

Graniph is a Japanese department store that collaborates with artists from all over the world. They commissioned us to create a range of images for use over various garments, including T-shirts. They organised the printing and did a great job, complete with swing tags and beautiful packaging.

21.2009

2009.22

Tate

Project
Christmas Home
and Kidswear

Discipline
Applied Graphics

After working with the Tate on numerous projects over the years, this was our first attempt at home and kidswear for them. We created a core set of repeat and placement prints based around art materials, splitting the patterns over a range of textiles, melamine, glass and limited edition artworks. The highlight of this project was having our framed screen prints hung between a Peter Blake and a Hockney - this is probably as close as we'll ever get to hanging in the Tate.

23.2009

Tate   Christmas Home
        and Kidswear

2009.24

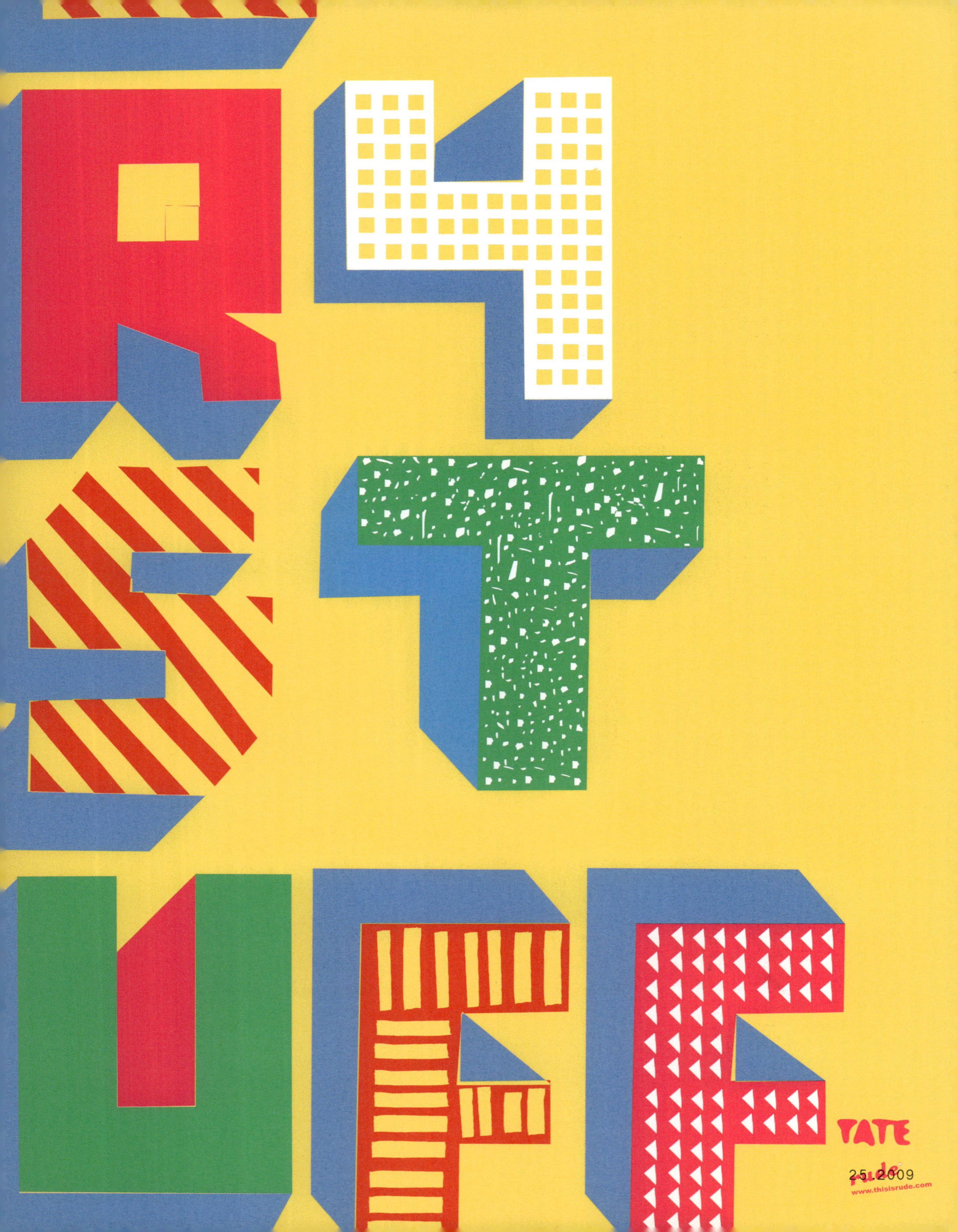
TATE
rude
www.thisisrude.com
25.2009

THIS VERY CHEAP BLEACH
100% OFF
FREE LIQUID
Only 1p
FLUSH
ALL PURPOSE
UR NOT SO FINE RANGE
CHEAP AS CHIPS
CHEAP AS CHIPS RANGE
ICING SUGAR
ONE MILLION TEA BAGS
CHEAP AS CHIPS
HORRIBLE KETCHUP
YUK
BUDGET BEANS
MARMALADE WITH CHEAP BITS
FREE
NO THANKS
GRAVY FOR CHICKEN
BASIC HANDWASH
SUPER CRAP TOOTHPASTE

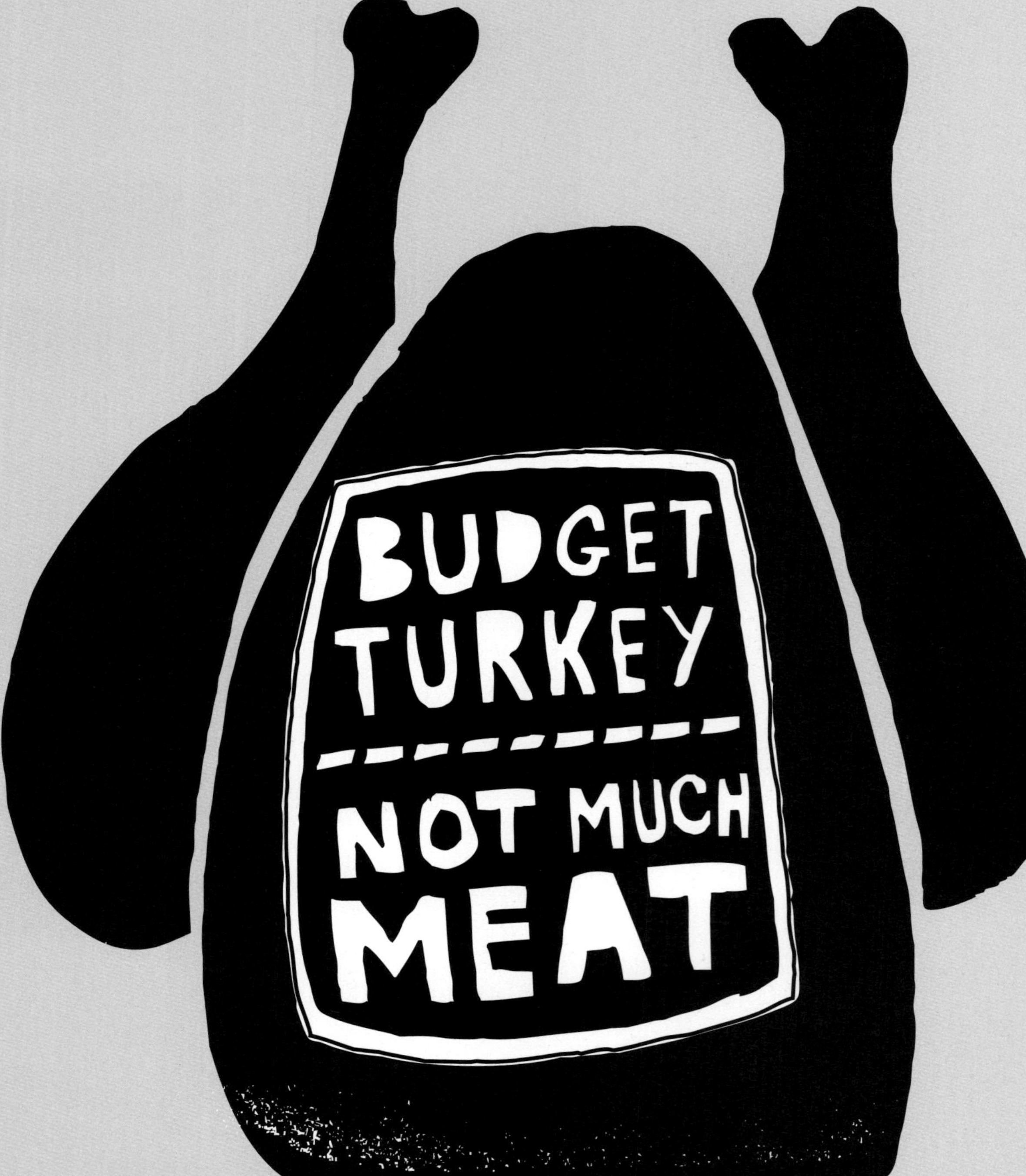
BUDGET
TURKEY
NOT MUCH
MEAT

IT'S JUST A

THE HOMIE AS TIMES

After running a shop in 2003, we began to feel the urge to create more retail environments. We embarked on a series of pop-up shops, for which we created our own bespoke product. For our Christmas shop, we took over an old Jewish dance hall, turning it into a department store selling vintage furniture and art alongside our own collections. We even made a Santa's grotto, which was great fun. We toured our shop around a series of advertising agencies, disused retail spaces and galleries.

We continued to develop our large format work and created murals in studios, on walls and in business receptions. We took lots of photographs of these artworks, later using them in moving image pieces and applying them onto product.

2010

31.2010

<u>Project</u>
Advertising

<u>Discipline</u>
Model Making

Before moving into a new arena or commiting to an idea that we haven't used for a client before, we sometimes do a self-initiated test project to check it works.

In this instance, we made 3D signage including 'Dinner in the Bin' and 'Home is Where Your Stuff Is'. Rupert hand drew various household electrical items and we assembled them into a photograph that our friend Luke Kirwan shot for us.

Eventually, we'd take this idea further down the line in a video we would make for Manchester International Festival. It all gets used eventually.

Rude

2010.32

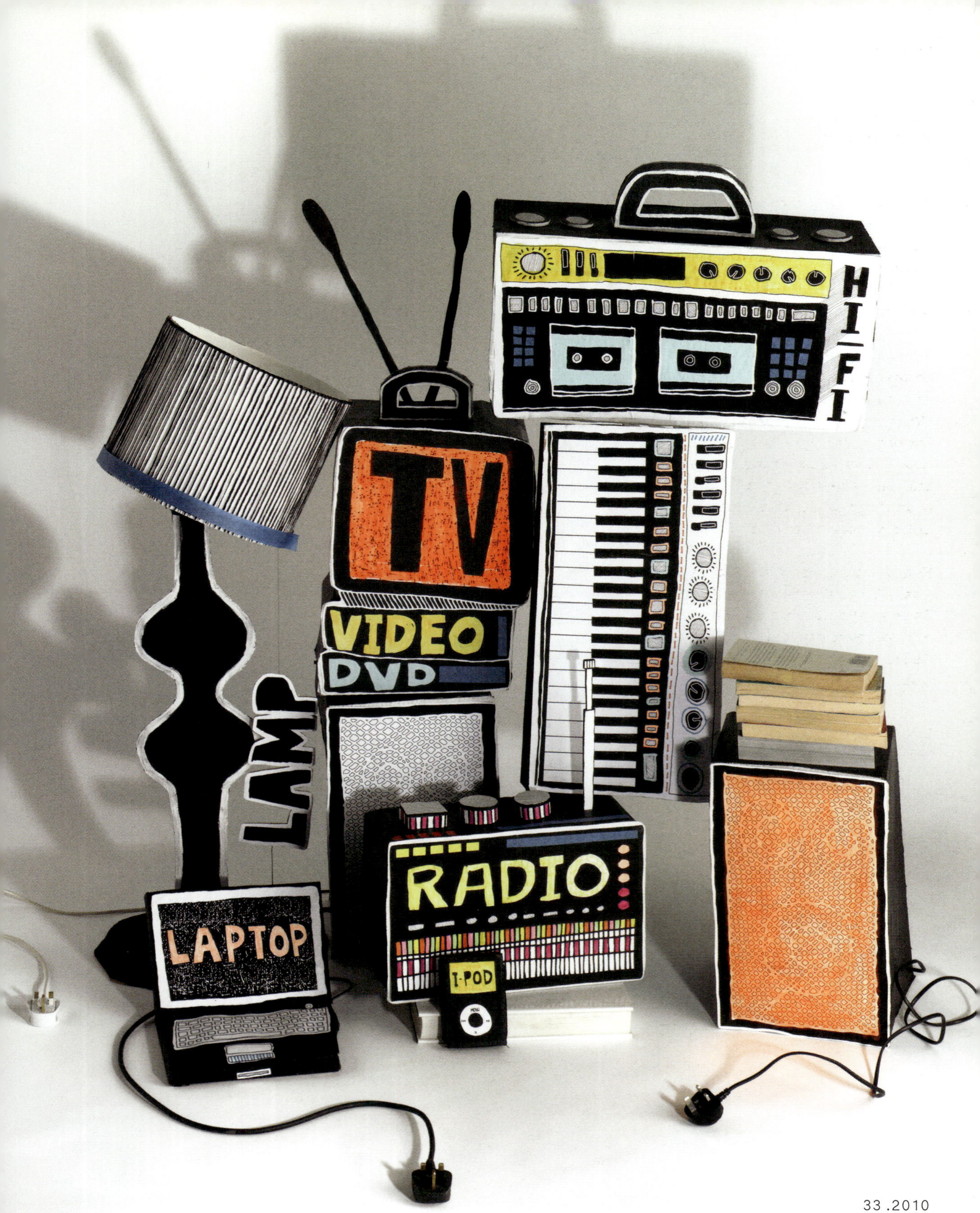
HI-FI
TV
VIDEO
DVD
LAMP
RADIO
LAPTOP
I-POD

Rude   Advertising

2010.34

35.2010

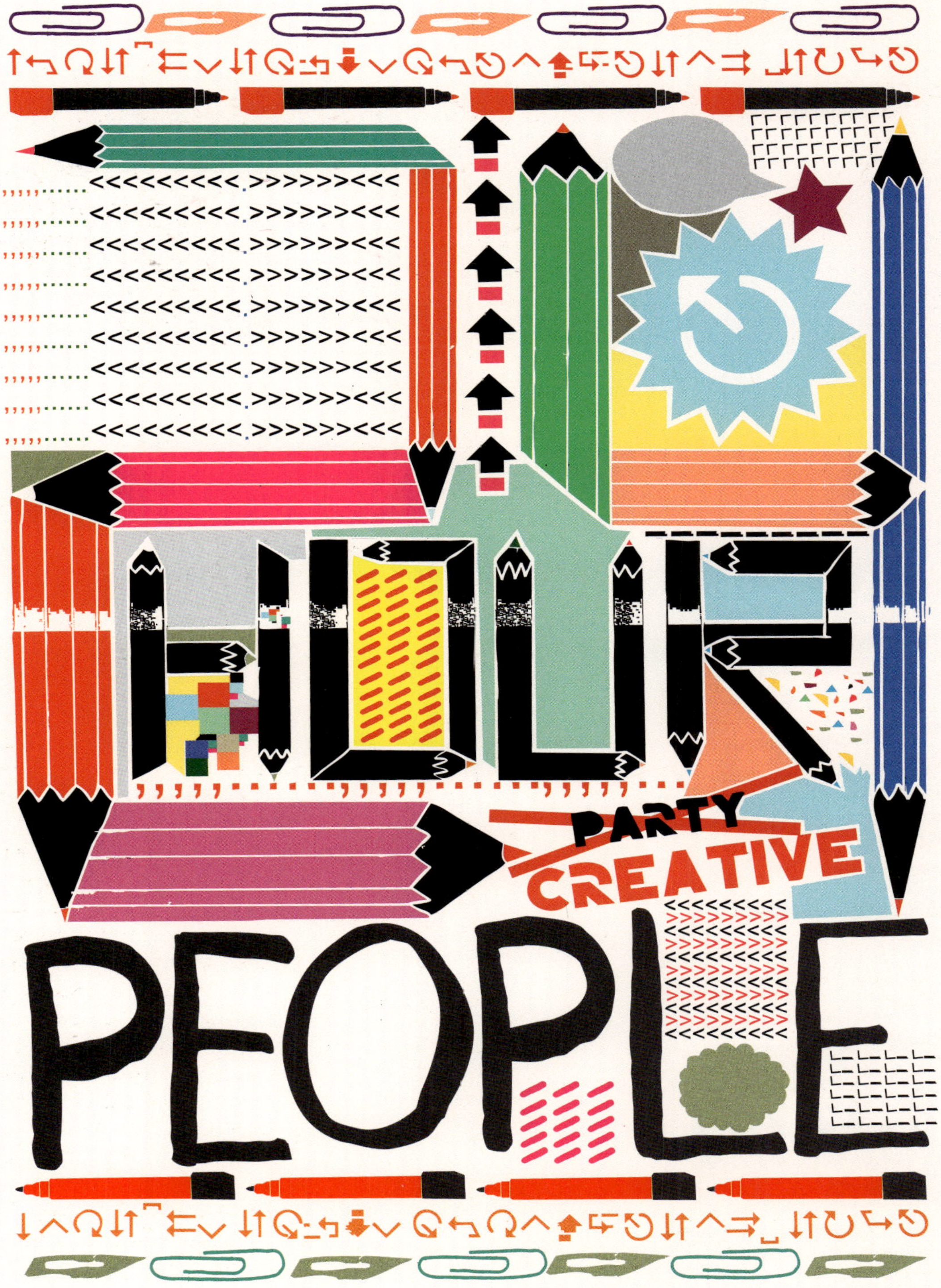

2010.36

Project
Editorial

Discipline
Illustration

Oh Comely

Oh Comely Magazine is a gorgeous arts and crafts based publication, produced with women in mind but open and inclusive to men also. They devote themselves to the artists, brands and outsiders that they deem worthy of talking about and also commission fantastic illustrations and photography. We were delighted to be commissioned for a piece called '24 Hour Creative People', which described the almost obsessive and consuming nature of creativity, something we instantly related to.

Project
The Great Indoors

Discipline
Illustration

The Great Indoors was an annual event held in the stunning surroundings of Manchester Town Hall.

Part of Manchester International Festival, the free event was aimed at children from three to eleven, and hosted fantastic international performances alongside arts and crafts for children. Rude created the poster to advertise the event, with the same image used as press ads. Large poster formats were found around Manchester and the North West of England.

Manchester International Festival

2010.38

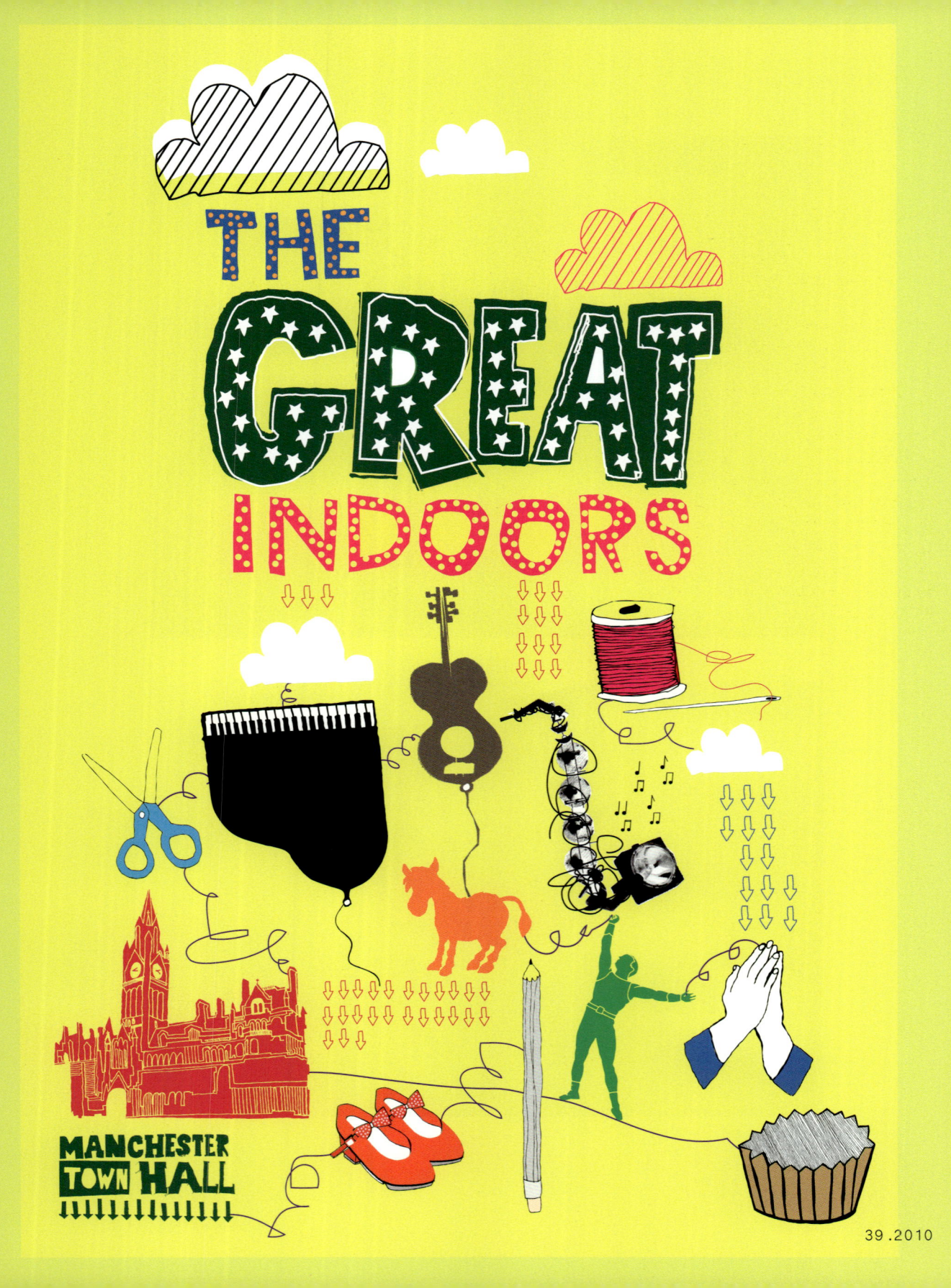

THE GREAT INDOORS

MANCHESTER TOWN HALL

39.2010

2010.40

Project
This is Now Mural

Discipline
Paint and Illustration

Root

London design agency Root asked us to create some artwork for their new identity. The illustration was used for a set of limited edition prints, their website and a mural in their reception. Made from tape, paint and marker pens, the mural looked great in black and white.

Picador

Project
Viral Book Promo

Discipline
Moving Image

In 2010, acclaimed Australian author Tim Winton released a novel entitled Breath, through his publisher Picador. Tim draws his prime inspiration from landscape and place, mainly coastal western Australia and this was set in the surfing fraternity of the seventies.

Rude provided some rich online content for their marketing department. Filmed on Super 8 in Sydney, the footage was re-shot through a projector with plenty of dust and scratches included and anything that didn't look like it was from the seventies omitted. The outcome was an authentic looking three minute piece with layered type and Kodachrome colour.

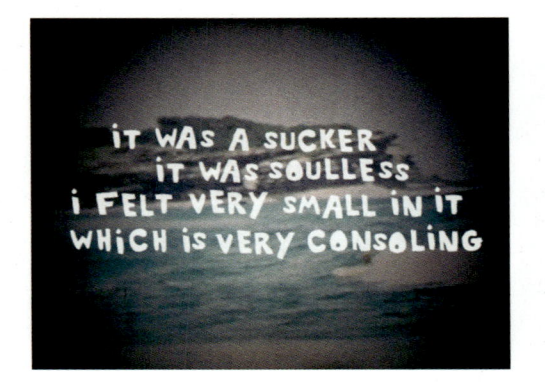

it was a sucker
it was soulless
i felt very small in it
which is very consoling

i could walk away
with a surf board
under my arm and
know i hadn't
wrecked it
or left any
marks on it

...uld harness its p...
and sail on it,
swim in it
or surf it

i don't know if
the sea felt any better
but i certainly did

43.2010

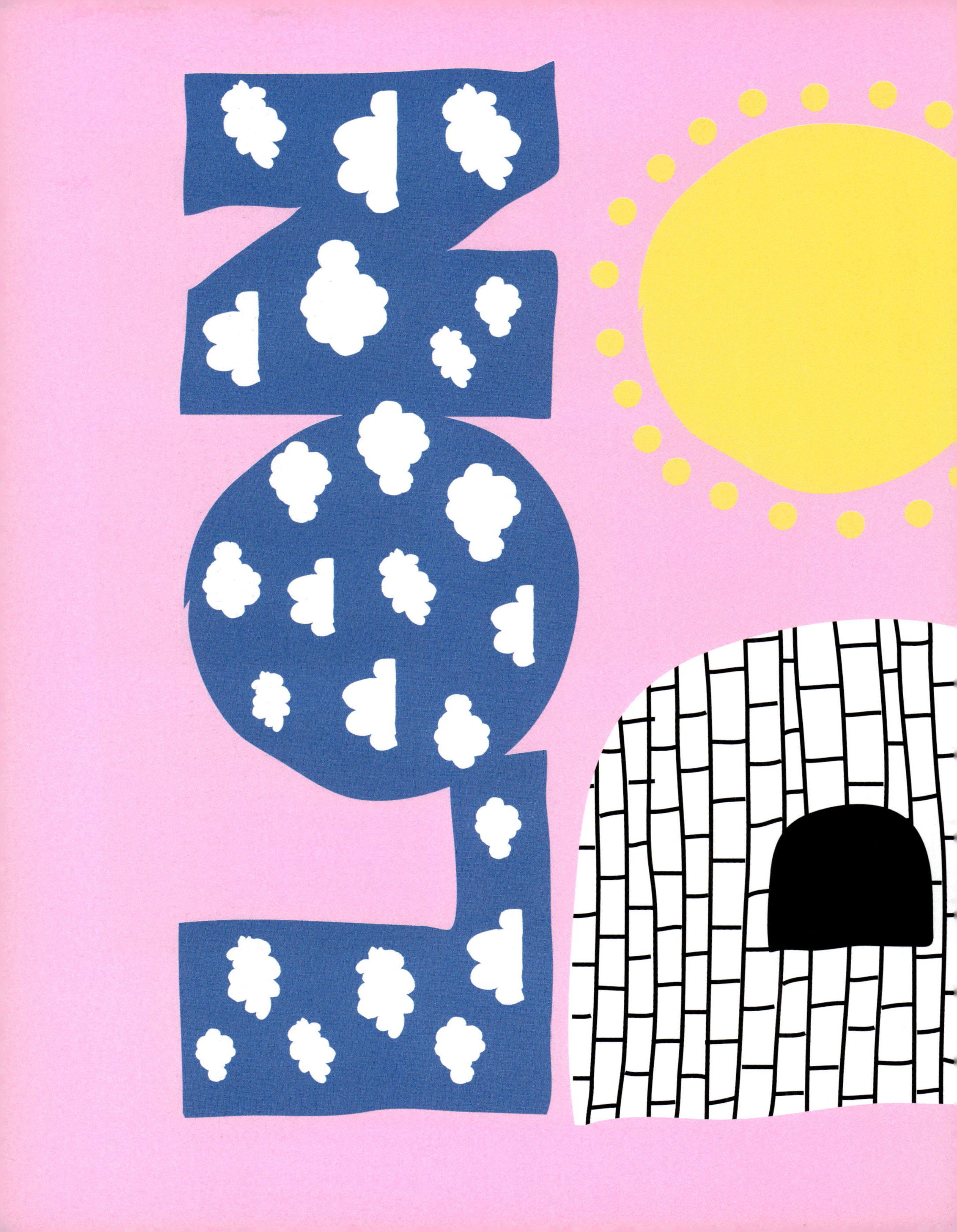

N

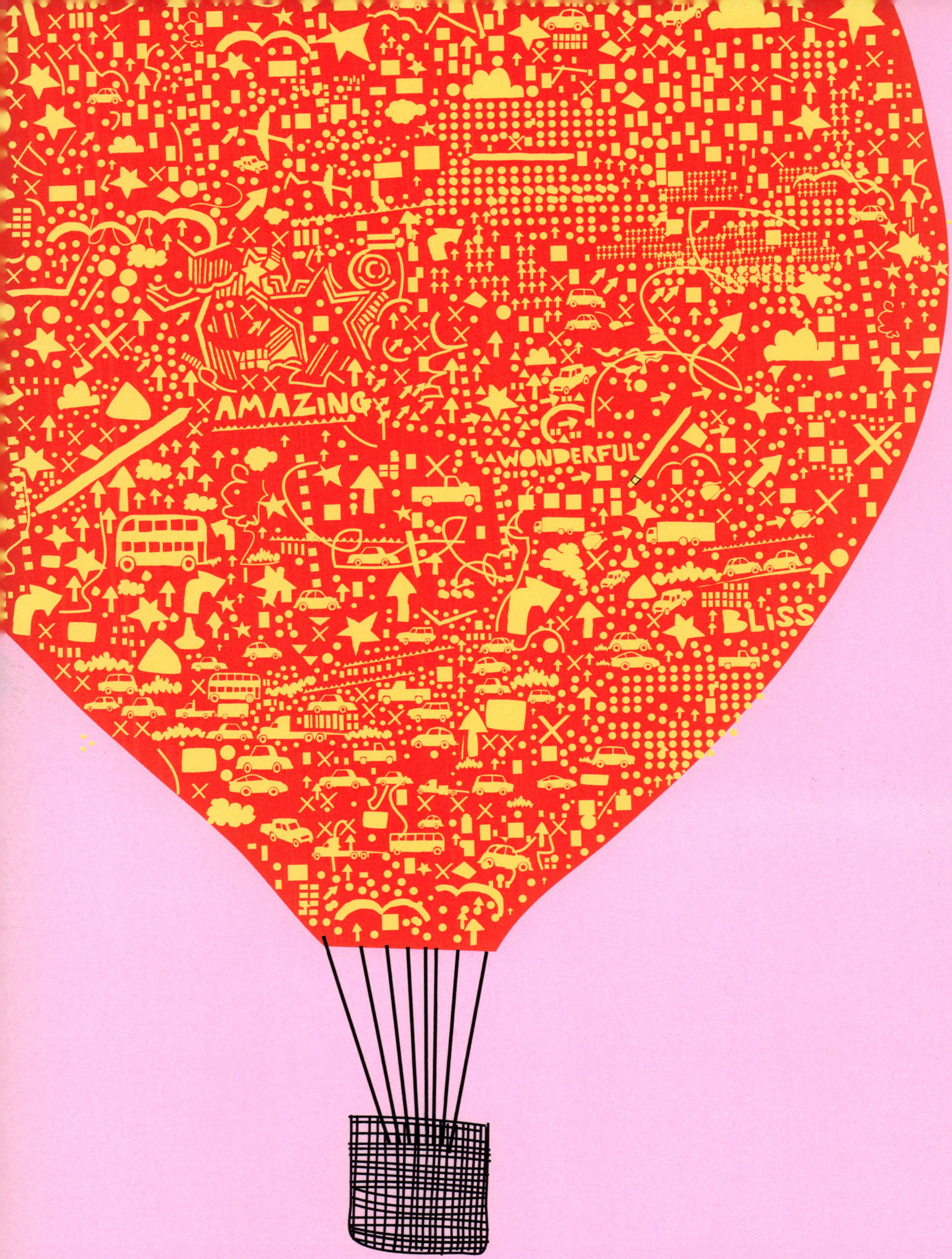
AMAZING
WONDERFUL
BLISS

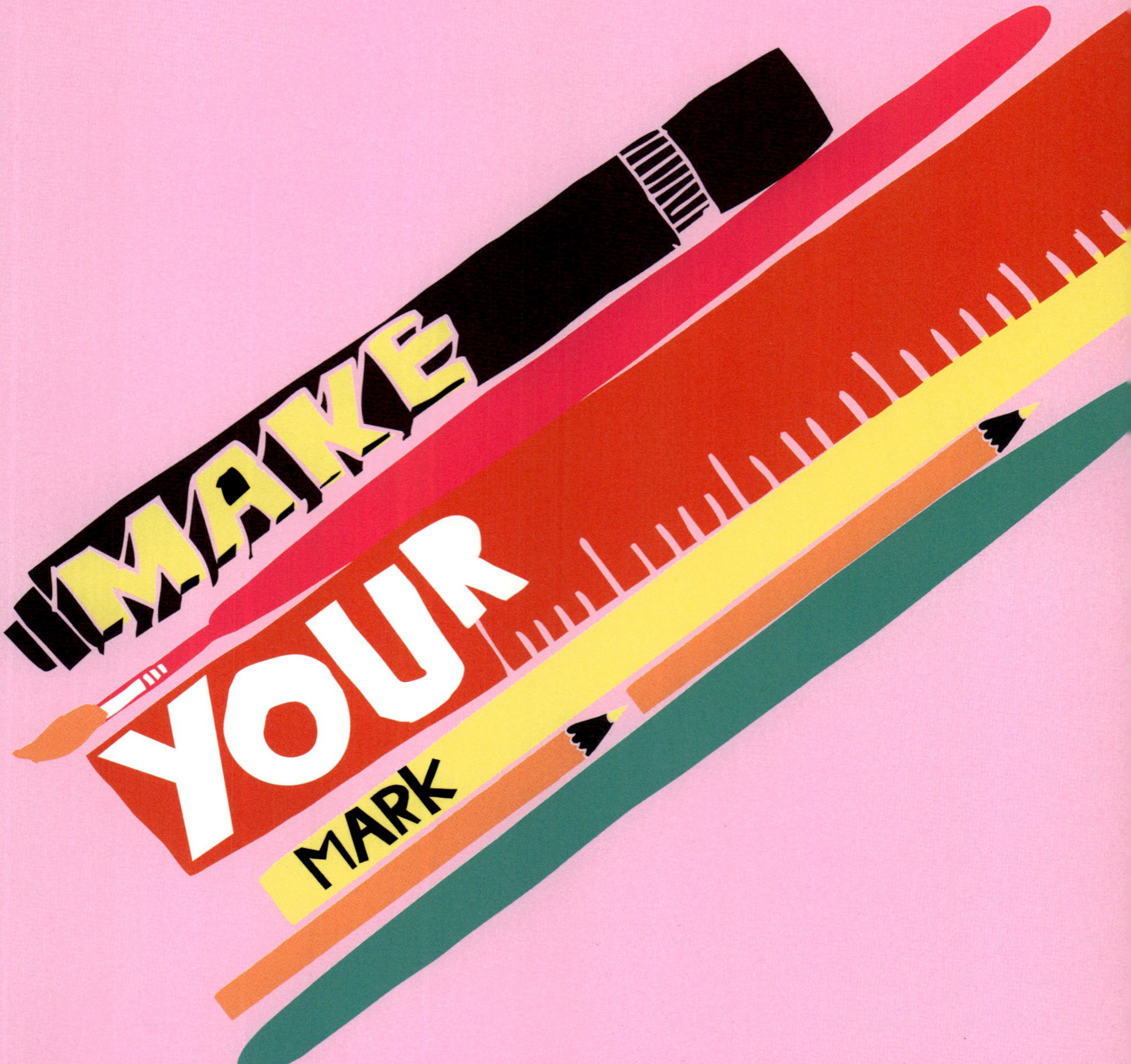
MAKE
YOUR
MARK

This was a year bursting with productivity. We were busy with our paints and markers, pushing and refining our illustration style and picking up some nice new clients.

It was also a year of experimental design, when we worked with schools and held animation workshops. A more permanent move into designing was made, as well as producing collections for museum-based clients and own brand labels.

Our factory database was expanded for production purposes and Rude started to investigate the world of licensing.

2 0
1 1

49.2011

Hodder Publishing

Project
Book Cover

Discipline
Illustration

In 2011, Hodder Publishing commissioned book covers for two of their new titles.

The first was NIV Soul Survivor Bible in One Year, a condensed version of the bible crammed into one year. Aimed at teens, it breaks the text down into sizeable chunks that are to be read each day. Our brief was to portray a contemporary take on the Bible to appeal to younger readers who might not have accessed religion before.

Signs of Life was written by twenty-four-year-old Natalie Taylor who had a fulfilling job, a wonderful husband, a new house and a baby on the way. This all changes when she gets the news that her husband has died in a freak accident, four months before the birth of her son. This true story describes a journey of loss, grief, motherhood and new-found friends, some of the essence of which we tried to capture on the front cover.

2011.50

NEW INTERNATIONAL VERSION
BIBLE
in ONE YEAR

51.2011

Kay and Dave Buchan

Project
Wedding Invite

Discipline
Eight Colour Screen prints

When our great friends Kay
and Dave asked us to design
and illustrate the invites
to their French wedding,
we were honoured.

We created an intricate eight
colour screen printed poster
that was produced by London-
based printers Eight Bob Bit.

The posters were rich
in colour, with the
illustrations featuring
K's and D's along with
lots of 3D lettering,
shading and detailing.

2011.52

2010
CELEBRER
AVEC
NOUS
K et D
au
Chateau de Lartigolle
28-29 août

53 .2011

MUSIC BOXES

FREE!

Manchester International Festival

Project
Music Boxes Poster

Discipline
Illustration and Graphics

Manchester International Festival (MIF) is a wonderful organisation that brings together a cultural fusion of live music, theatre and literary events taking place all over the city, every year.

We had worked previously with MIF, but this time they commissioned us to design the branding and poster for a new kid's event called Music Boxes. The concept was to build an interactive music-based experience outside the BBC centre in Salford. The construction was made from shipping containers, piled on top of each other.

Each Music Box had an experience inside, from an orchestra that you conducted yourself, to a Zingzillas production by the BBC.

Rude was also asked to create an experience and a pop video, which are shown on the following pages.
The poster itself was a montage-based piece with black and white images of children, musical props and instruments. The artwork was used over printed literature, posters, banners and buses.

Project
What Did the Hippie Have in His Bag?

Discipline
Animation

As part of the Music Boxes experience, Rude were asked to hold a workshop at Castle Hill School in Bolton, where we taught an animation class to year one. We teamed up with Tjinder from cult band Cornershop who held a lyric workshop at the same time.

The outcome was a fantastic song called 'What Did the Hippie Have in His Bag' that Tjinder and the children wrote and recorded together.

Next, Rude helped the children make a huge hippie from recycled objects, like eggboxes, buttons, wool and card. The hippie was held together with hinge pins that formed his joints and allowed us to create some stop frame animation with him.

Once we had gathered all the elements to make the animation, we went back to the studio to put the video together in Flash. The result is a really fun, bright promo, which we adapted into a desktop interactive app, ready for use at the Music Box experience.

Manchester International Festival

OK

YEAH

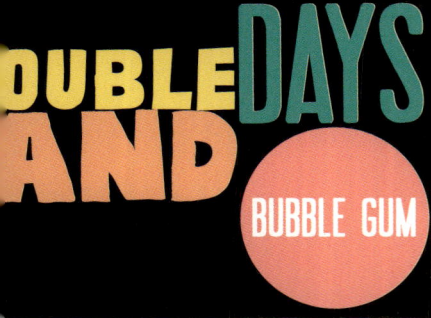

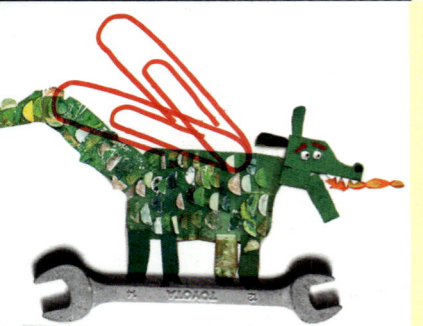

WHAT DID THE hippy HAVE IN HIS BAG?

DUBLE DAYS AND BUBBLE GUM

MARMALADE JAM FRESH OUT THE CAN

HOW THE STORY UNFOLDS

STEREO

WHAT DID THE hippie HAVE IN HIS BAG?

CRAYONS CRAYONS CRAYONS CRAYONS CRAYONS CRAYONS

pop'o'motion

MARMALADE JAM

57.2011

NATIONAL THEATRE

2011.58

National Theatre

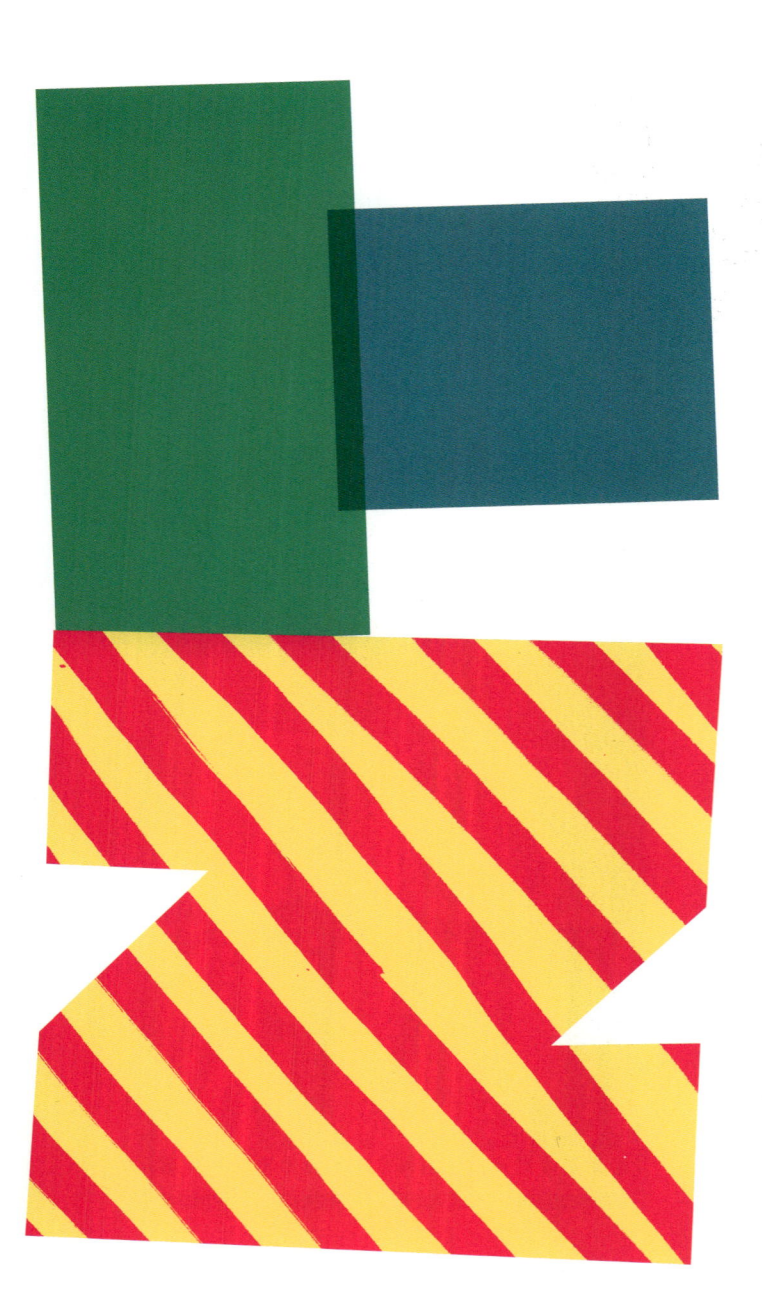

Project
In-store Merchandise

Discipline
Illustration and Product Range

This project started when we received a call from the art buyer at the National Theatre who wanted to buy a print for herself. We cheekily turned this opportunity into a portfolio showing, which in turn led to us picking up a lovely job. We started with some in-store T-shirts and merchandise which extended to staff uniforms and a range of greetings cards. The product sold well and the relationship led on to a variety of projects.

The graphics included theatre related slogans such as 'Break a leg' and 'Learn your lines'.

59.2011

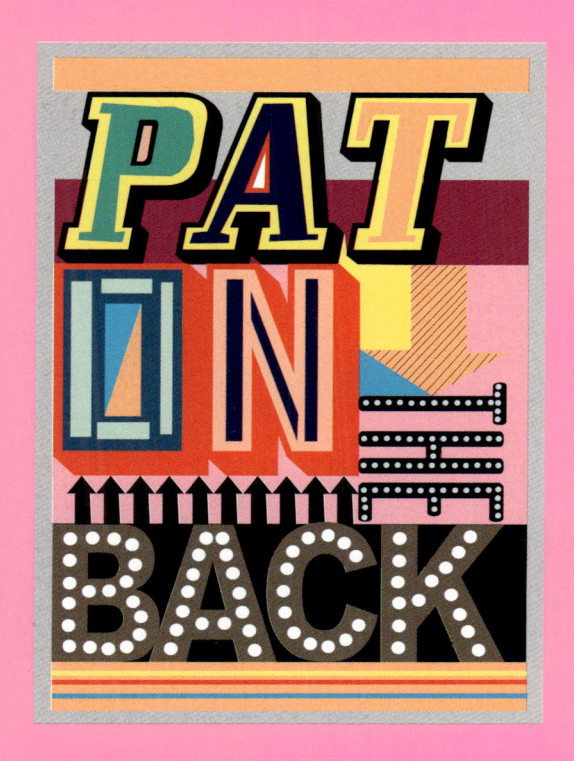

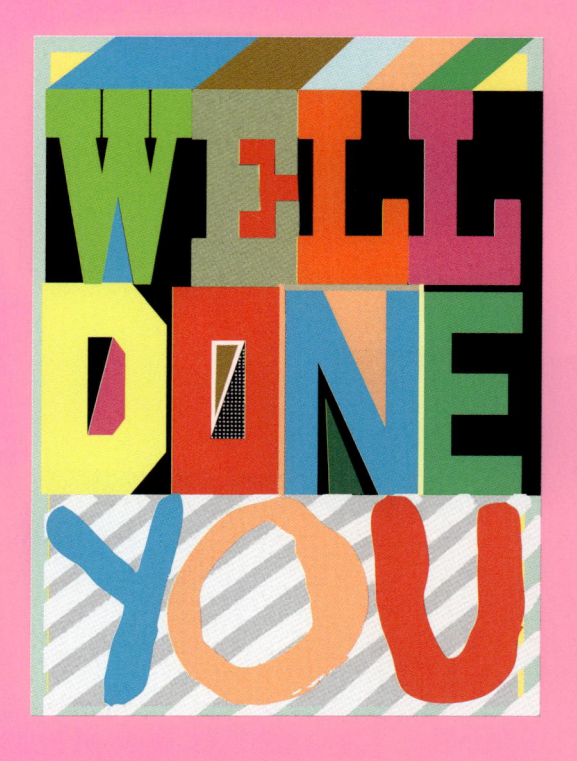

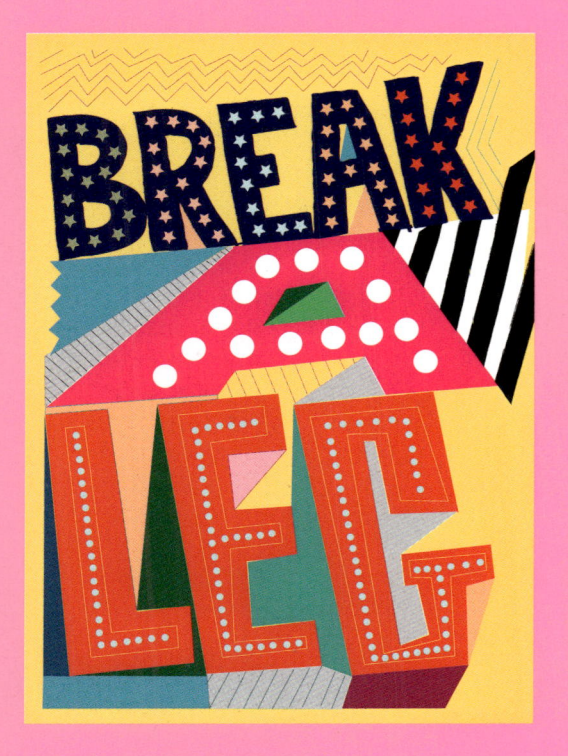

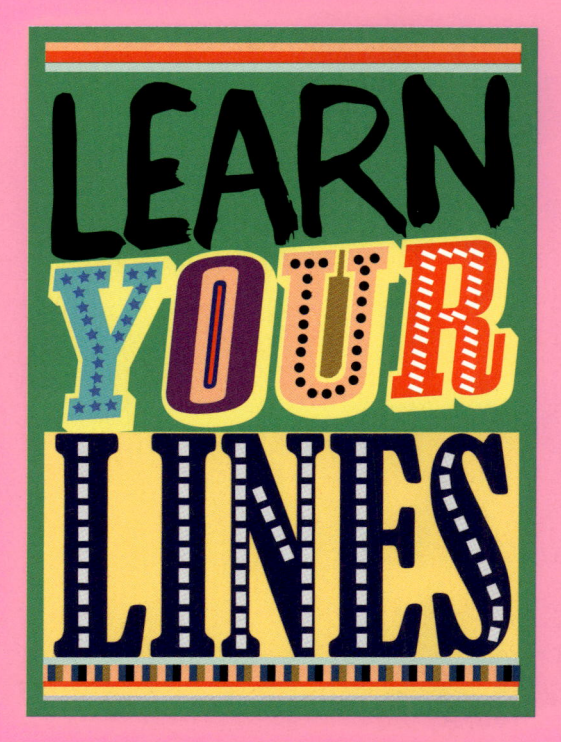

National Theatre — In-store Merchandise

2011.60

61.2011

Project
One Man, Two Guvnors
Merchandise

Discipline
Illustration and
Product Range

One Man, Two Guvnors is a show of great acclaim, originally starring James Corden at the National Theatre before moving to the West End. The production is based on a play by Richard Bean and is an English adaptation of Servant of Two Masters, a Venetian comedy penned in 1743.

The NT commissioned Rude to produce a typographic print based around dialogue from the show and apply it across a collection of merchandise.

National Theatre

2011.62

OCK & CHIPS
D MUSHY
S! A PUB THAT
↑ ONE ↓
AN,
GUVNORS
THE CRICKETERS' ARMS

63.2011

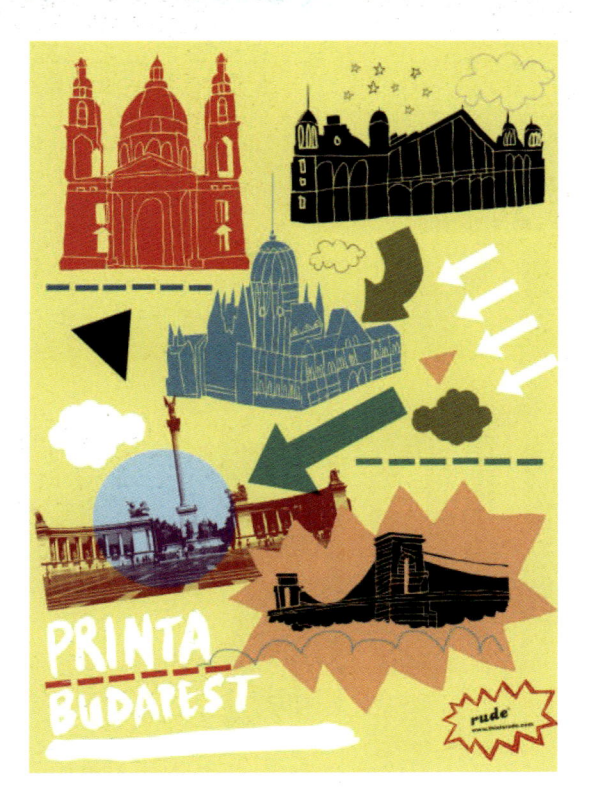

Project
Print Exhibition

Discipline
Illustration

Printa is a screen printing shop and gallery in the heart of Budapest, run by enthusiastic owners Claudia Martins and Zita Majaros. Printa's business model invites artists to submit work which is printed on the premises and then exhibited.

To this end, Rude created a new body of work based around the city of Budapest. It was a good opportunity to experiment with new illustration ideas and move our style on. We were delighted with the results and Printa went on to sell the limited edition screen prints.

Printa

65.201

Printa   Print Exhibition

2011.66

67.2011

Project
House of Cards Poster

Discipline
Illustration

Shelter is a brilliant charity that has been raising money and awareness for the homeless for many years. To help fundraise, their advertising agency Leo Burnett came up with an idea to auction off unique artworks at a celebrity endorsed event at the Royal Academy.

The project was called House of Cards and they invited famous artists like the Chapman Brothers to create original art on playing cards.

To publicise the event, Rude was asked to draw the poster in a live environment, while being filmed for the online promotion. The original set of posters were exhibited outside the Royal Academy and reproduced for advertising purposes.

Shelter

Rimmel

Project
Advertising Campaign

Discipline
Illustration

We got this call when our illustration agent Blunt was briefed by advertising agency J. Walter Thompson; their client, Rimmel, needed a painting in gloss pinks and reds to advertise a new nail polish range. The painting was created as a large canvas which was photographed and reproduced for Rimmel's latest advertising campaign.

GREEK ISLANDS

HOW to AVOID HUGE SHIPS

LONDON A-Z

HOW TO COOK WHEN NAKED

WORLD ATLAS.

The Book of MARMALADE

ALWAYS LOOK ON THE BRIGHT SIDE OF LIFE

NEVER JUDGE A BOOK BY IT'S COVER

Think and Grow Rich

Never Ending Story

JOY OF STATIONERY

LIFE... EVERYTHING you NEED TO KNOW

It's GREAT TO BE ME

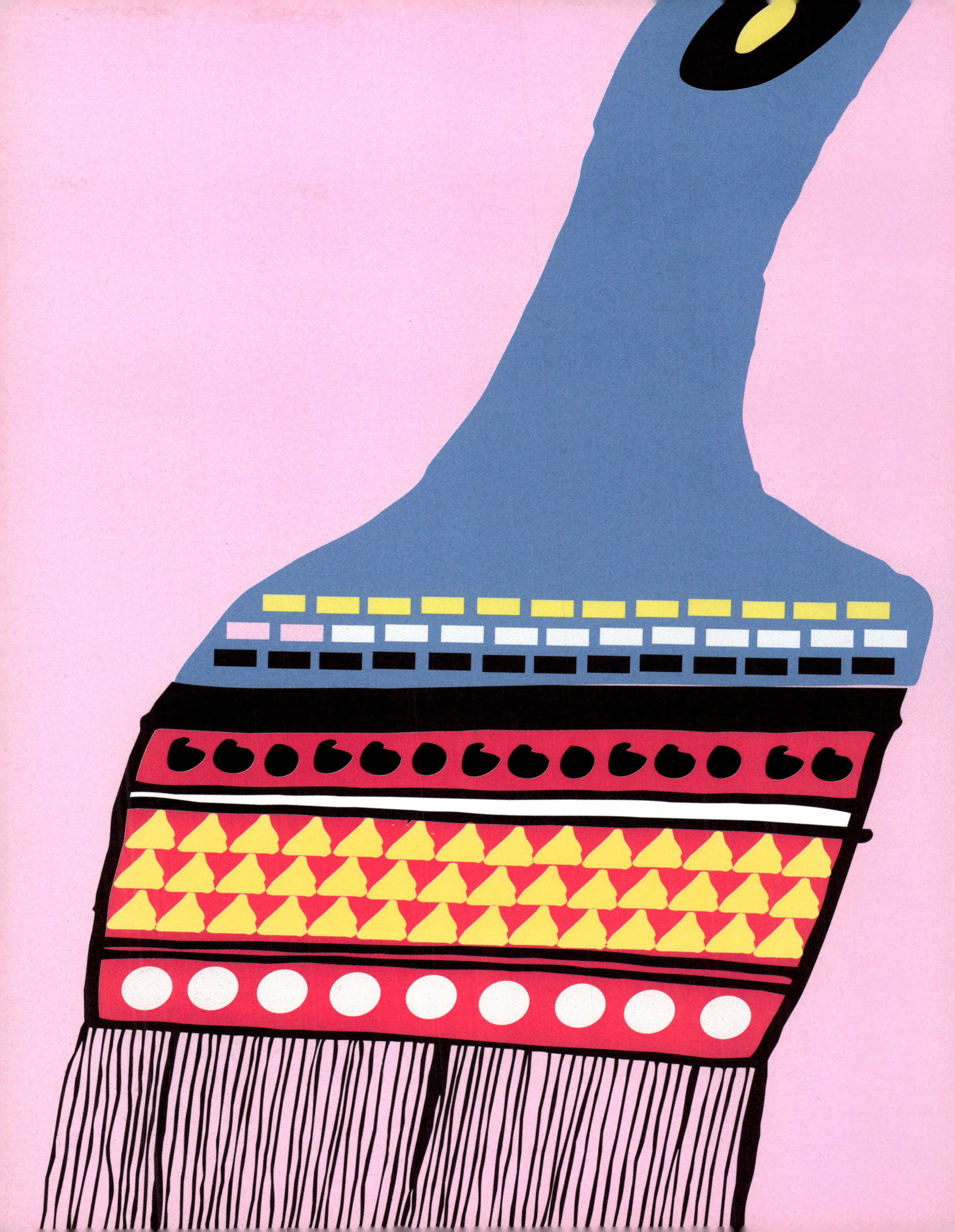

YOU'RE ALWAYS ON mind.

NIC

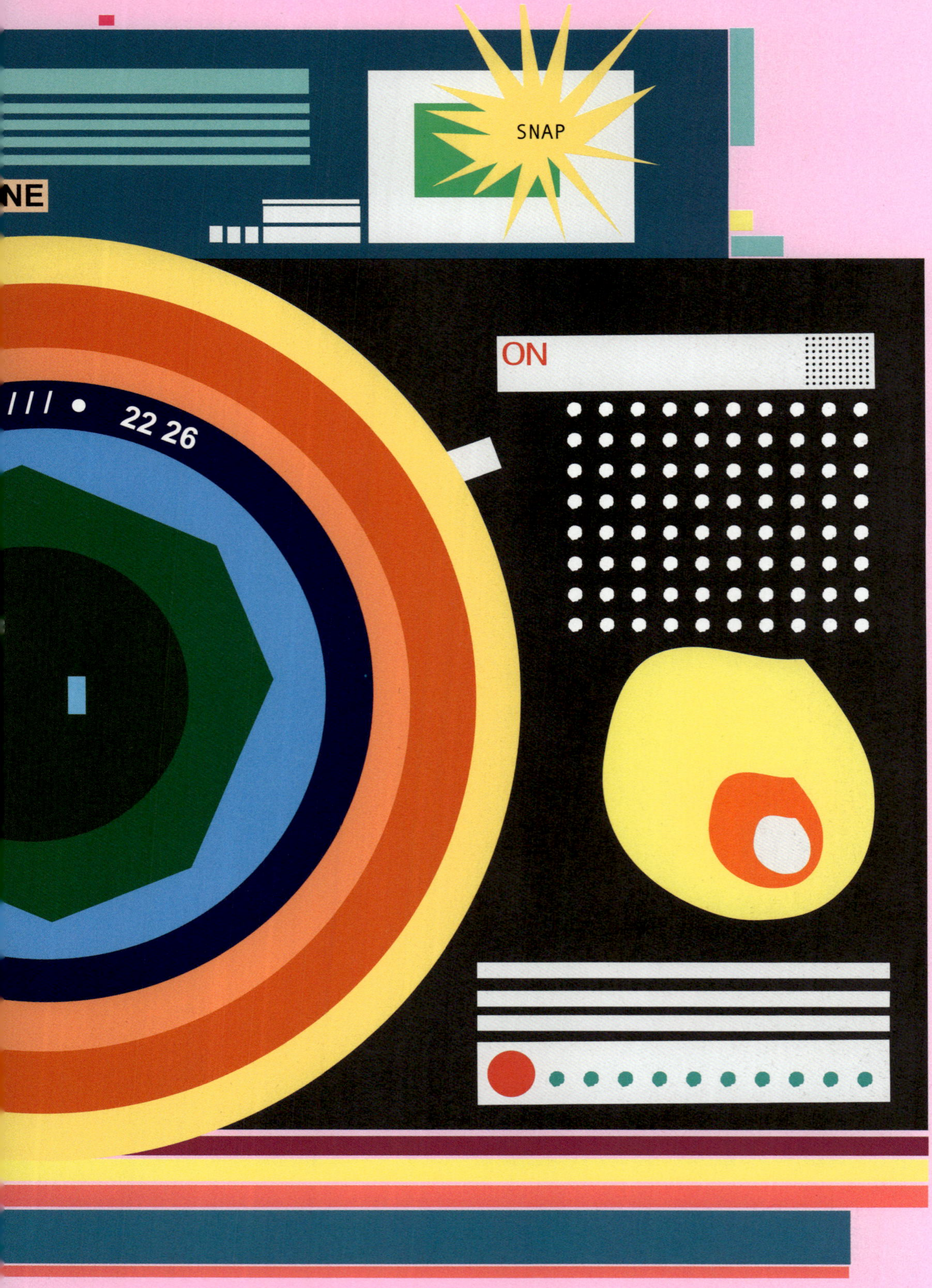
SNAP
NE
ON
22 26

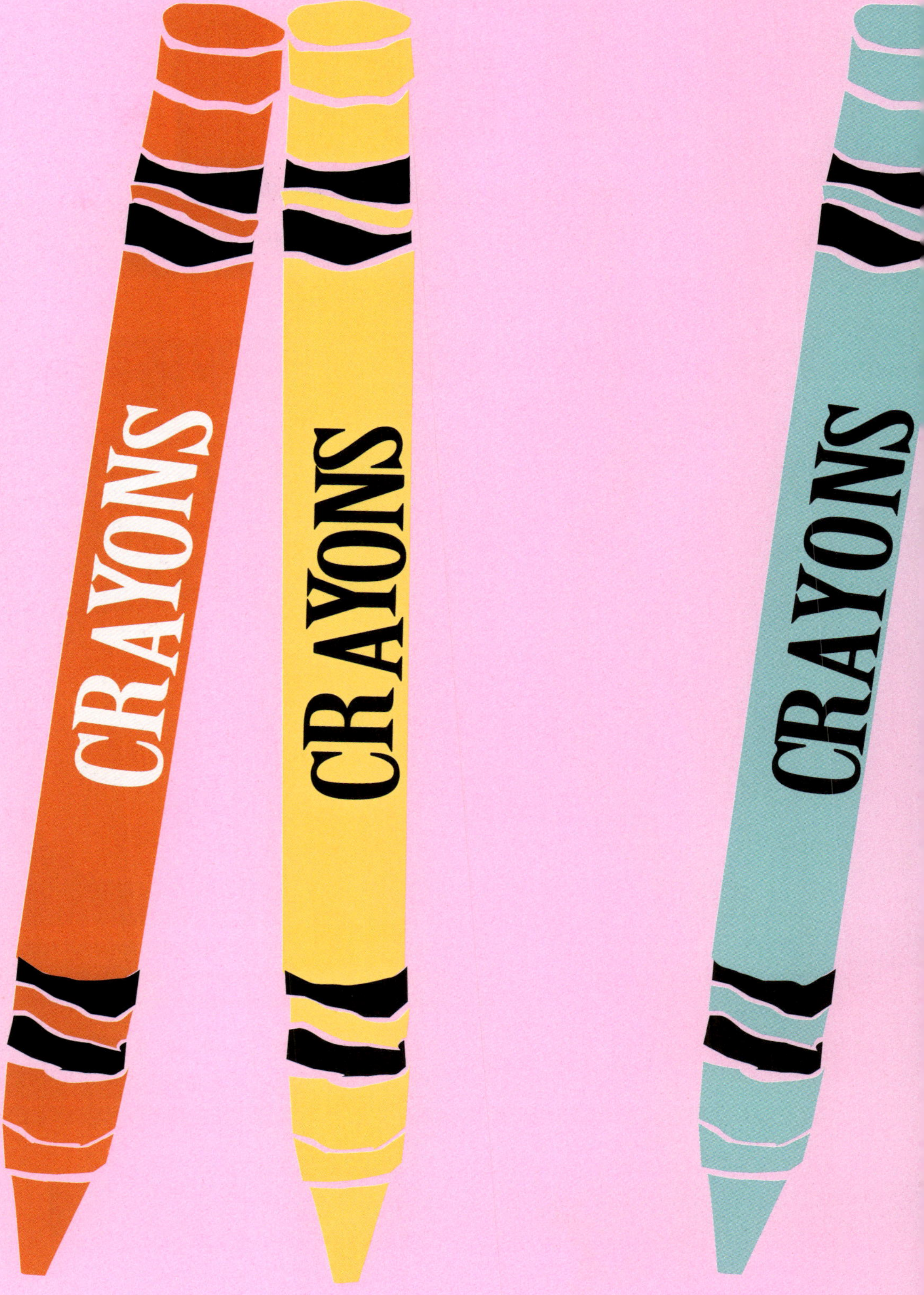
CRAYONS
CRAYONS
CRAYONS

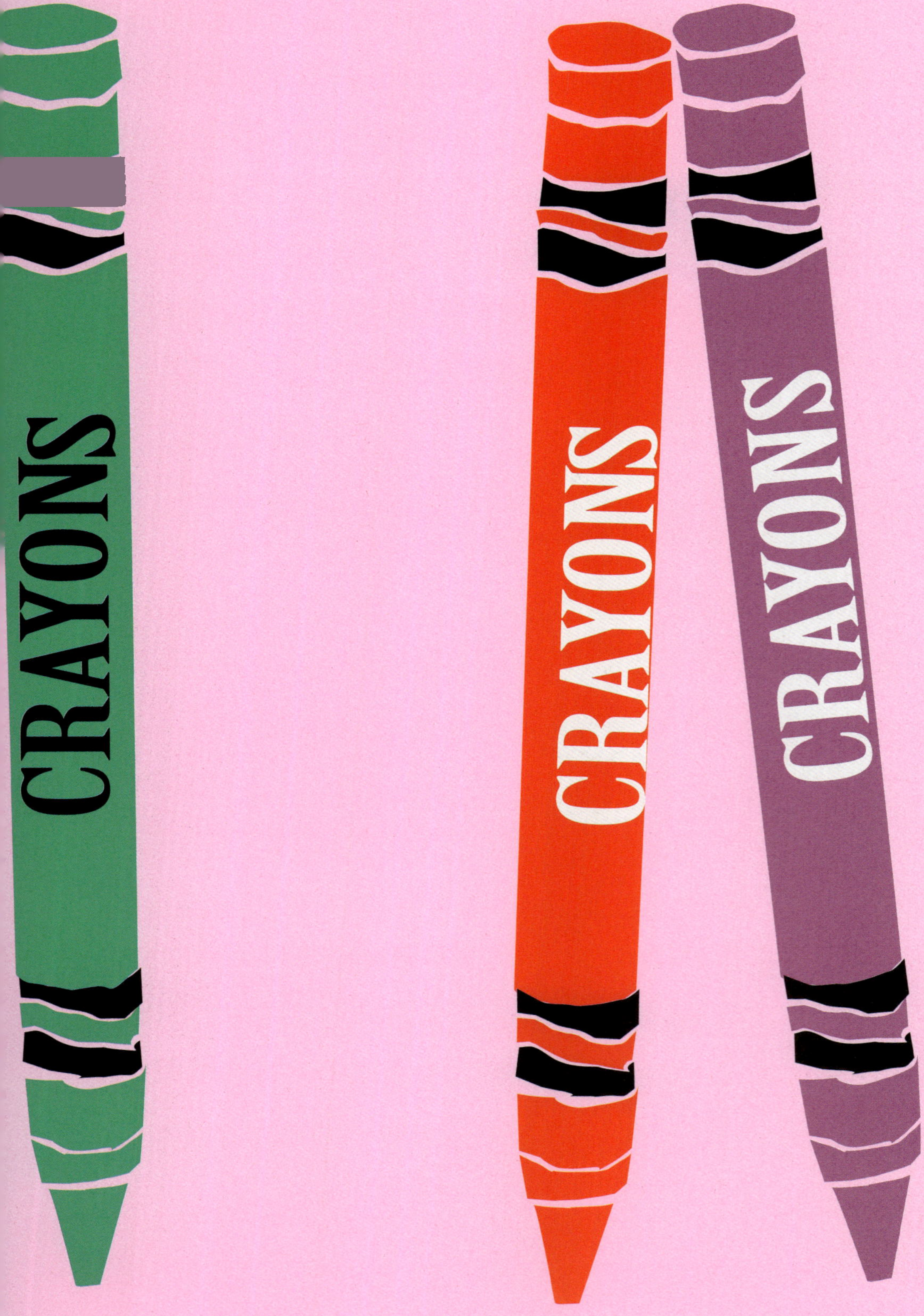
CRAYONS
CRAYONS
CRAYONS

In times of difficult trading on the high street, museum shops always seemed to prosper. By playing to their niche audiences who wanted tokens of their experience, the buyers were creating bespoke product to accompany their exhibitions. By working with designer makers like Rude, they were able to create reactive collections and refreshed product on an ongoing basis.

Licensees were also moving in a similar direction by looking at clever ways of expanding the life span of their brands and reinvigorating tired approaches.

Rather than creating product that looked like merchandise, there was a need to design and produce high quality branded collections that approached fans and non-fans alike. This was the direction that Rude would take this year.

2012.78

2012

79.2012

Project
Doctor Who Homeware Collection

Discipline
Textiles, Ceramics and Illustration

The BBC's ever popular sci-fi show Doctor Who was turning 50 in 2013. To mark the occasion we were commissioned to design and produce a homeware collection celebrating its longevity and appeal across all ages and genders.

Working alongside licensing specialists Skew, we researched, designed and manufactured a ceramic, textile and stationery range.

The challenge was to appeal to the fan (or 'Whovian') and non-fan simultaneously. Our consumer research told us that everyone in the UK was familiar with Doctor Who, even if they didn't watch the show.

The concept was to treat the iconic imagery in a contemporary way, with the focus on attracting a design savvy audience that wouldn't normally associate themselves with the show. The range was launched at a trade show aimed at high end gift and homeware stores and the result was a very well received collection, selling to a wide mix of retailers.

BBC

81.2012

2012.82

ITV

Project
Thunderbirds
Menswear Collection

Discipline
Graphics

'Brains' was the name we gave to the menswear and accessory label we created for ITV's Thunderbirds later this year.

Our inspiration came from the geeky scientist of the same name, created by Gerry and Sylvia Anderson in the 1960s. We imagined that Brains had devised the collection around his needs, like the T-shirt with a long test tube shaped pocket that he could pop his glasses into.

Although we used some graphics of Brains himself, we wanted the collection to be more subversive and based around his precise nature. Rude curated the whole project, covering all aspects needed for a successful launch.

This included the design and manufacture of the collection, a viral film and lookbook, press day attendance and an e-commerce site to sell direct to consumers. The label had immediate lift off and sold out at selected stores.

83 .2012

ITV Thunderbirds
Menswear Collection

2012.84

85.2012

AMV

Project
Plan Charity Booklet

Discipline
Illustration and
Printed Literature

One in three girls around the world is denied an education by the daily realities of poverty, conflict and discrimination. In 2012, the Because I am a Girl campaign was launched by Plan, a global childreen's charity, to enable girls to get the education they need.

Plan's advertising agency AMV commissioned this beautifully produced booklet, requesting that the illustrations suggested a naivety that conveys the vulnerability of the subject matter.

2012.86

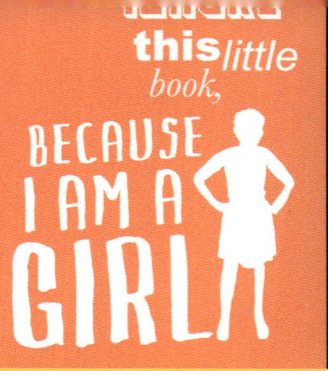

this little book,
BECAUSE I AM A GIRL

Er Excuse me I'm over here

YES YOU

Disadvantage

Project
Children's
Merchandise

Discipline
Illustration, Apparel
and Accessories

This was also the year in which London's Science Museum gave us a cracking brief to design and produce a range of products to encourage children and parents to get involved with science.

Rude has an inherent love for test tubes, litmus paper and petri dishes, so we got straight to work on some science lab repeat prints.

T-shirts, pin badges, notebooks, Oyster wallets and tote bags all bore the slogans 'What goes up must come down' and 'Great minds think a lot'.

Science Museum

2012.88

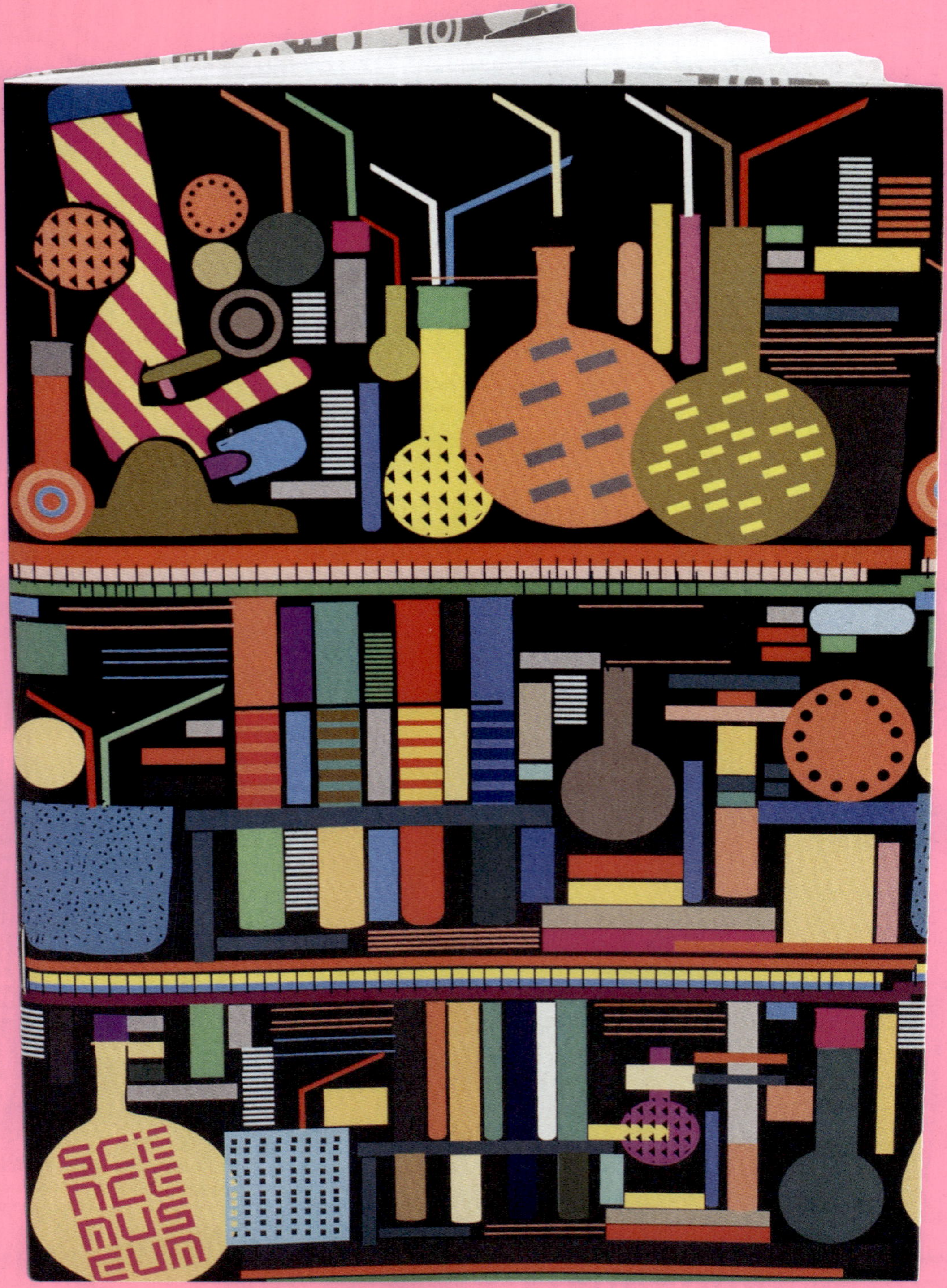

89 .2012

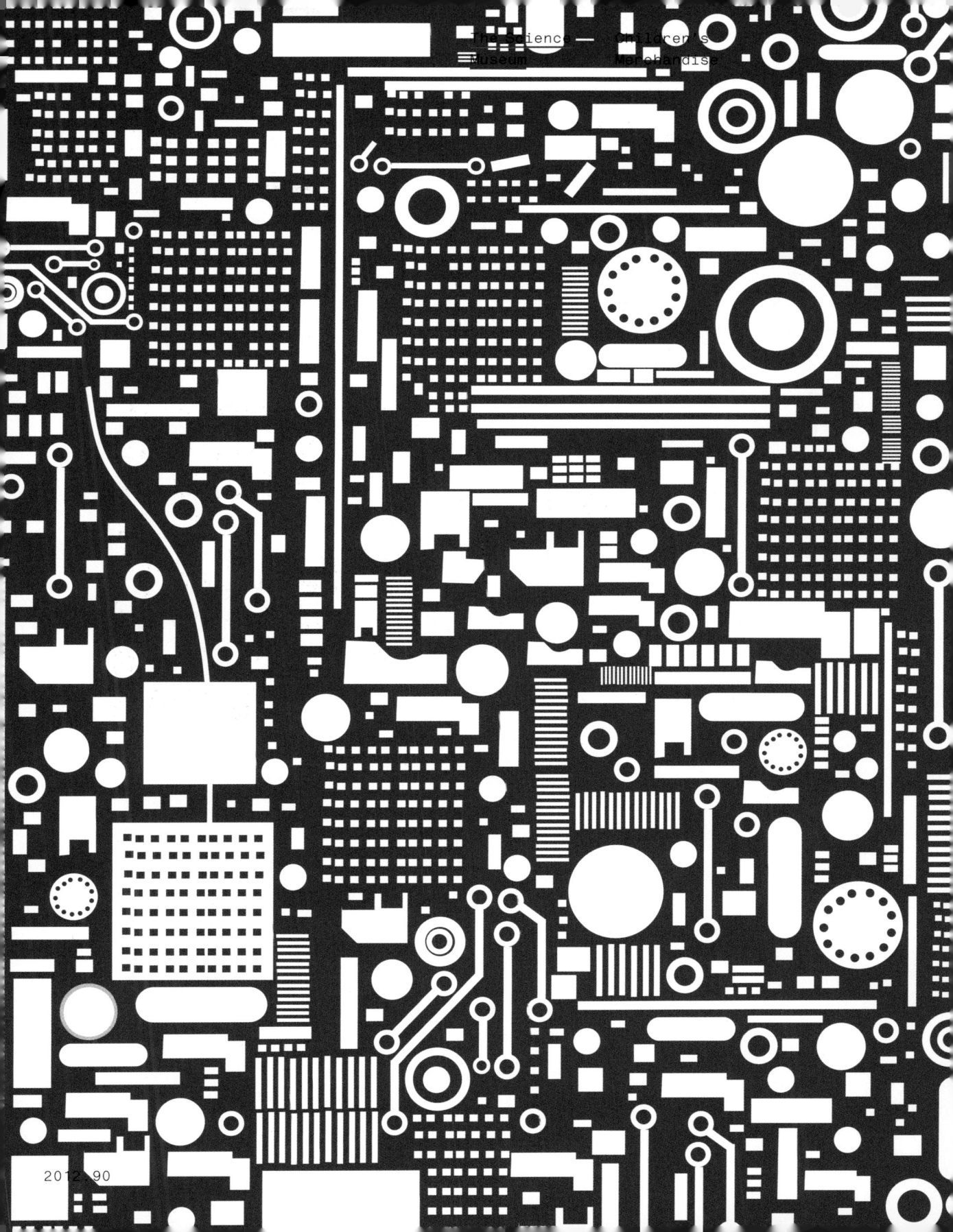

The Science— Children's
Museum   Merchandise

2012.90

91.2012

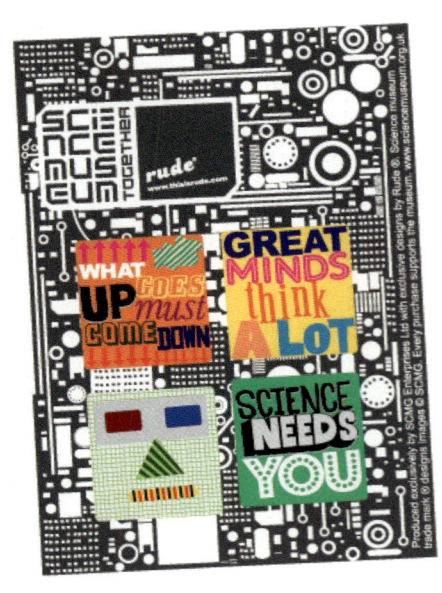

SPARKLY

Project
Window Mural

Discipline
Applied Design

Our friends over at AMV thought they'd treat their staff to a Christmas pop-up shop to save them the hassle of venturing out into the cold to buy presents.

We came up with a bespoke AMV wrapping paper and Christmas cards and set up shop in their foyer for a day.

The pattern we'd created for the wrap was turned into window transfers and stuck to the outside of their office, to create a Christmassy stained glass effect. If we had read the instructions on how to apply the transfers, we wouldn't have had to pull them all down and start again once we realised they had tiny bubbles rippling through them.

AMV

NOËL
WALKING IN THE AIR
CHRISTMAS AMV NEW YEAR
NEW YEAR
A CRACKING TOASTY
AMV
SPARKLY
LOVE XMAS LOVE
LOVE NEW YEAR LOVE AMV
CHRISTMAS AMV
XMAS 2012 XMAS
XMAS PUD
SPARKLY
WOW XMAS LOVE
LOVE CHRISTMAS
LOVE CHRISTMAS
XMAS 2012 XMAS
XMAS
SPARKLY
XMAS 2012
LOVE CHRISTMAS
LOVE CHRISTMAS
EATING LOADS
JOYEUX XMAS to you
JOYEUX NOËL LOVE AMV
CHRISTMAS SONGS ON THE RADIO
THE MUPPET CHRISTMAS CAROL
NEW YEAR
LOVE XMAS
A CRACKING
AMV
XMAS to you
SECRETLY PLAYING CAROLS FROM OCTOBER
XMAS 2012 XMAS
XMAS
THE MUPPET CHRISTMAS CAROL
SNUG AS A BUG
THE MUPPET CHRISTMAS CAROL
NEW YEAR
XMAS 2012 XMAS
SNUG NEW YEAR
LOVE XMAS OVERDONE SPROUTS
TOASTY
TOASTY
TINSELY LOVELINESS
BAND AID
MISTLETOE
NOËL
AMV XMAS
AMV
AMV LOVE
A CRACKING
XMAS 2012
DING DONG DING DONG BAHHHH HUM BUG
BAND AID
BEING A KID AGAIN
LOVE CHRISTMAS
XMAS
AMV
XMAS PUD
LOVE JOYEUX NOËL
AMV
TOASTY, ROASTY, MOSTLY FULL.........
PASS THE GRAVY!
A CRACKING
MISTLETOE
AMV
XMAS 2012 XMAS
DICKENS
XMAS to you
JOYEUX NOËL LOVE CHRISTMAS
AMV
OVERDONE SPROUTS
AMV
XMAS to you
JOYEUX NOËL AMV
XMAS 2012 XMAS
XMAS
DICKENS
FUN NEW YEAR
AMV
AMV
XMAS CRACKERS XMAS CRACKERS
WOW
TOASTY
AMV XMAS 2012
CHRISTMAS CRACKERS NEW YEAR
LOVE AMV XMAS
EATING LOADS
CRACKERS
LOVE CHRISTMAS LOVE CHRISTMAS
A CRACKING TOASTY
AMV
SPARKLY
SECRETLY PLAYING CAROLS FROM OCTOBER
XMAS 2012 XMAS
SPARKLY
OVERDONE SPROUTS
XMAS
XMAS 2012
BING CROSBY, JAMES STEWART, BOND, JAMES BOND
EATING LOADS
NEW YEAR
DICKENS XMAS to you
SNUG XMAS
CRACKING
BBQ XMAS DINNER—YUM
A CRACKING
MISTLETOE

AMV   Window Mural

2012.94

95.2012

Tetley Tea

Project
Heritage Collection

Discipline
Ceramic Applied Graphics

In the depths of the Tata Global Beverages office is an archive stuffed with old tea packets, tins and ephemera dating back to when Tetley was owned by Lyons tea.

It was with great pleasure that Rude collaborated once again with licensing design agency Skew to produce a heritage inspired drink and storage range.

The artwork and typography from the original packaging lends itself to being wrapped around porcelain and vintage-looking tea tins. The result was a charming but eclectic take on afternoon tea.

97.2012

ACE
GREAT
BRILLIANT
FANTASTIC
WONDERFUL
LOVELY
PERFECT
AMAZING

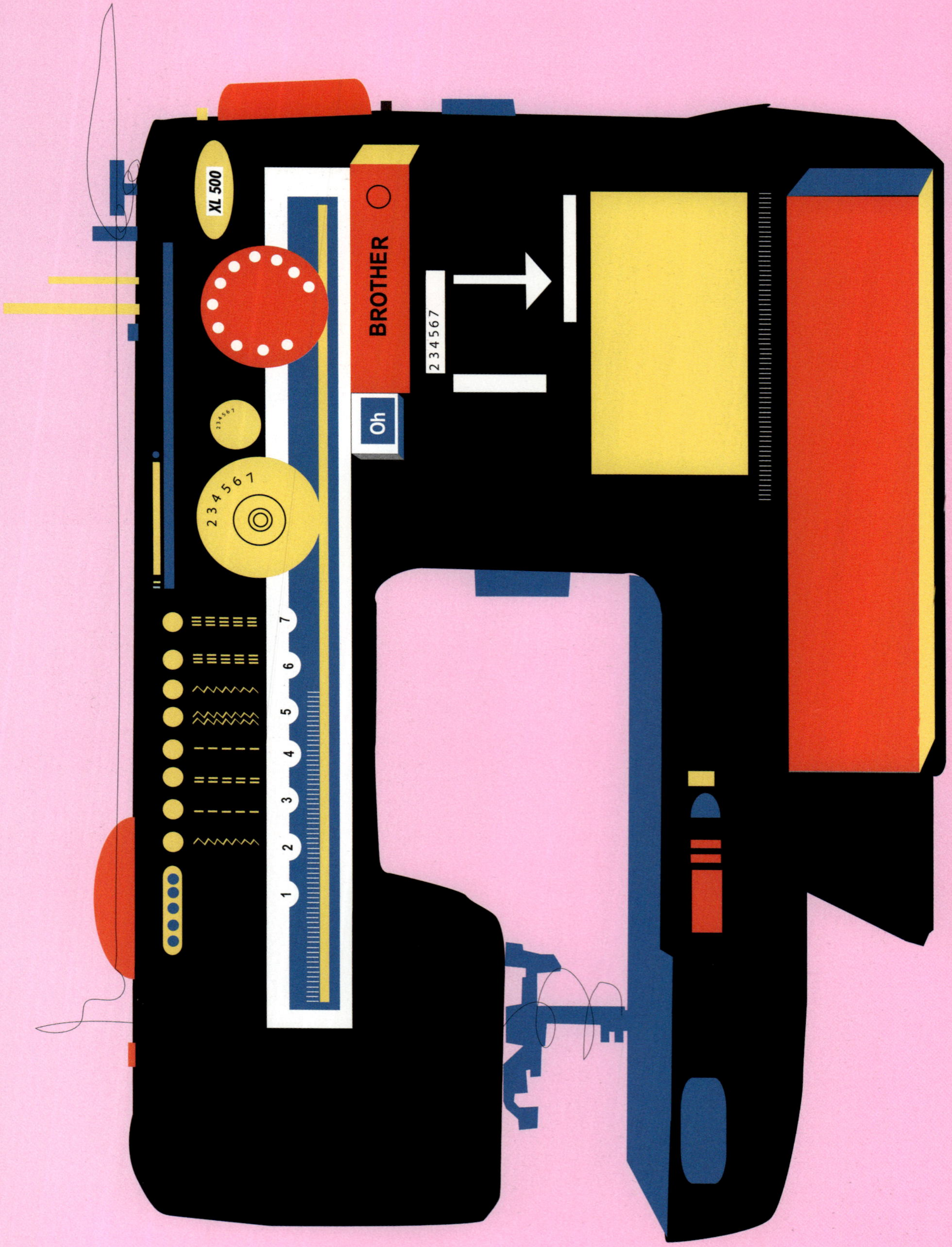
XL 500
BROTHER
234567
Oh
1 2 3 4 5 6 7

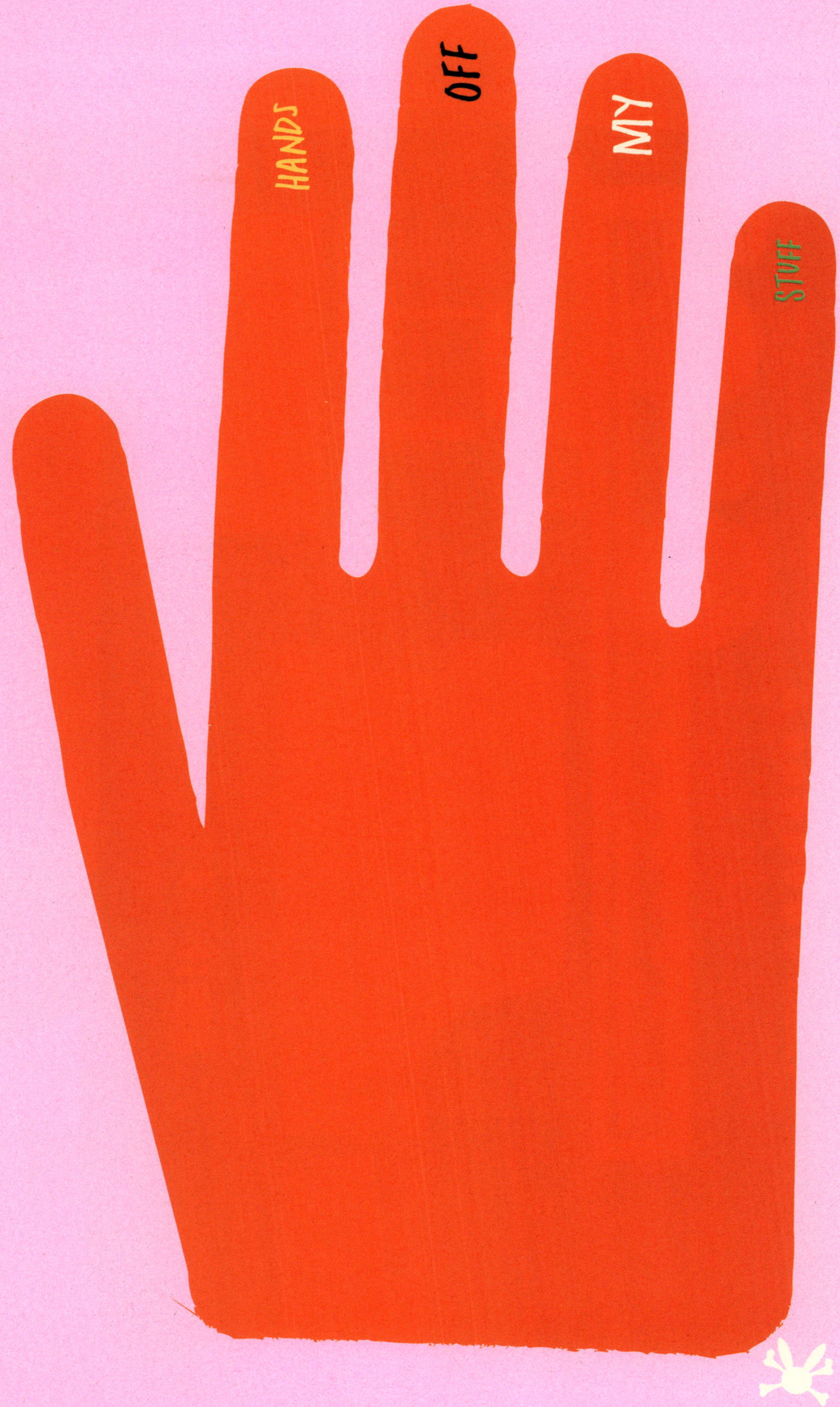
HANDS
OFF
MY
STUFF

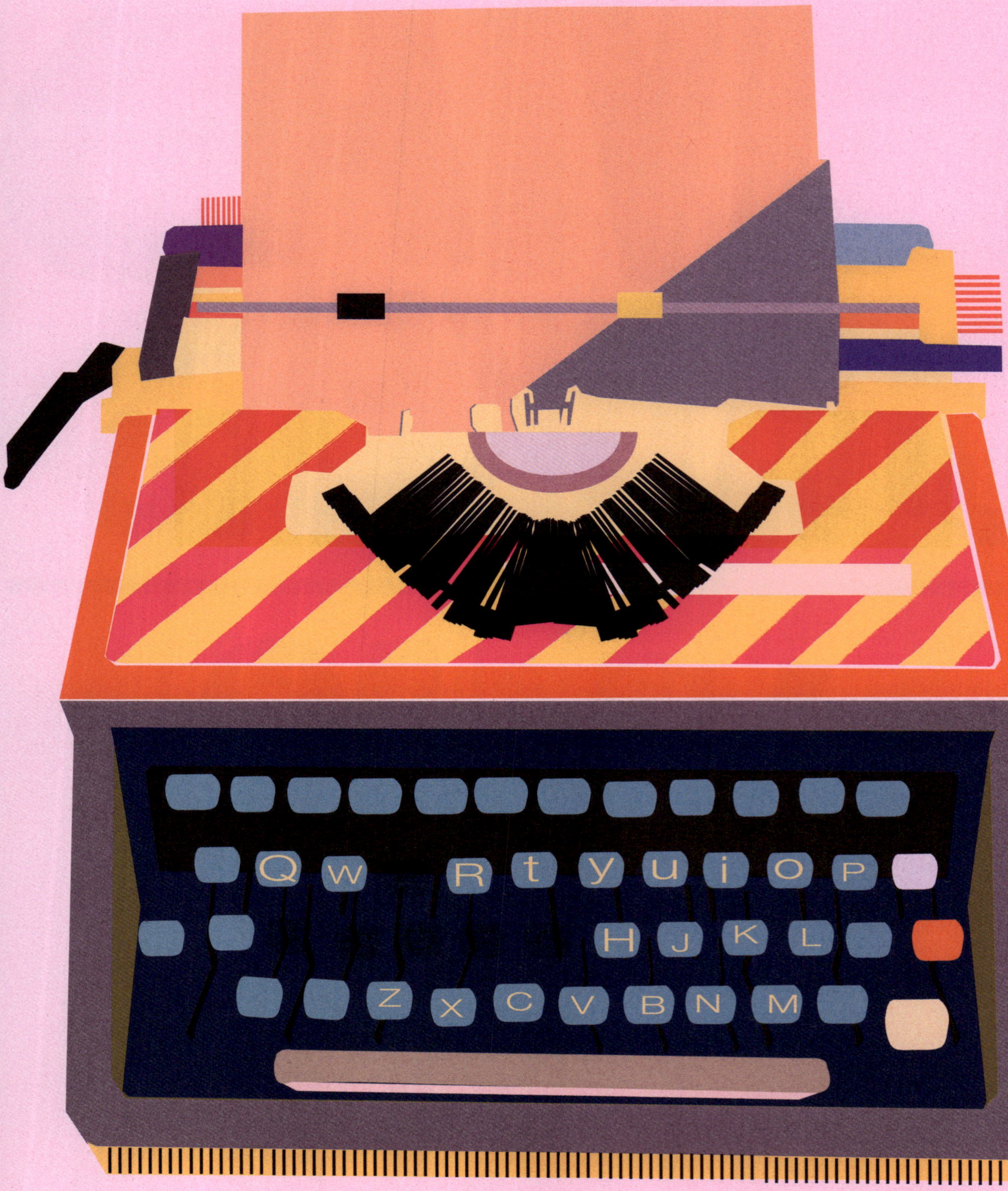
Q W R t y u i O P
H J K L
Z X C V B N M

XMAS CRACKERS

XMAS CRACKERS

BECOME BOLDER MARKETING LEADERS

MARKETING SOCIETY

This year, Rude would finally return to designing and producing our own collections. With bags of ideas, new products and kick ass graphics, we set to work. Where we had formerly sold apparel, this time we moved into the home, stationery and furniture department. We continually keep an eye on what's selling at retail, new brands and product development, whether we're designing for ourselves or a client, so we had plenty of inspiration.

We wanted to make sure our return collection stood apart in an already crowded market. The launch of this collection not only put us back on the map as a brand but also prompted some great clients with interesting projects to approach us.

2 0
1 3

105 .2013

Rude

Project
Homeware Collection

Discipline
Print and Product Design

We were determined that Rude Home would be a vibrant, trendsetting brand, making its mark with a unique and directional approach to design. Hopefully our confident use of colour and audacious designs have combined to offer something new and exciting.

Thanks to a fantastic production department, we've kept the production quality high and pushed ourselves into a new direction.

The Rude Home collection covers printed cushions, laptop cases, stationery and furniture.

107.2013

2013.108

Project
Furniture

Discipline
Print and Furniture Design

Rude

This range was a new
departure for us - a flat
packed, easy-to-assemble
collection of digitally
printed plywood furniture.
Stools, coffee tables and
coat racks come complete with
their own branded carry bags,
making storage neat and tidy.

Rude   Furniture

2013.110

111.2013

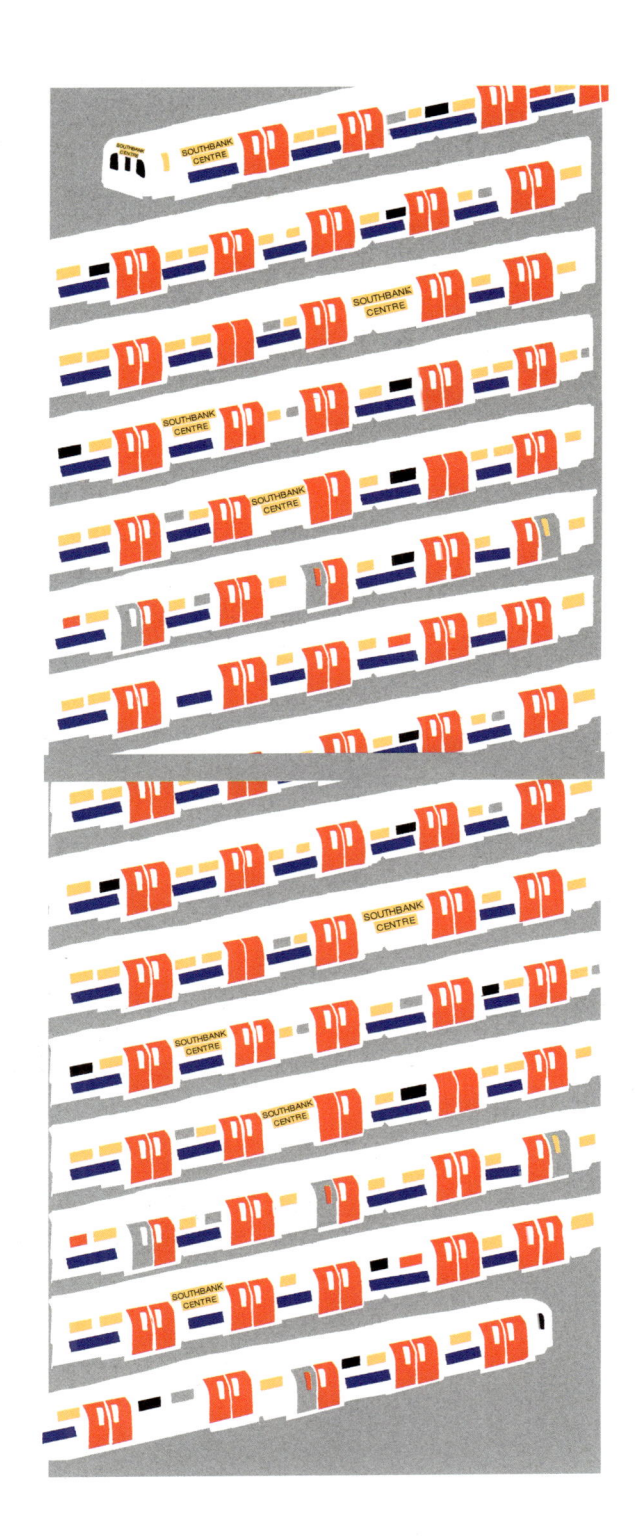

Project
Southbank Collection

Discipline
Illustration, Product Design and Production

We have always wanted to work with the Southbank Centre, Europe's largest centre for the arts. It comprises three main buildings, the Royal Festival Hall, the Queen Elizabeth Hall and the Hayward Gallery.

In 2013 Rude was commissioned to develop, design and produce a collection using illustrations that appeal to children and tourists alike. We developed a range of A2 prints, bowls, magnet sets and T-shirts that perfectly sum up the fun that families can have at the Southbank Centre.

Southbank Centre

2013.112

113.2013

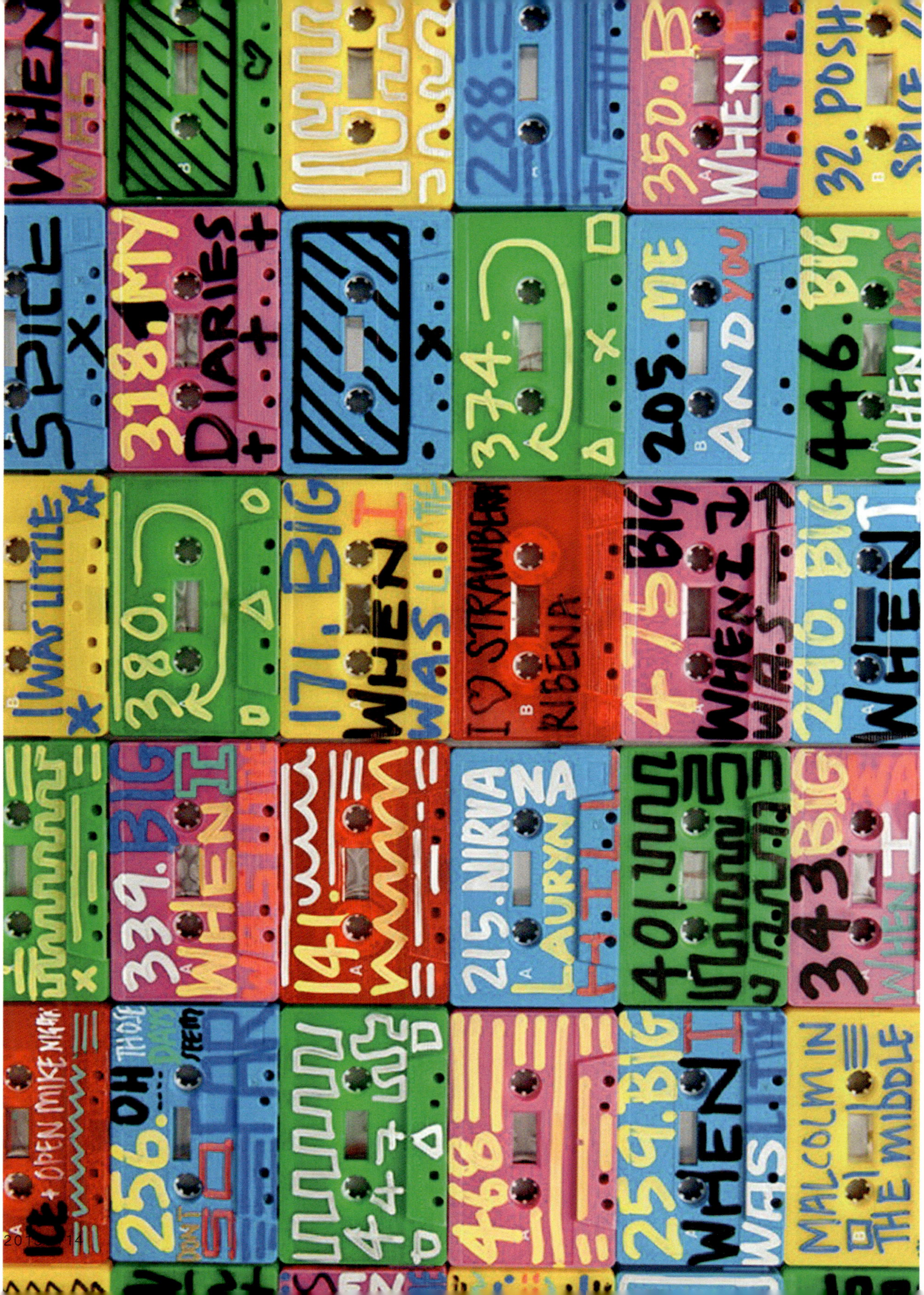

Project
Eliza Doolittle Tapes

Discipline
Illustration

When record label Parlophone kindly asked us to get our felt tips out and create five-hundred individually illustrated and numbered cassettes to promote artist Eliza Doolittle's latest release, we were delighted. The lyrics were written onto both sides of the tapes and shot as part of the album's launch campaign. They were available to buy, but we like to believe they sold out like hot tapes.

Parlophone

115.2013

Project
Magazine Cover

Discipline
Illustration

We were honoured in this year
to be commissioned by French
Elle to illustrate their
cover announcing the birth
of the royal baby, Prince
George. The magazine rarely
uses illustration on their
covers, so we whipped out
the pens and got scribbling
before they could stop us.
Hoorah! (That's in French.)

French Elle

ELLE

www.elle.fr

LA BEAUTÉ
C'EST DANS
LA TÊTE...
ET DANS
L'ASSIETTE

AMOUR
EN VACANCES
DEVENEZ UNE
DRAGUE QUEEN

SO VERY BRITISH

SPÉCIAL **été** 2€

mode
PREPPY
MÊME
EN ÉTÉ

HE'S THE DADDY

THE QUEEN IS GAGA FOR THE BABY

KATE SUPERMUM
LE ROYAL BABY, LA REINE-MÈRE,
LES PAPARAZZIS, WILLIAM...
OH MY GOD!

HOURRA!

HEBDOMADAIRE.XX JUIN 2013
FRANCE MÉTROPOLITAINE. AND. 2 €. BEL: 2,30 €. CAN$: 5.50 CND A: 4,60 €. D: 4,20 €. DOMA: 4,70 €. CH: 3,90 FS. ESP: 3,30 €. FIN: 5,60 €. GR: 4,20 €. ITA: 3,30 €. LUX: 2,30 €. MAR: 30 MAD PORTcont: 3,30 €. NL: 4,20 €. NCAL: 450 CFP. POLY S: 500 CFP TUN: 4,60 DNT

117.2013

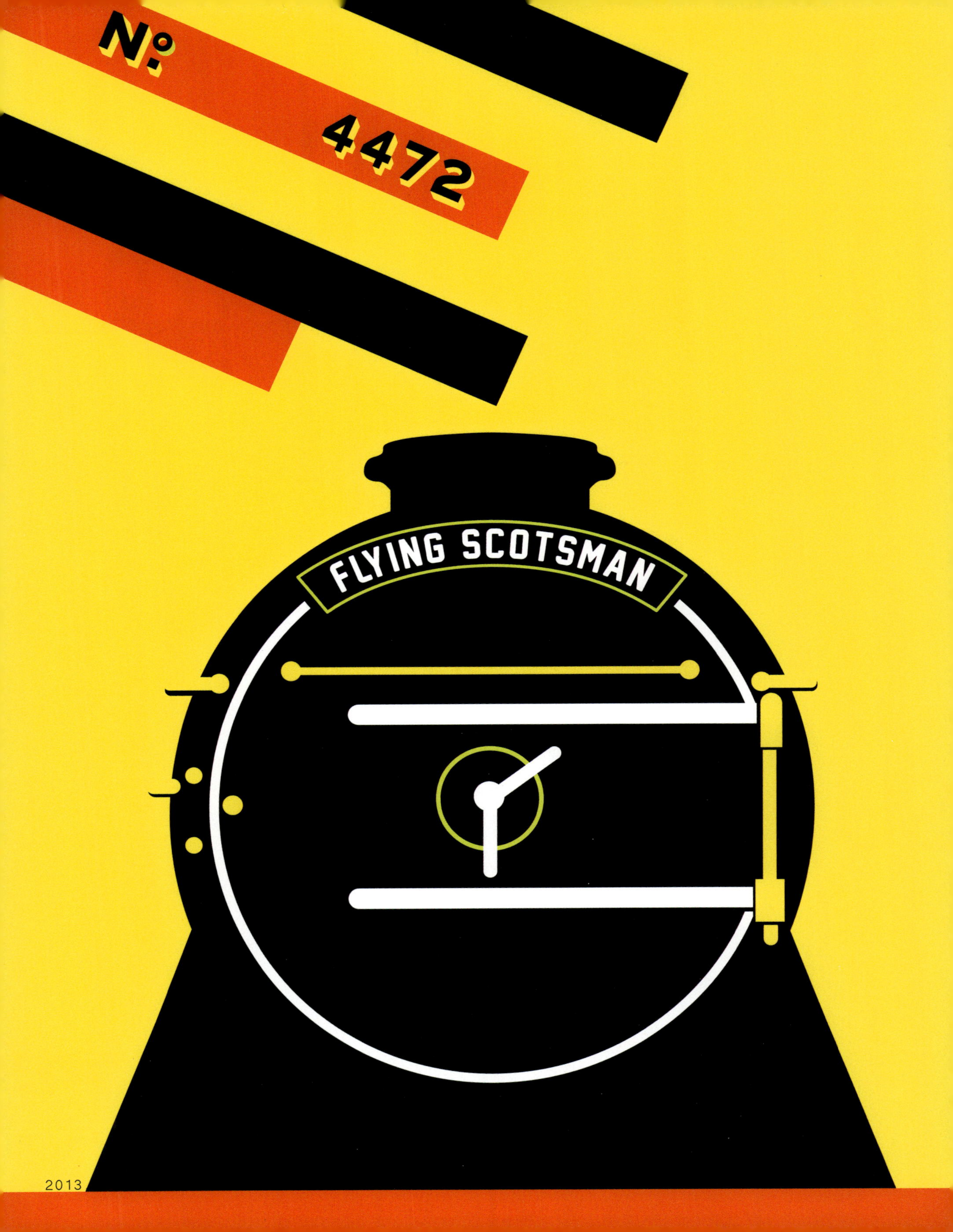

2013

FLYING SCOTSMAN

HERE'S YOUR TRAIN CRUISE OF OVER 1,000 MILES

Project
Flying Scotsman

Discipline
Illustration, Product Design and Production

The National Railway museum is part of the Science Museum Group and therefore has the same buying team as the Science Museum Shop, who we worked with previously on a kids' collection.

After the success of the previous range, they commissioned Rude to design a succinct range of vector illustrations for the Flying Scotsman, the famous train and route of the same name.

We applied the graphics across a well-sourced and produced range of product, including textiles, ceramics and stationery.

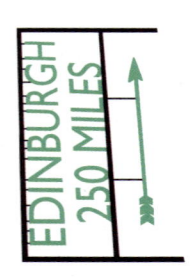

The National Railway Museum

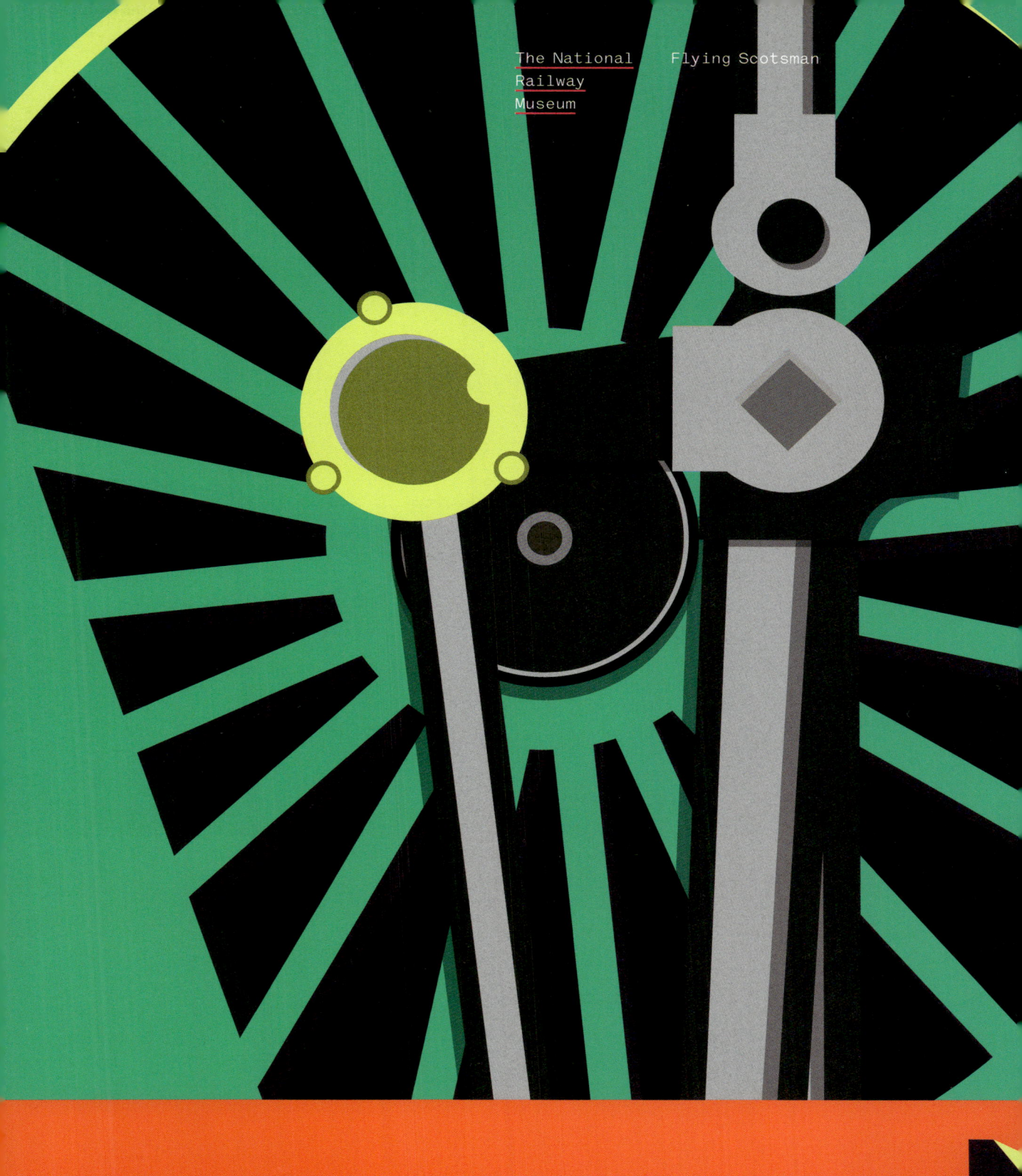

The National Flying Scotsman
Railway
Museum

2013.120

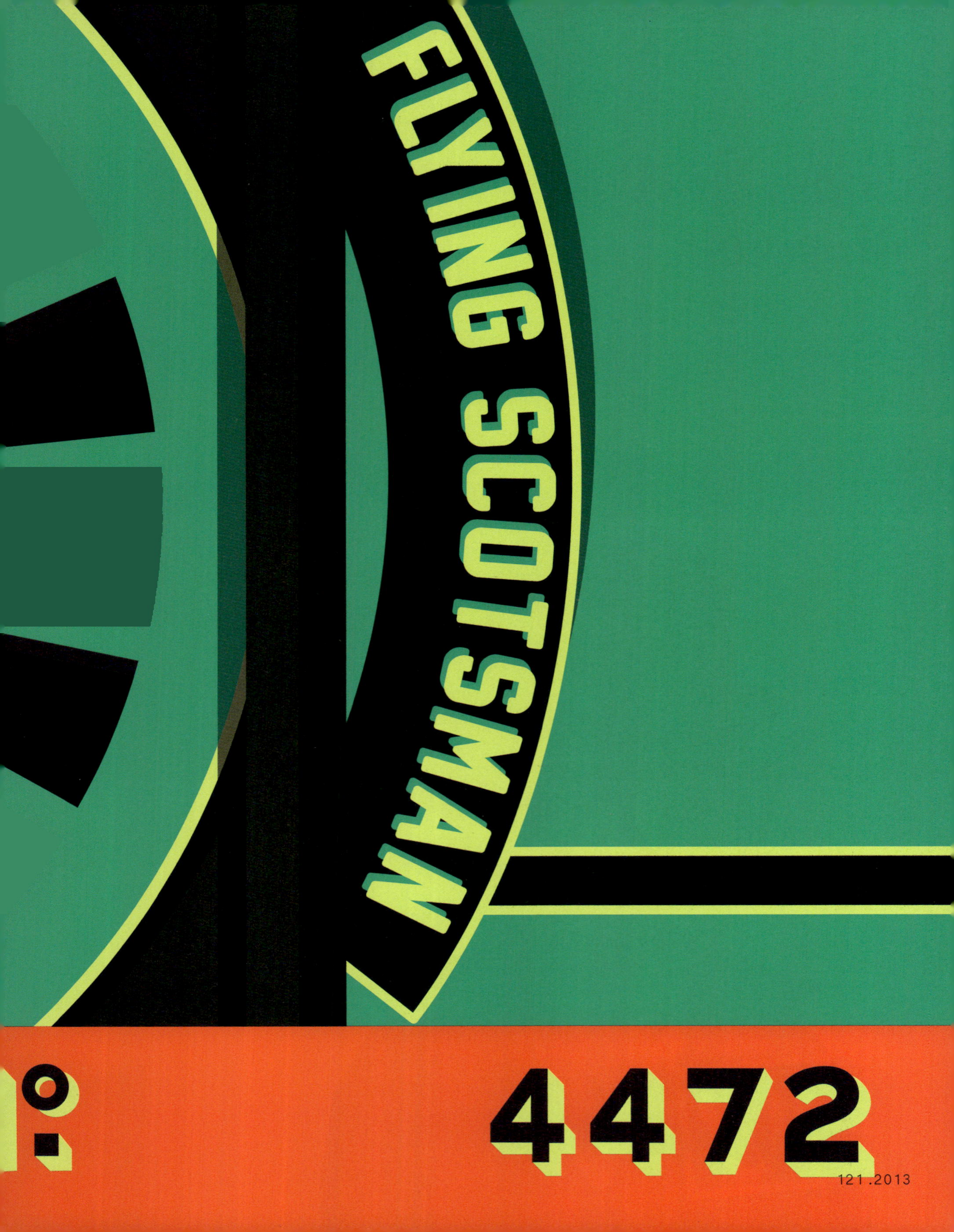
FLYING SCOTSMAN
4472
121.2013

Project
Spy Merchandise

Discipline
Applied Illustration

Imperial War Museum

In preparation for this job, the Imperial War Museum sent us to the Churchill War Rooms to immerse ourselves in the environment. It's a fantastic exhibition and it set us up perfectly for the job.

The brief was to devise a range of spy inspired packages and product aimed specifically at kids. We took the opportunity to use our son Herbie as the main image for the packs and adorned him with a hat, glasses and classic spy moustache. The graphics work over open and closed boxes, swing tags, blister packs and header cards, alongside T-shirts, pin badges, notebooks and Oyster card wallets with x-ray images of espionage equipment.

123.2013

Boxfresh

Project
Teenage Cancer Trust Poster

Discipline
Illustration

After seeing the illustrational work that Rupert had created for an Art and Sole sneaker design project, Boxfresh, a British fashion label, approached us to help promote a competition they were running with Teenage Cancer Trust.

The competition encouraged entrants of all ages to submit a trainer design onto one of their preexisting trainer templates. The winner saw their artwork go into production and into the Boxfresh stores. From each trainer sale, 10% went towards the cancer charity.

Rude's poster artwork was used as part of their on and offline advertising campaign.

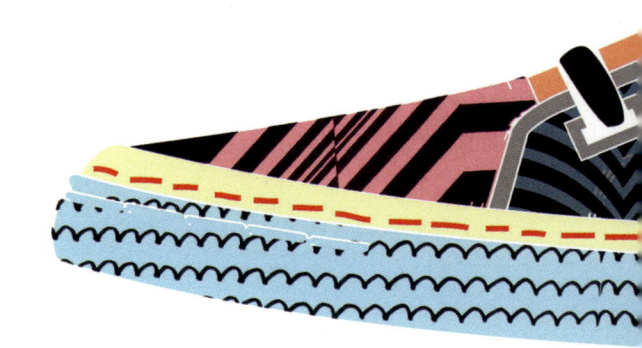

125 .2013

Project
Anniversary Poster

Discipline
Typography

National Theatre

The National Theatre turned fifty in 2013 and decided to celebrate and promote all the skills that are involved with theatre, not just acting. To do this, they commissioned Rude's artwork as a birthday present to themselves. The print is sent in poster format to all secondary and comprehensive schools in the UK to promote all the skills and arts that make theatre happen.

To mark the occasion, the National Theatre called in Mary Portas and the talented Kit Grover to create a new retail space called Shopping and Eating. Situated on the Southbank, the shop sells bespoke ranges designed by a great group of artists including Jamie Reid, Graphic Thought Facility and David Carson.

2013.126

127.2013

National Theatre — Anniversary Poster

129.2013

ico Design

Project
Taste Magazine

Discipline
Illustration

ico Design is the London based studio behind designing and making this very book happen. We have worked and been friends with ico since the inception of Rude and our collaborative method continues. In this instance, they asked us to illustrate the cover of their new flavoursome publication entitled Taste.

Taste is a free publication dedicated to the pleasure and business of food and reflects ico's interest in the sector. Through photography, illustration, interviews and analysis, they explore the ups and downs of an industry that's constantly evolving. It's available at selected restaurants, cafés and retailers.

TASTE

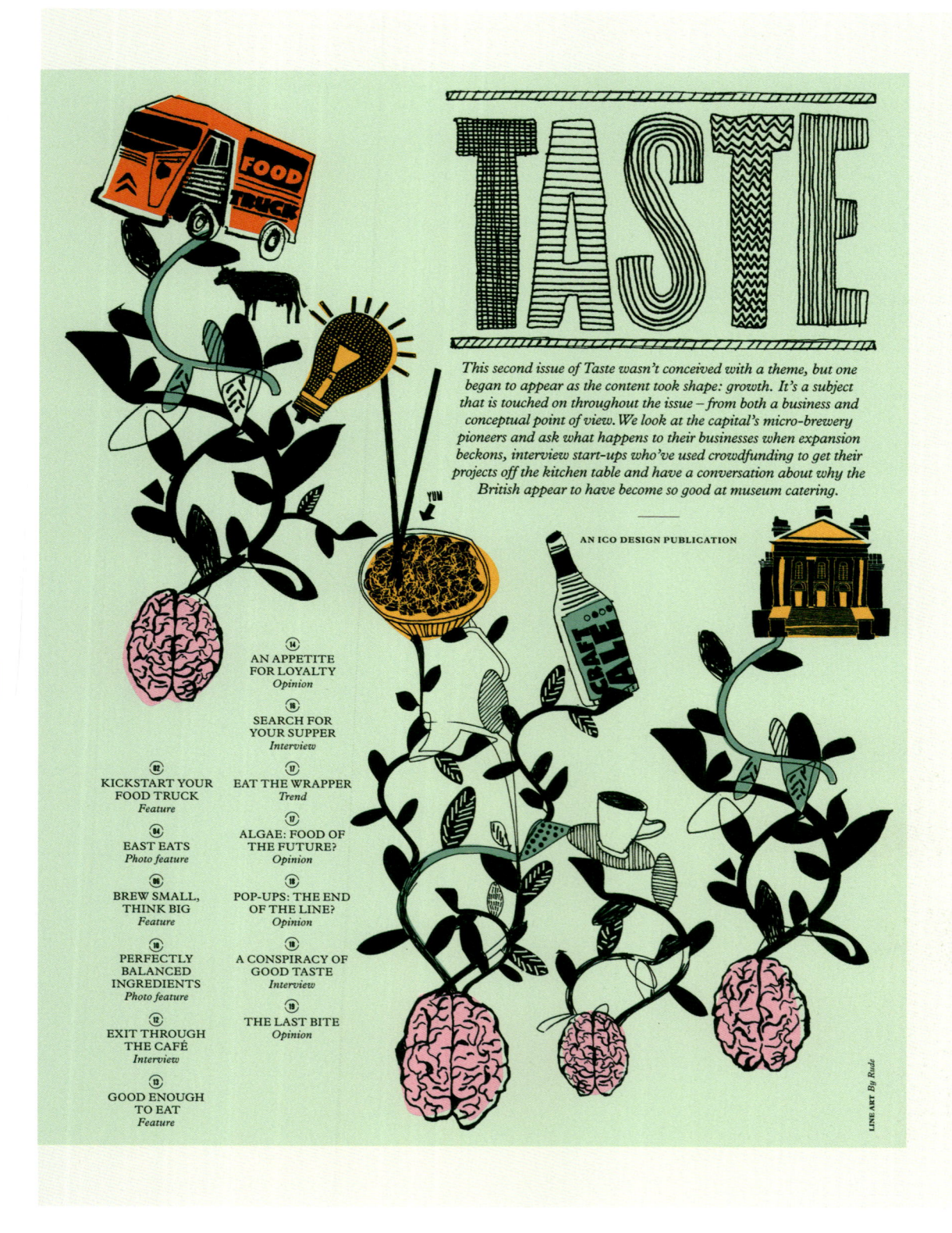

This second issue of Taste wasn't conceived with a theme, but one began to appear as the content took shape: growth. It's a subject that is touched on throughout the issue – from both a business and conceptual point of view. We look at the capital's micro-brewery pioneers and ask what happens to their businesses when expansion beckons, interview start-ups who've used crowdfunding to get their projects off the kitchen table and have a conversation about why the British appear to have become so good at museum catering.

AN ICO DESIGN PUBLICATION

KICKSTART YOUR FOOD TRUCK
Feature

EAST EATS
Photo feature

BREW SMALL, THINK BIG
Feature

PERFECTLY BALANCED INGREDIENTS
Photo feature

EXIT THROUGH THE CAFÉ
Interview

GOOD ENOUGH TO EAT
Feature

AN APPETITE FOR LOYALTY
Opinion

SEARCH FOR YOUR SUPPER
Interview

EAT THE WRAPPER
Trend

ALGAE: FOOD OF THE FUTURE?
Opinion

POP-UPS: THE END OF THE LINE?
Opinion

A CONSPIRACY OF GOOD TASTE
Interview

THE LAST BITE
Opinion

LINE ART By Rude

Project
In-store Merchandise

Discipline
Illustration, Product Design
and Production

Cass Art is by far our favourite art shop, established by Mark Cass over thirty years ago. Mark is totally commited to encouraging everyone to realise their creative talents, believing strongly that art brings freedom through creative expression.

We second that, and for this collection of bespoke art products, we let our creative juices flow… Launching for Christmas 2014 is a collection that includes storage and stationery.

Cass Art

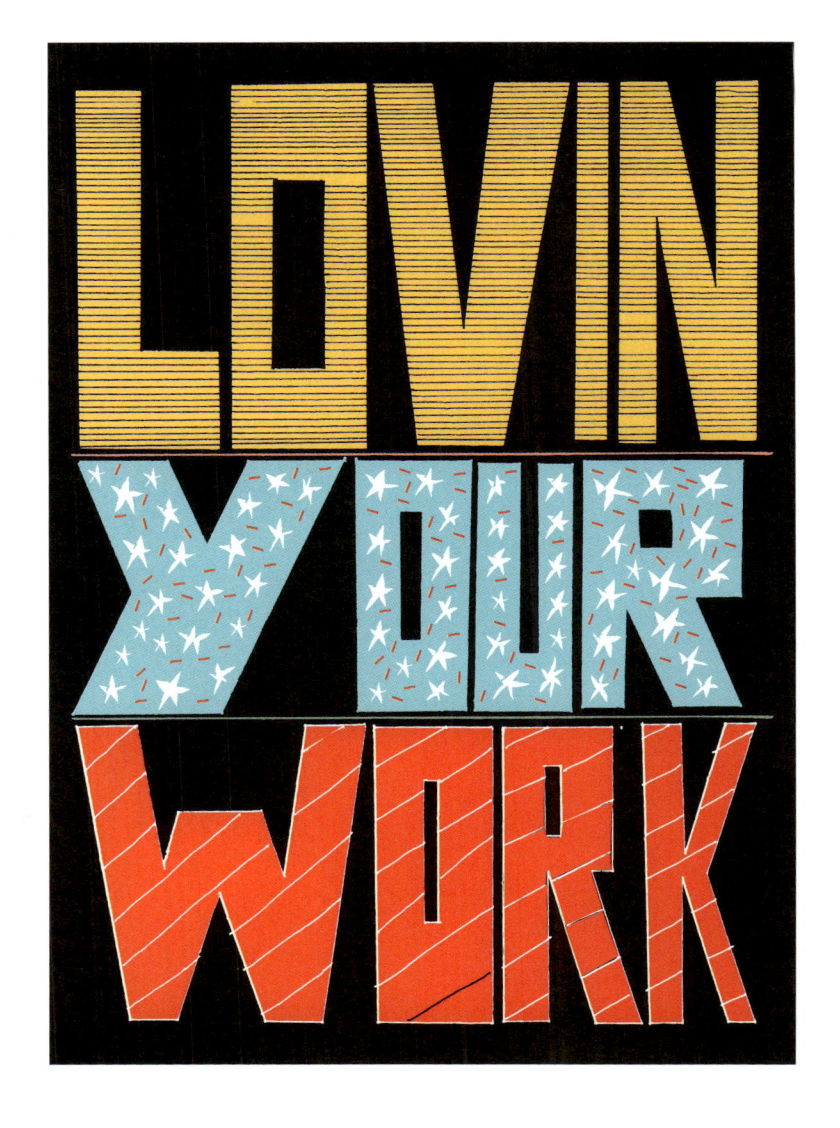

2013.132

WHEN YOU'VE GOTTA PAINT, YOU'VE GOTTA PAINT

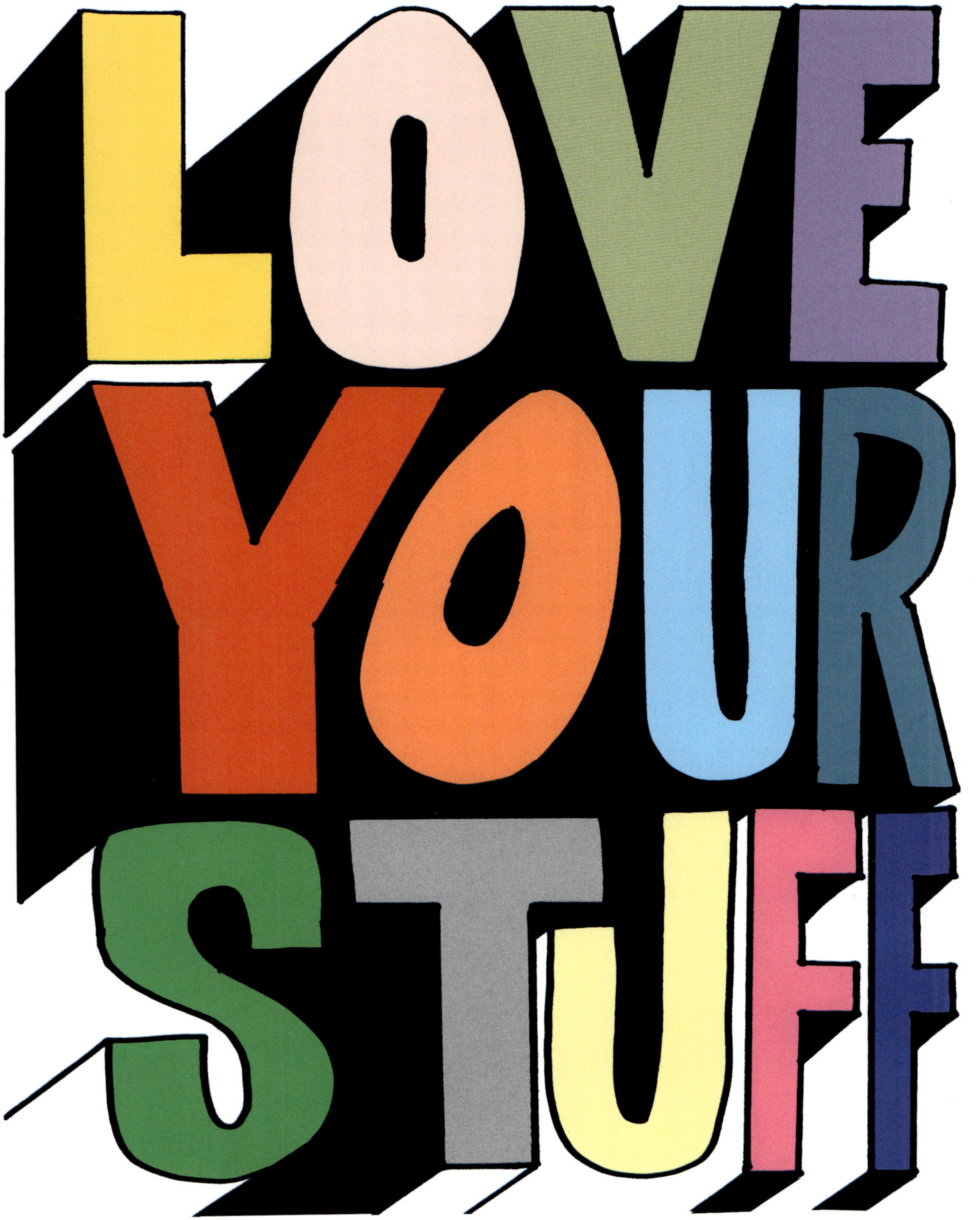

2013.134

Urban Outfitters

Project
Homeware

Discipline
Illustration, Product Design and Production

It seems fitting that as we conclude the book we feature a client that we have worked with right from the very beginning. Urban Outfitters opened their first UK store in High St Kensington and we were fortunate enough to launch our brand there.

This project sees Rude designing a specific homeware collection for Urban, called 'Home is where your Stuff Is'. We've always felt that Rude shares a similar design style to Urban and although their target audience is now a lot younger than we are, we still rock the same aesthetic we always have. Therefore our product is still as relevant today as it was fifteen years ago.

The collection includes bespoke prints applied to ceramics, textiles, stationery, storage and glassware.

2013.136

Urban Outfitters
Homeware

TELL ME, WHAT'S YOUR TYPE

SMiLE

Urban Outfitters Homeware

2013.138

HOME IS WHERE YOUR STUFF IS.
LOTS OF BOOKS
LOTS OF OLD TAPES
RADIO
CD'S
OLD DUSTY RECORDS
MORE DVD'S
PHOTO
LAMP
ANOTHER PHOTO
TV
VIDEO
MAGAZINES
DVD
DIGITAL—

139 .2013

2013.140

Urban Outfitters

Homeware

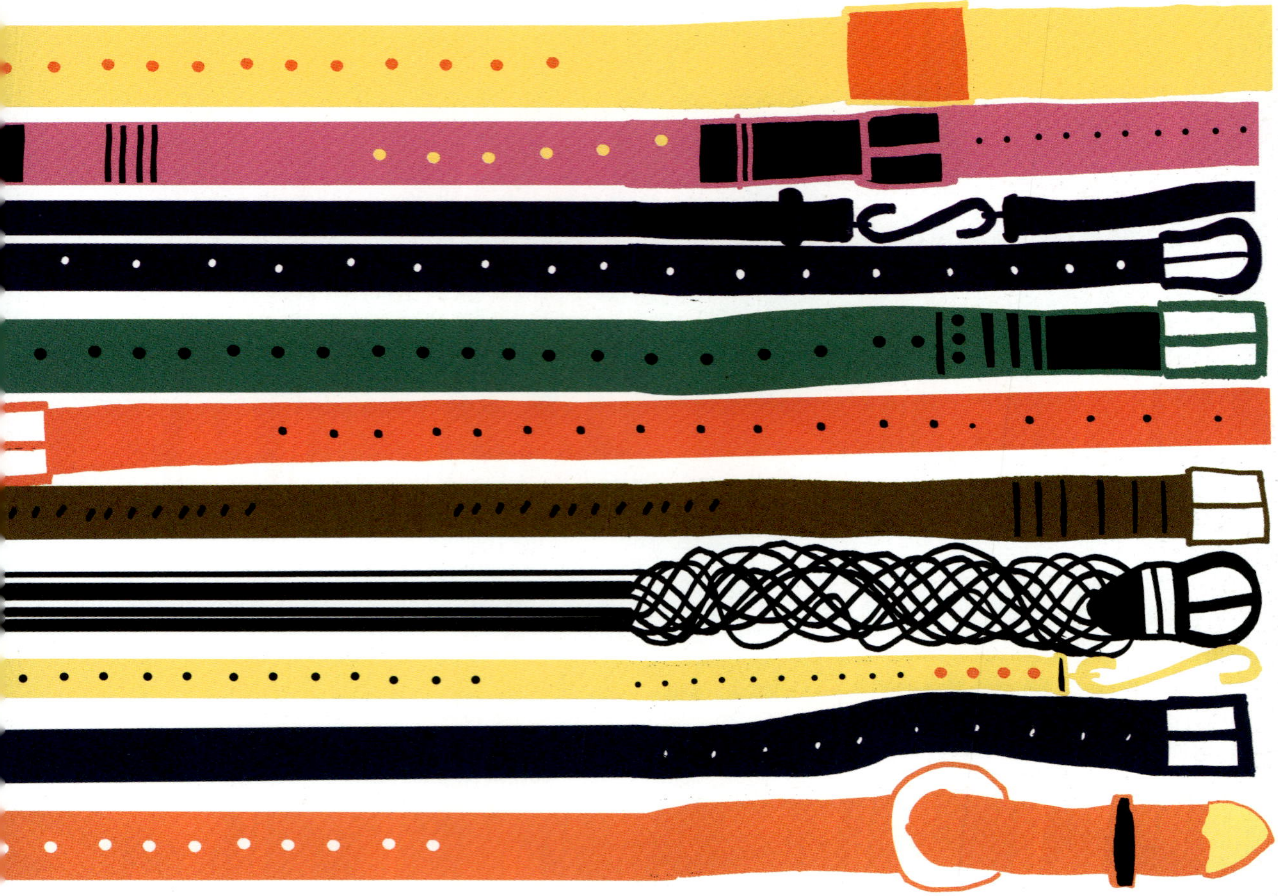

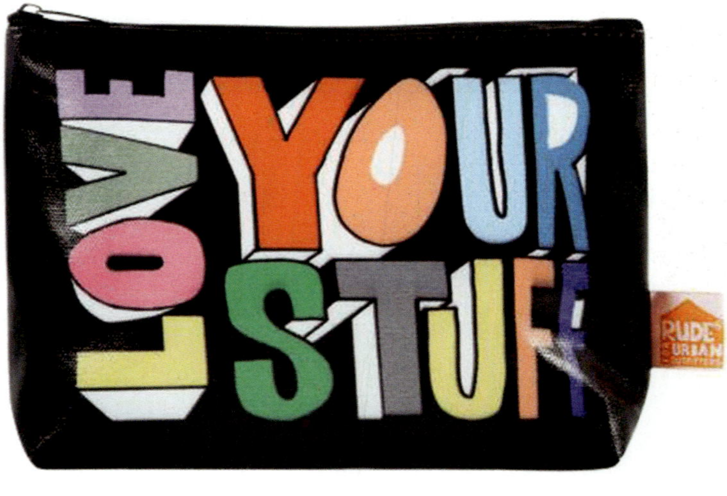

141.2013

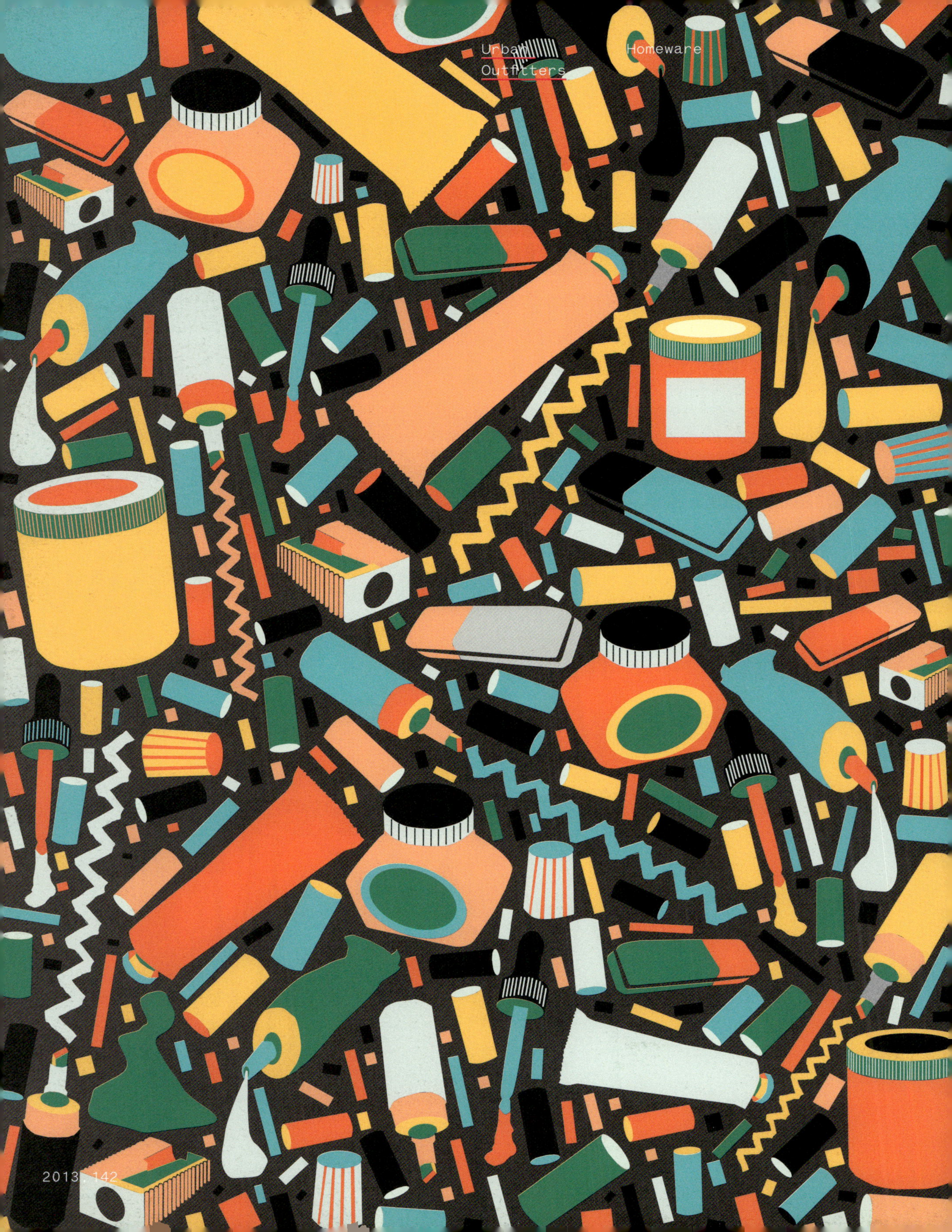
Urban
Outfitters
Homeware
2013.142

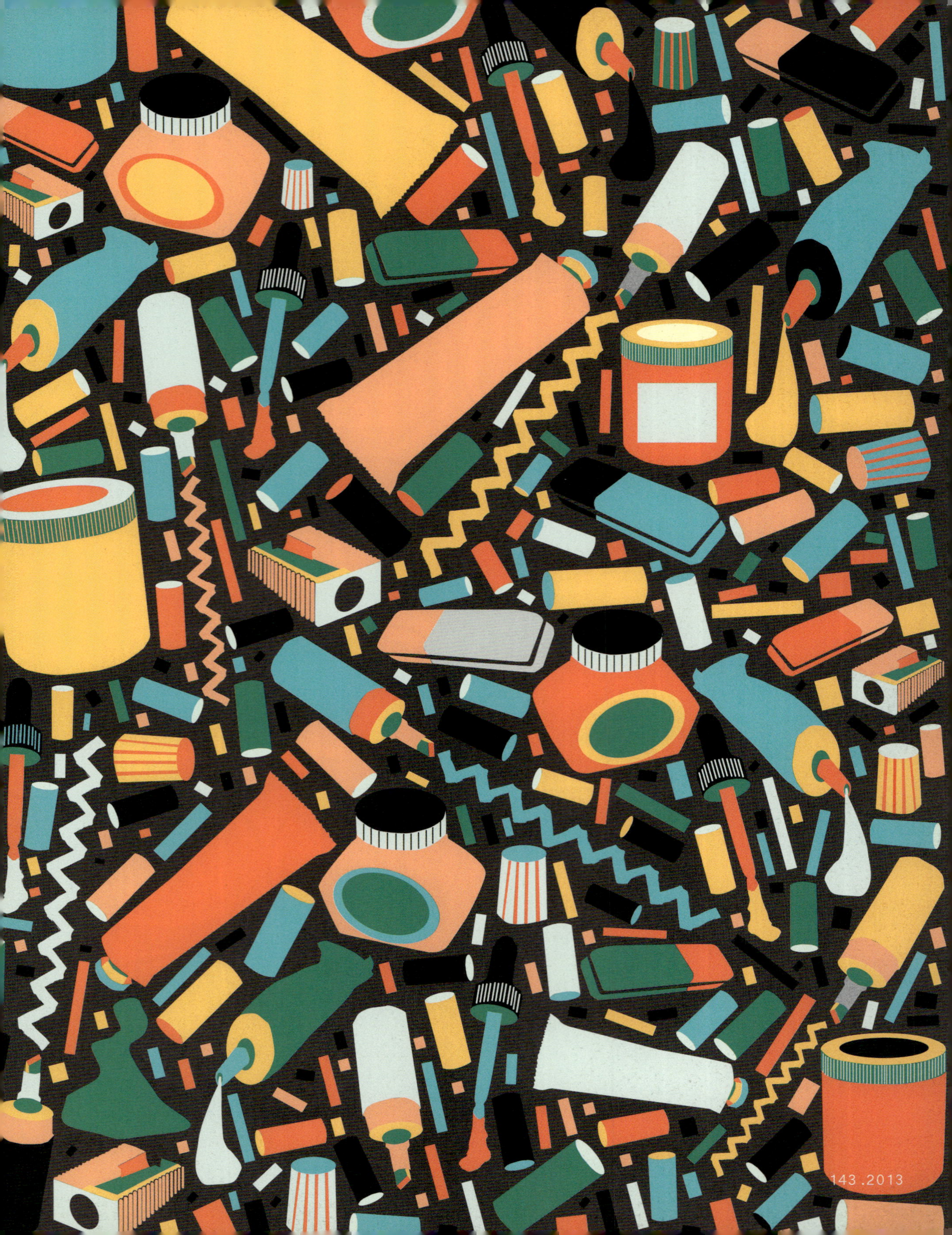
143 .2013

2013.144

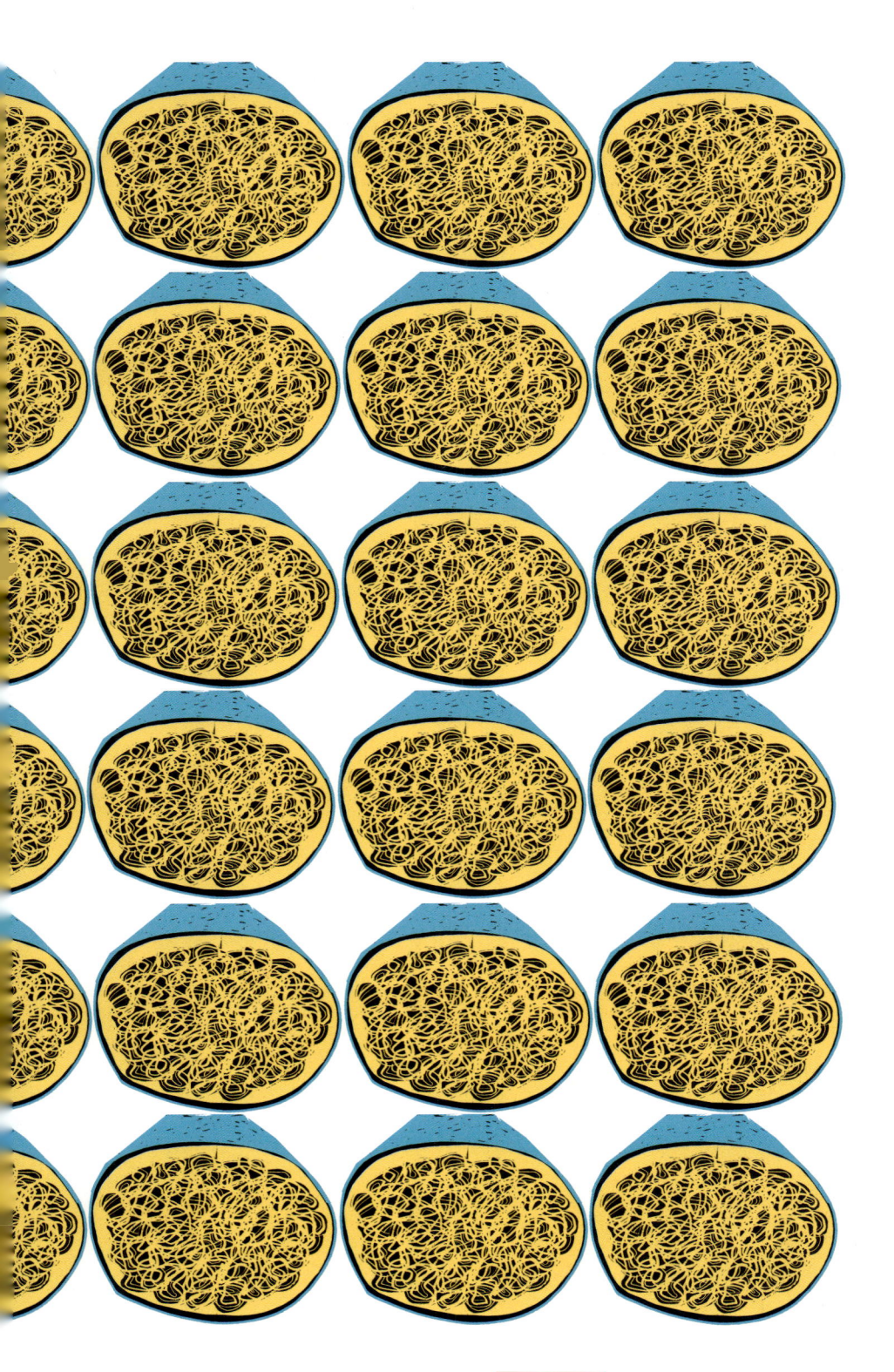

Urban Outfitters Homeware

145.2013

Ressourcer le monde

Havas Worldwide

Project
Veolia

Discipline
Illustration and Advertising

We have just started working with advertising company Havas Worldwide in Paris. Their client Veolia helps cities and industries to manage, optimise and make the most of their resources. The company provides an array of solutions related to water, energy and materials – with a focus on waste recovery – to promote the transition toward a circular economy.

2013.148

I LOVE MANCHESTER

Museum of Science and Industry

Project
I Love Manchester

Discipline
Illustration, Product Design and Production

The Museum of Science and Industry in Manchester is part of the Science Museum Group and therefore has the same buying team we worked with on the Flying Scotsman range.

The brief was a celebration of Manchester, to create a collection that pays tribute to all aspects of the first industrial city. From Boddingtons to Oasis it's all here...

IT ALL STARTED HERE IN MANCHESTER,
Name: The Lower Campfield Market. Architect: David Bellhouse Jr, Completed: 1882
Name: John Rylands Library. Architect: Basil Champneys, Completed: 1899
1714 FIRST PRINTING PRESS
1752 Manchester Mercury
(First Newspaper)
THE WORLDS
FIRST INDUSTRIAL CITY
1770 THE INDUSTRIAL REVOLUTION.
JOHN DALTON [1766–1844]
SHUDE HILL
1781
WORLD'S 1ST COTTON MILL FITTED WITH A STEAM STEAM ENGINE.
1842-THE FIRST PHOTO OF MANCHESTER
COTTONOPOLIS: TEXTILES IMPORTED ALL OVER THE WORLD.
MEE-MAWING
KISSING THE
GOOD IDEAS
SHUTTLE.
RIP William Huskisson
The LIVERPOOL MANCHESTER Railway
15th September 1830
1851 Clean water!
1840 JOULE'S FIRST LAW
AFFORDABLE POWER
ERNEST RUTHERFORD (1871-1937)
1870 'BODDINGTONS'
1889 LINOTYPE COMPANY
30,000 TYPE MACHINES
CENTRE OF THE UNIVERSE
BABY
MONDAY 21 JUNE
THE FIRST COMPUTER)
THE TIPPLER TOILET
1909 AVIATION
ADY MARY HEATH
(1897–1929)
££££
RICHARD ROBERTS
AUTOMATIC SLOT CUTTING MACHINE
Ford
MODEL T.
1908-1927
15 MILLION
EDINBURGH
NEWCASTLE
LIVERPOOL
MANCHESTER
BIRMINGHAM
BRISTOL
LONDON
1913-Mass Spectrometry
GAS ENGINES
1893 DICKINSON STREET STATION
Name: Chips. Architect: Will Alsop, Completed: 2009
Name: Central Library. Architect: Vincent Harris, Completed: 1934
1948 Manchester University's breakthrough
1817 'TOWN GAS'
1910 ELECTRICITY
Name: Town Hall. Architect: Alfred Waterhouse, Completed: 1877
1821 The Manchester Guardian
1959 The Guardian
1918 WOMEN VOTE
1922
1ST RADIO STATION
1951 'The Ferranti Mark 1"
1976 - MICROCHIP
THE LOWRY
DARESBURY
LABORATORY
1981 - 2008 1,200 PROTEINS MAPPED
Name: The Lowery. Architect: Michael Wilford, Completed: 2000
12th October 2000
1967
STAWBERRY STUDIOS
SALFORD
Architect: Alfred Waterhouse, Completed: 1877
Name: Chorlton New Mill. Architect: Unknown, Completed: 1813-15
1982
THE HACIENDA
OASIS
46 STOREY BEETHAM TOWER
THE STONE ROSES
WE LOVE
FACTORY RECORDS
MOSI
'THE STREET'
I LOVE MANCHESTER
BBC MEDIACITYUK

Education First

Project
T-shirts and Merchandise

Discipline
Illustration, Product Design and Production

Founded in 1965 by entrepreneur Bertil Hult, Education First is a privately-held company with fifteen divisions. They offer a range of educational programs from language training educational travel, and academic degrees to cultural exchanges. Rupert worked on a collection of T-shirt graphics for a children's collection, which will be in all stores worldwide soon. T-shirts, pin badges, notebooks and large purses carry the slogans 'The world's your oyster' and 'Mind your language'.

151.2013

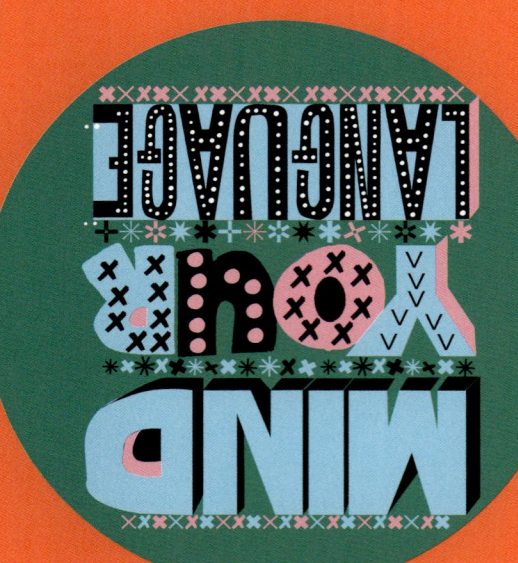

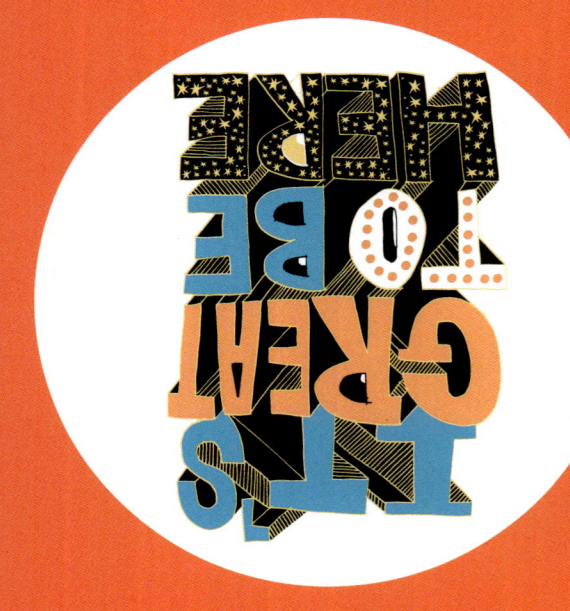

2013.152

Project
Building our house on Kyverdale Road

Discipline
Design

We have snuck this project in because we are so proud that this house has happened. We always wanted to build our own property and we finally achieved it by replacing an old garage in north east London for this white brick modern building. It's nestled between a Victorian terrace and a large synagogue.

Rude

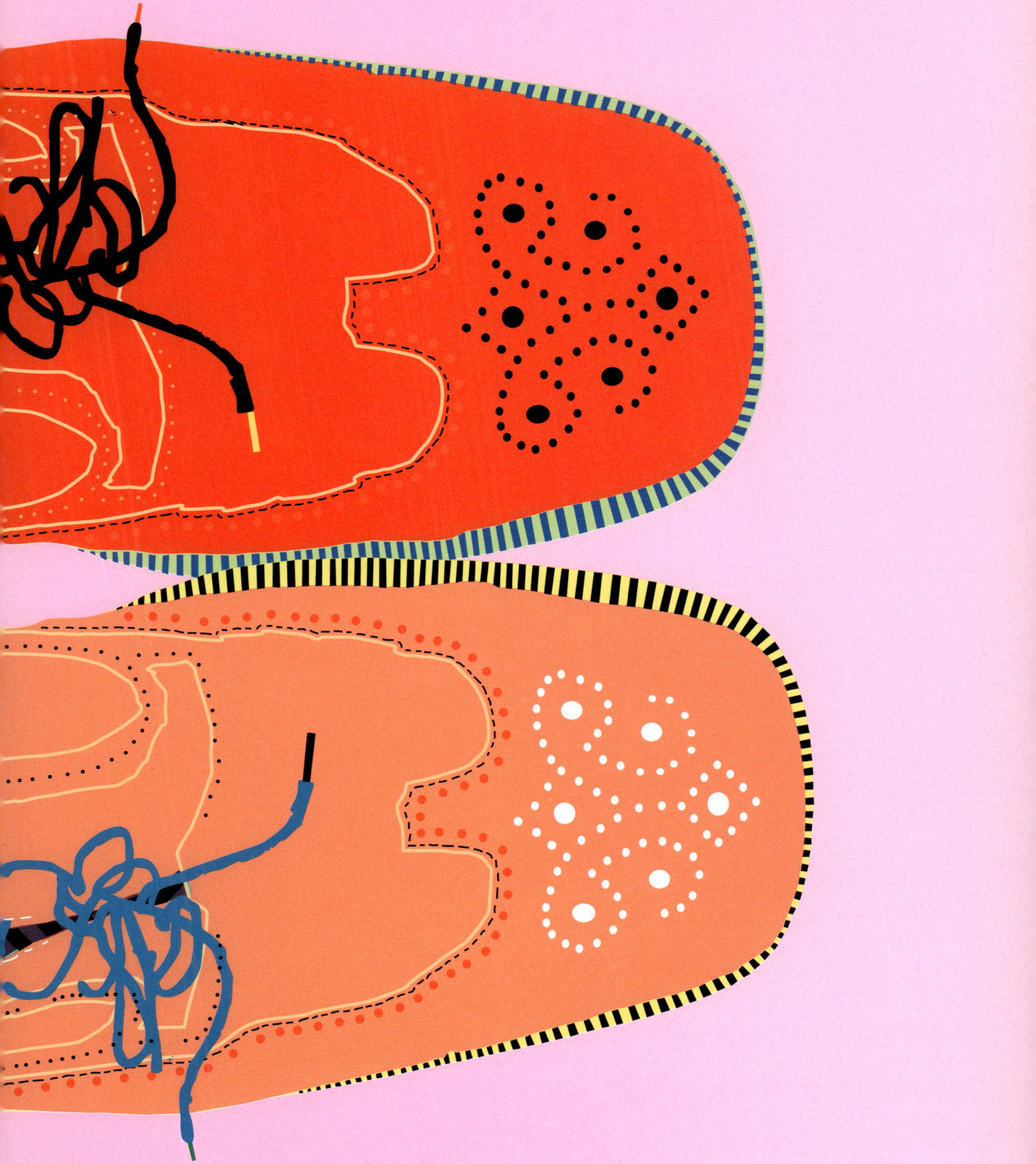

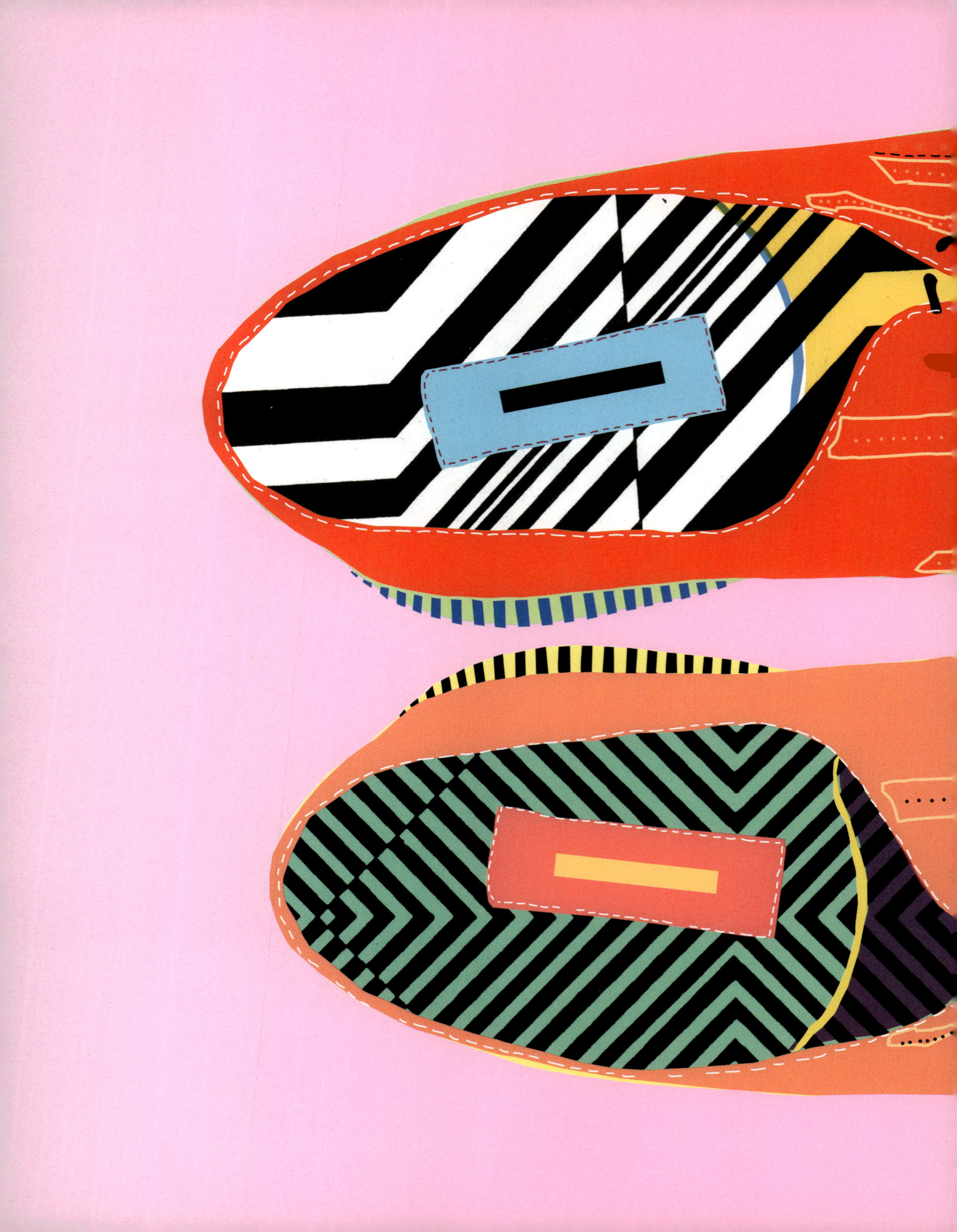

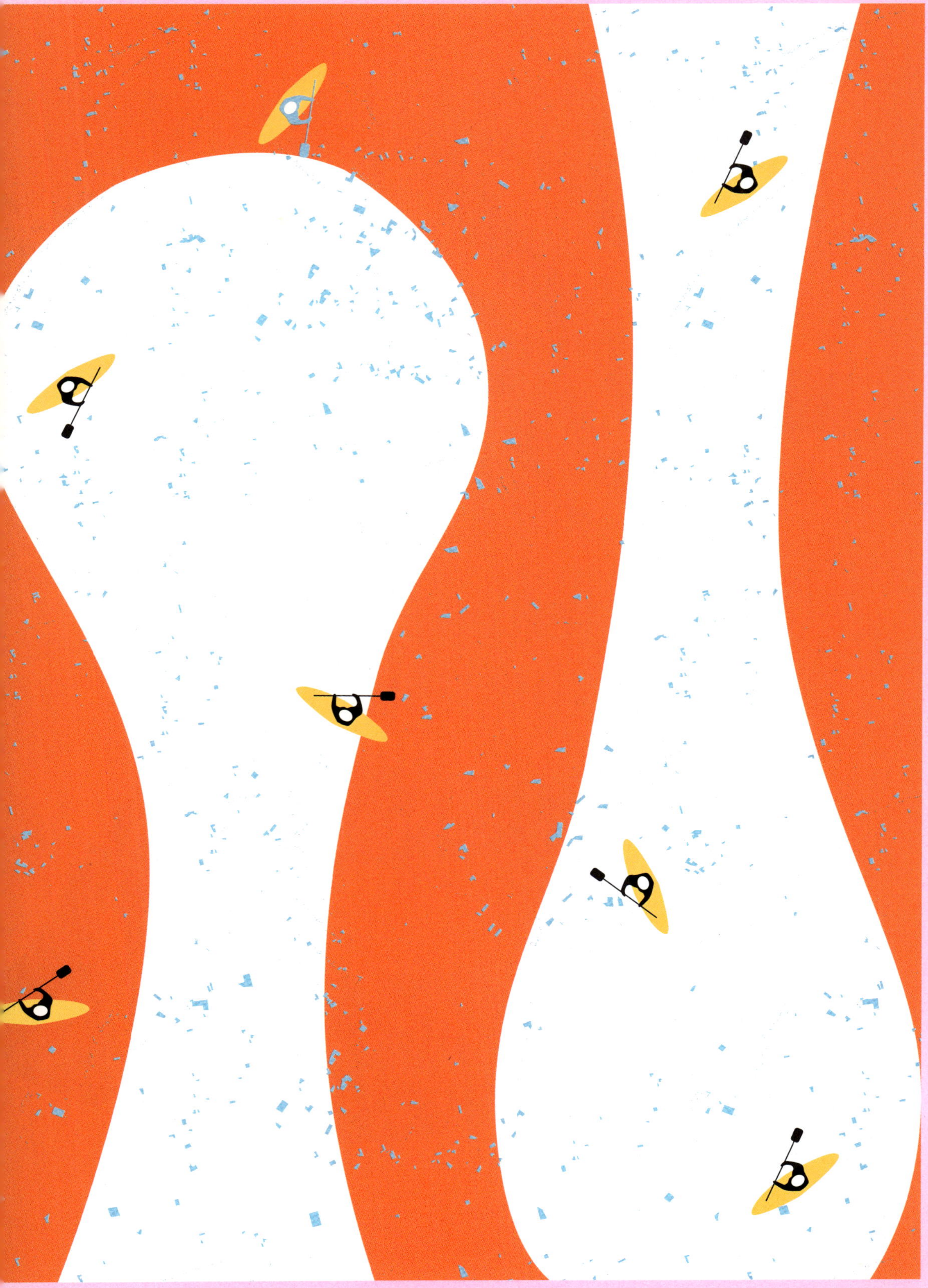

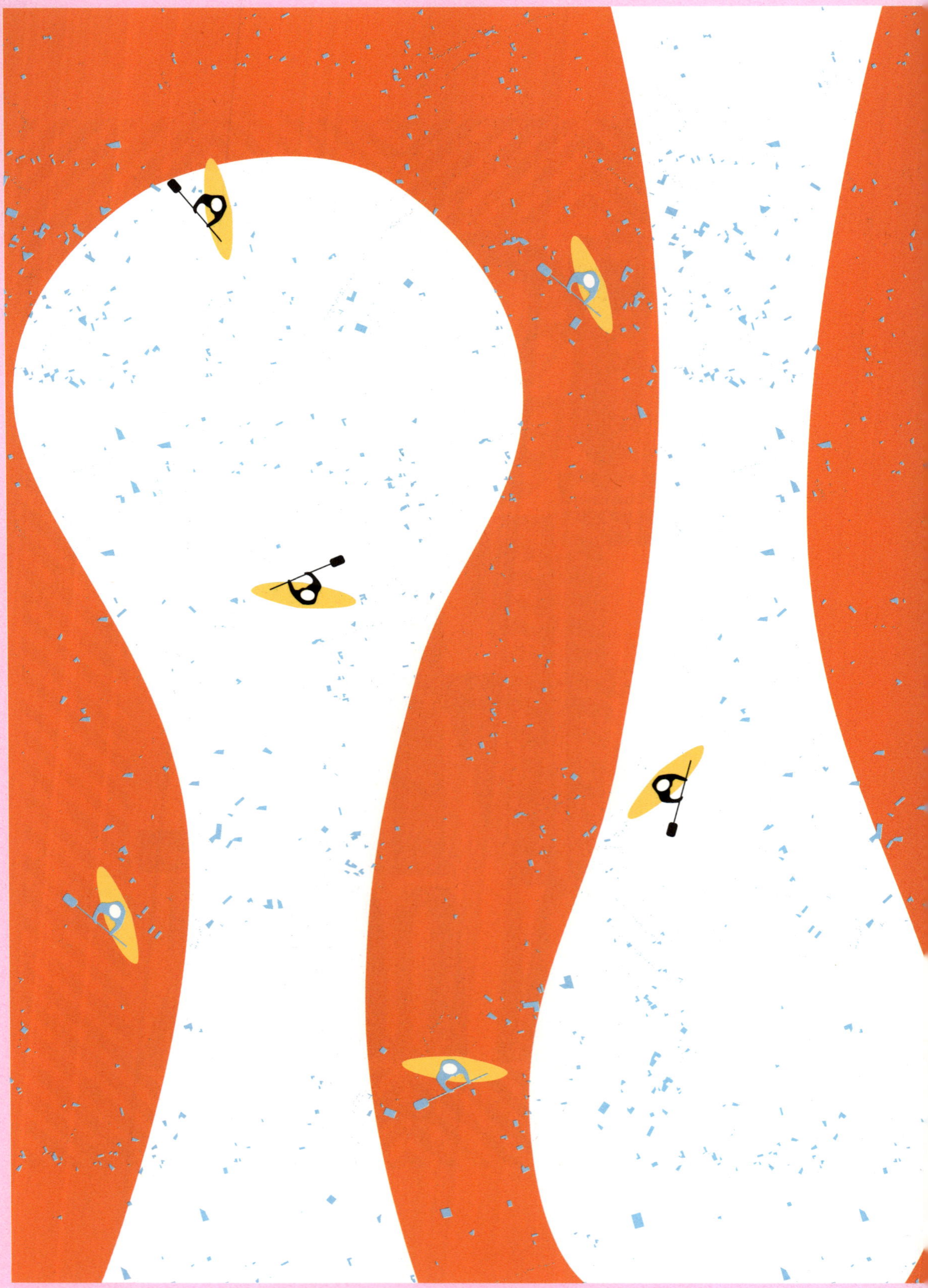

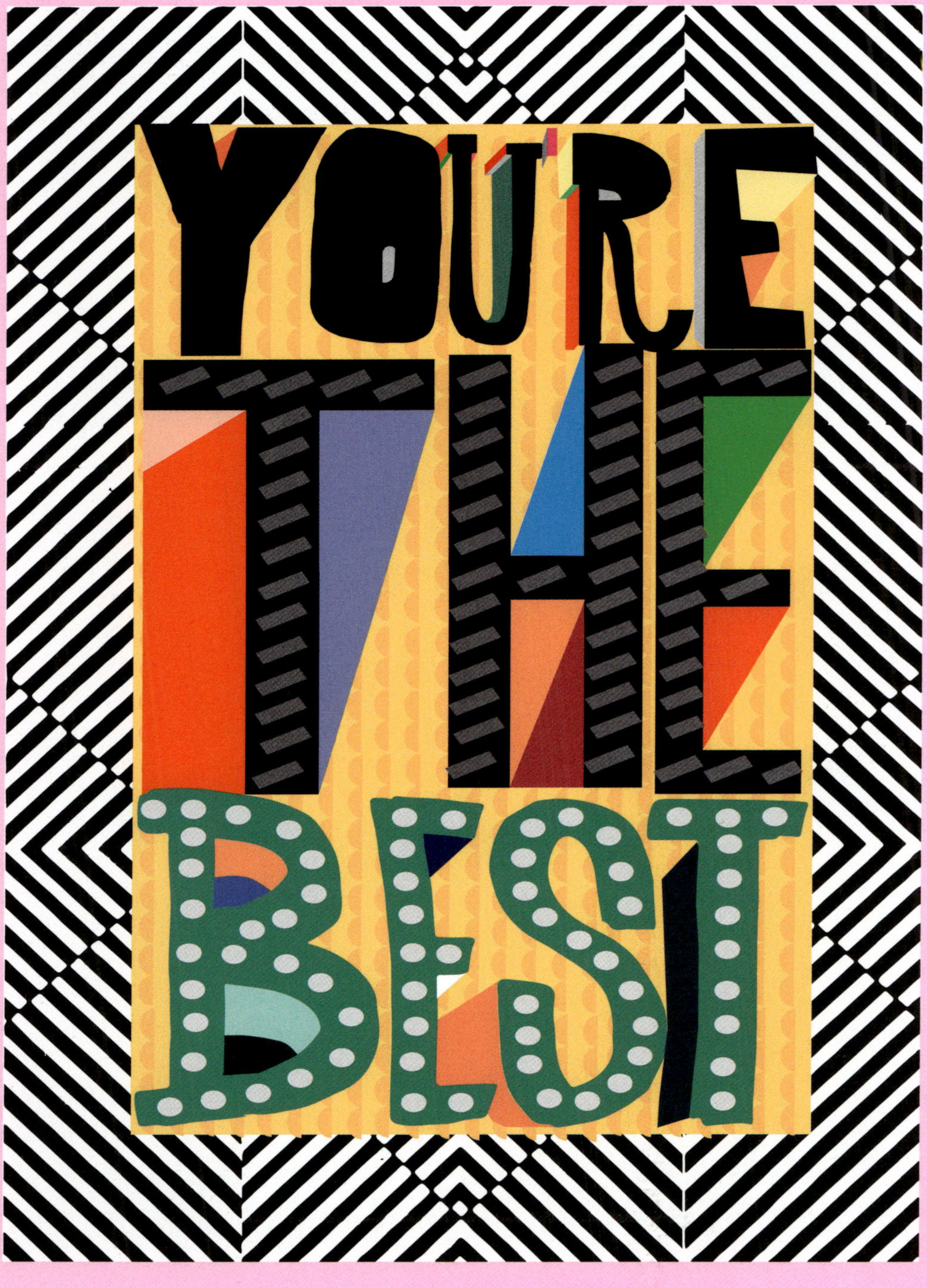
YOU'RE
THE
BEST

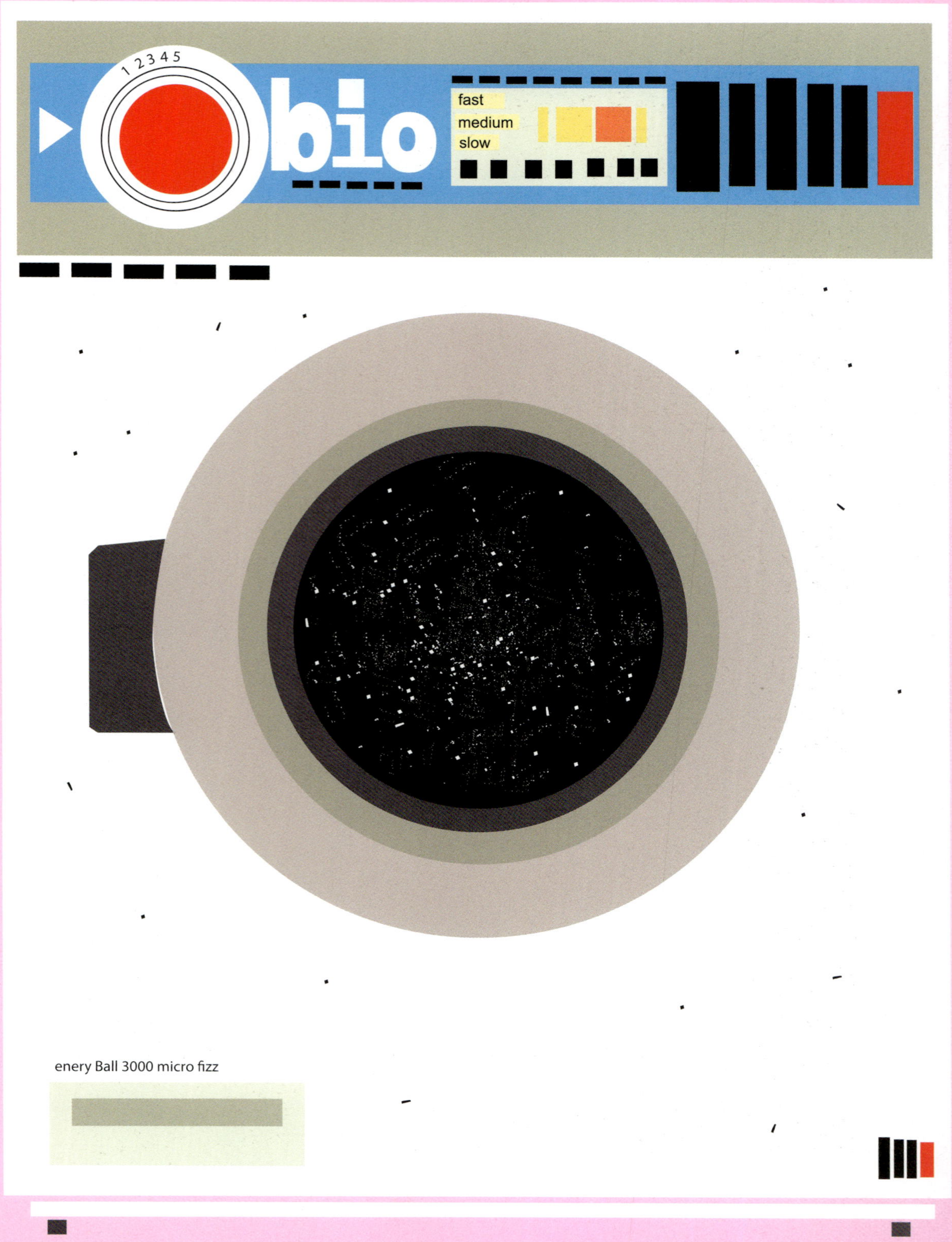
1 2 3 4 5
bio
fast
medium
slow
enery Ball 3000 micro fizz

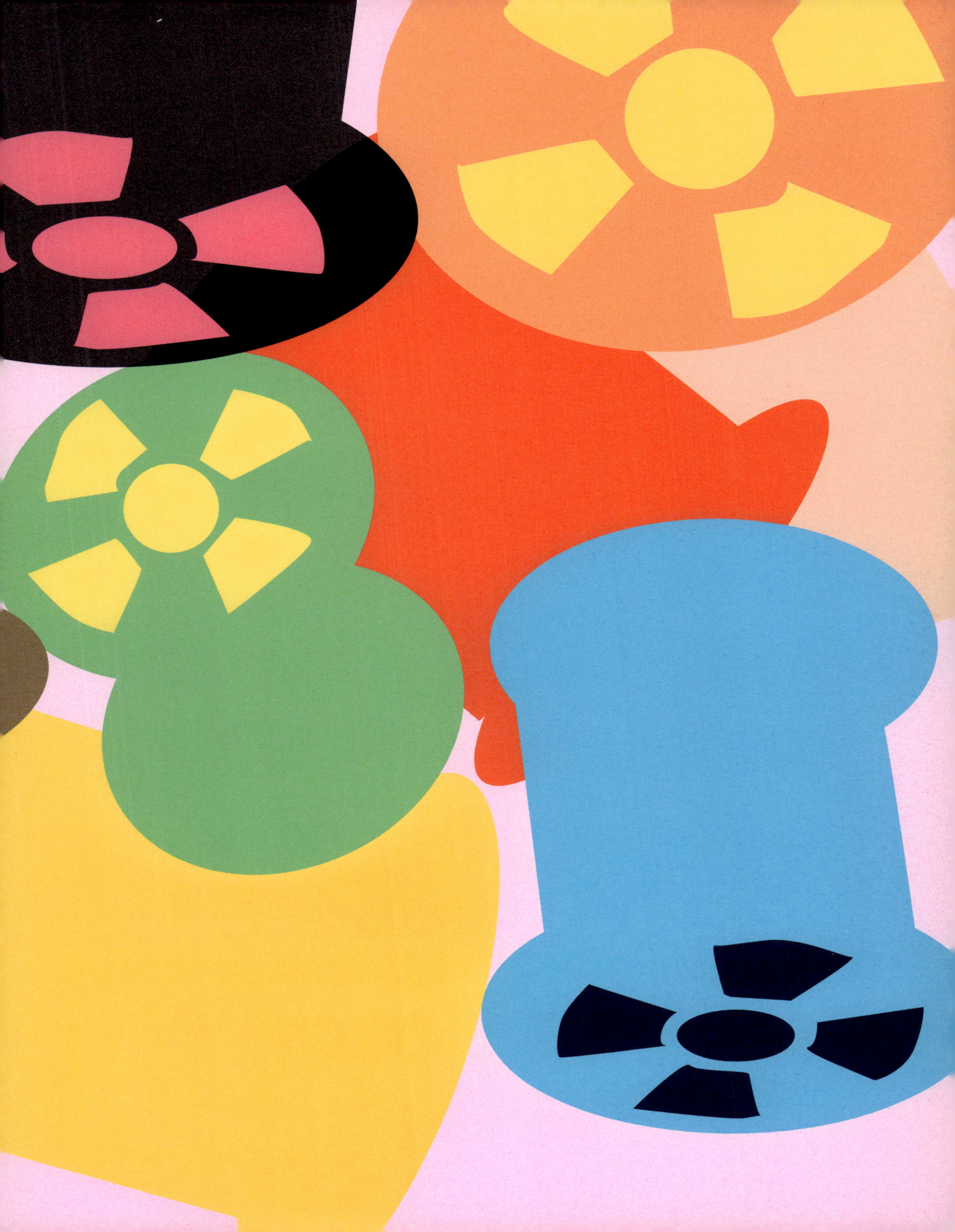

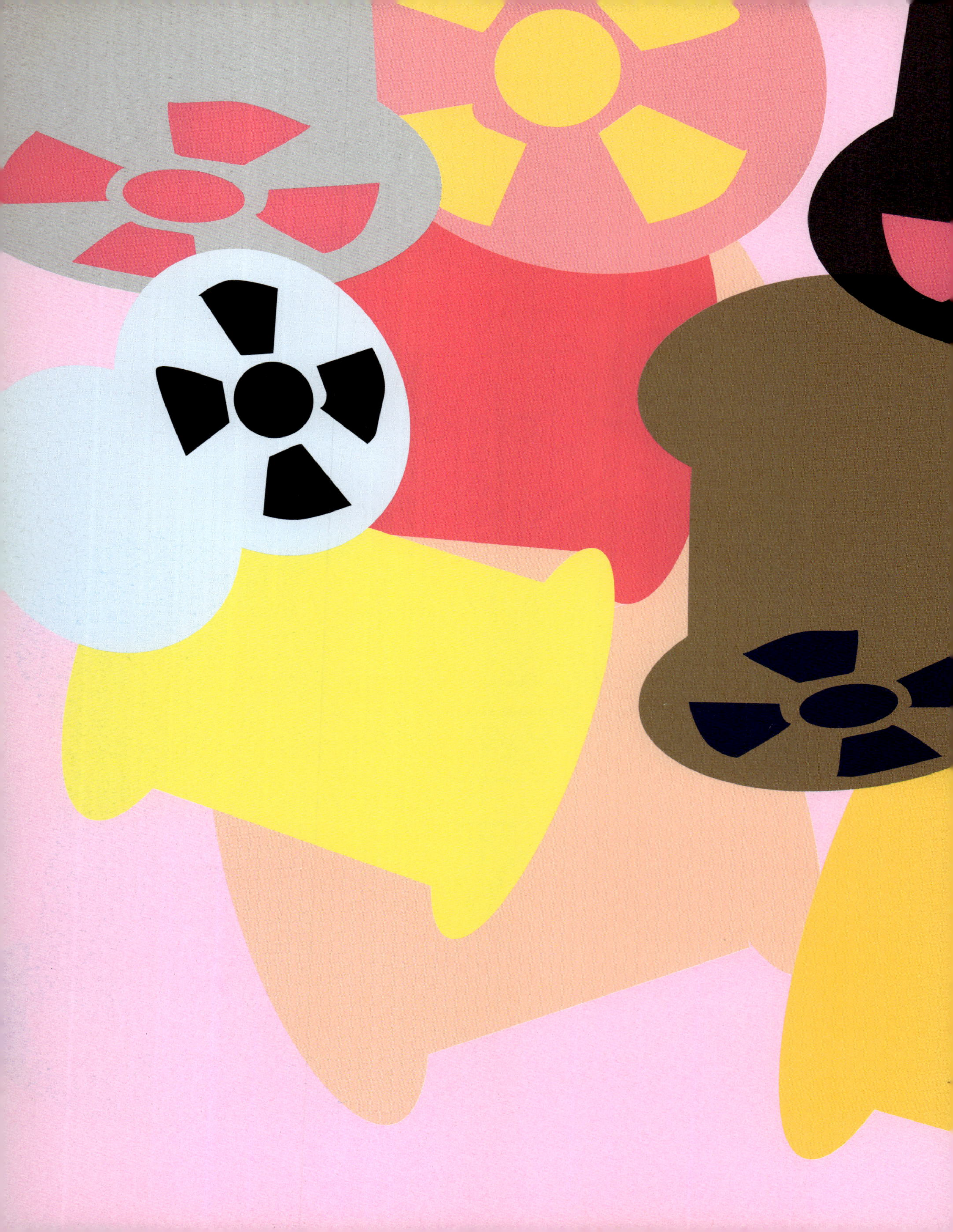

no added sugar

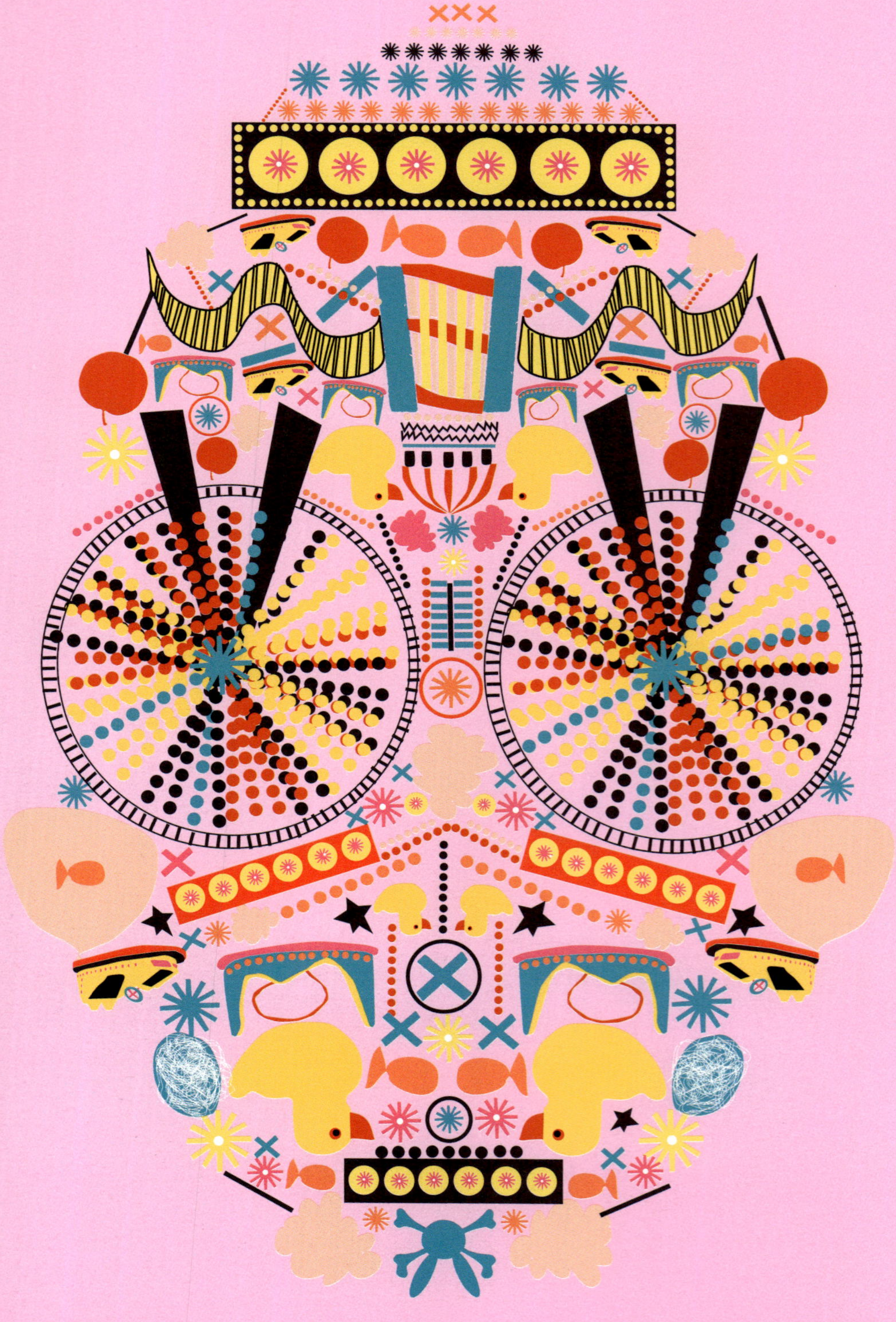

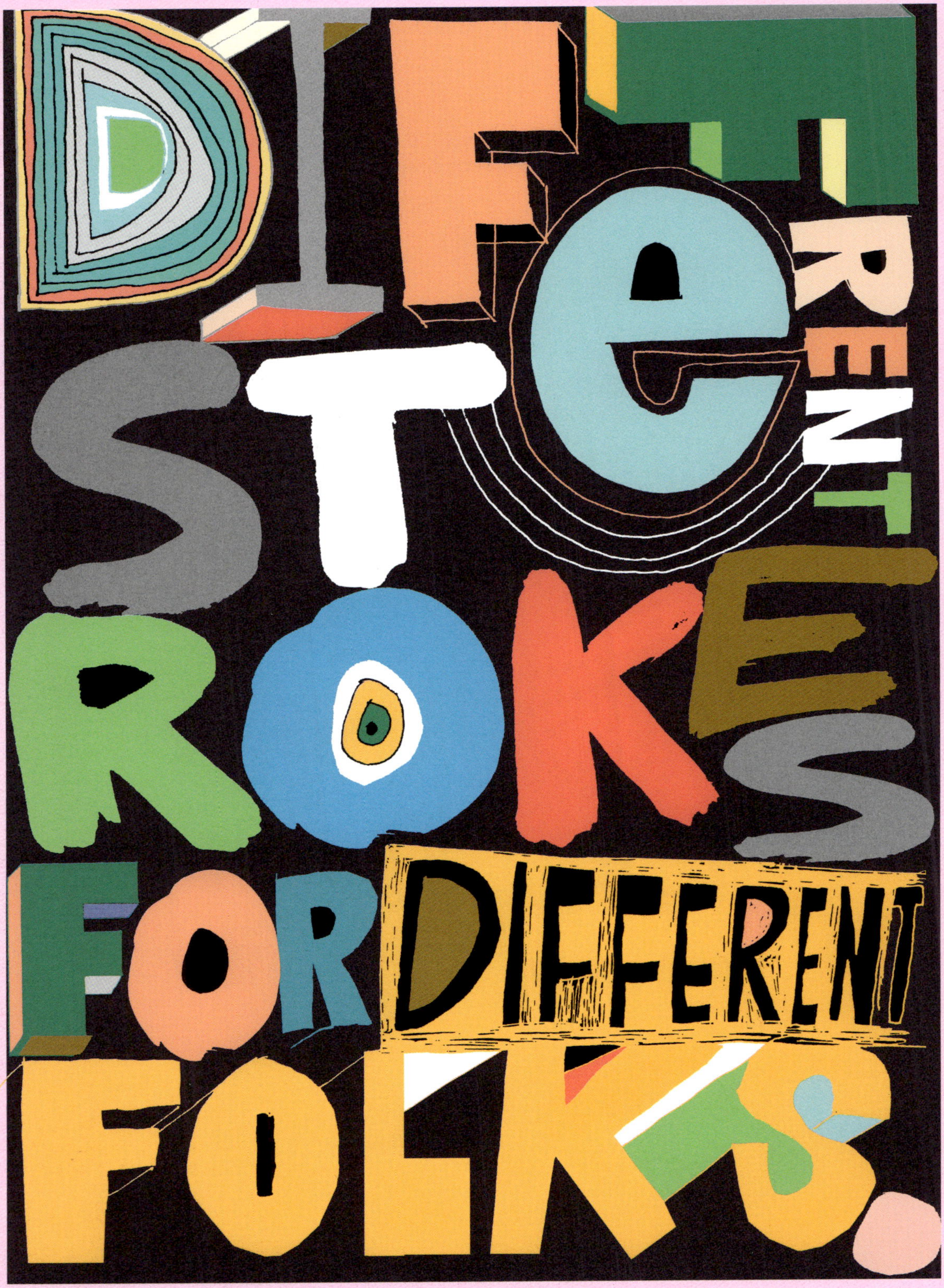
DIFFERENT STROKES FOR DIFFERENT FOLKS.

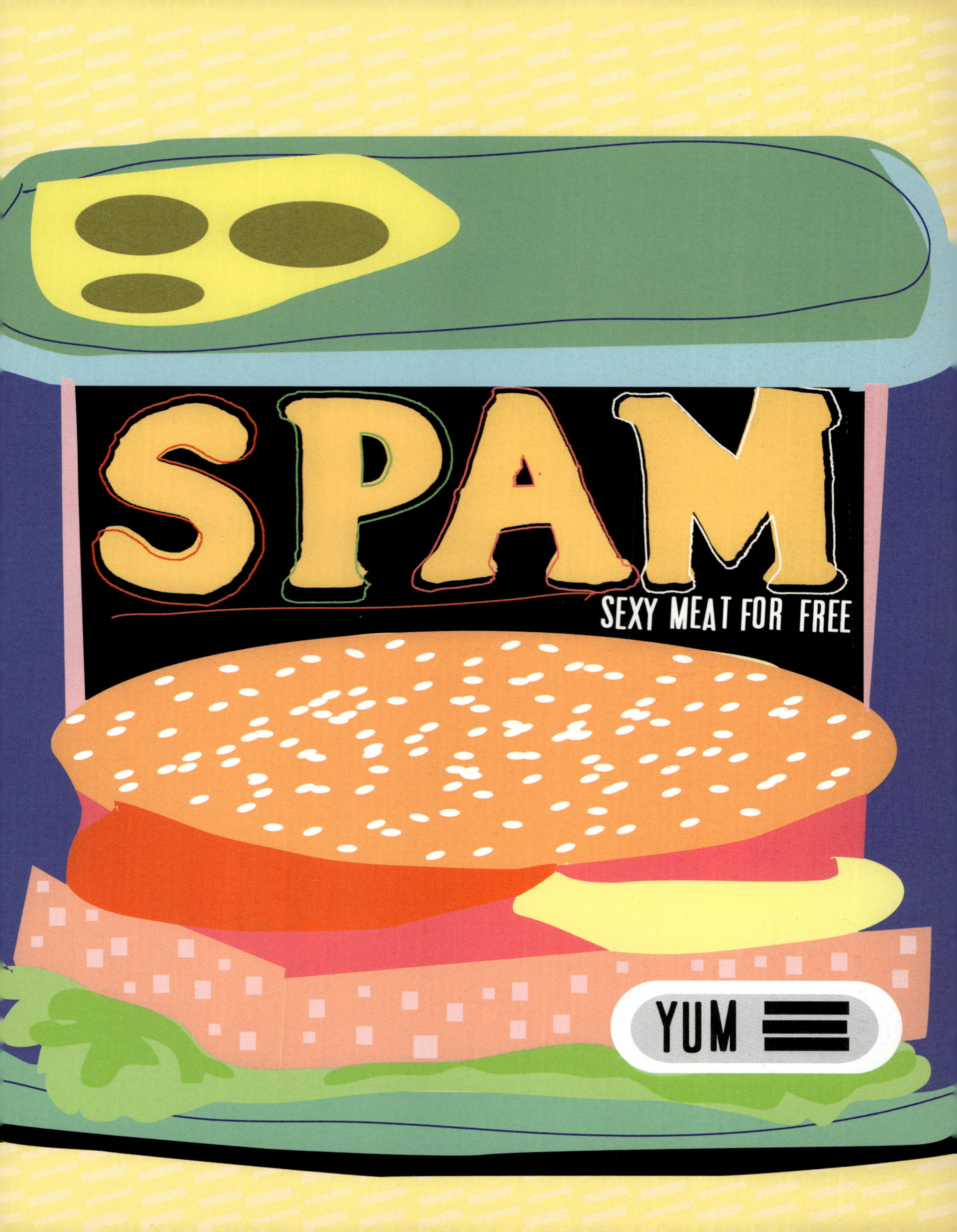
SPAM
SEXY MEAT FOR FREE
YUM

MIND

LANGUAGE

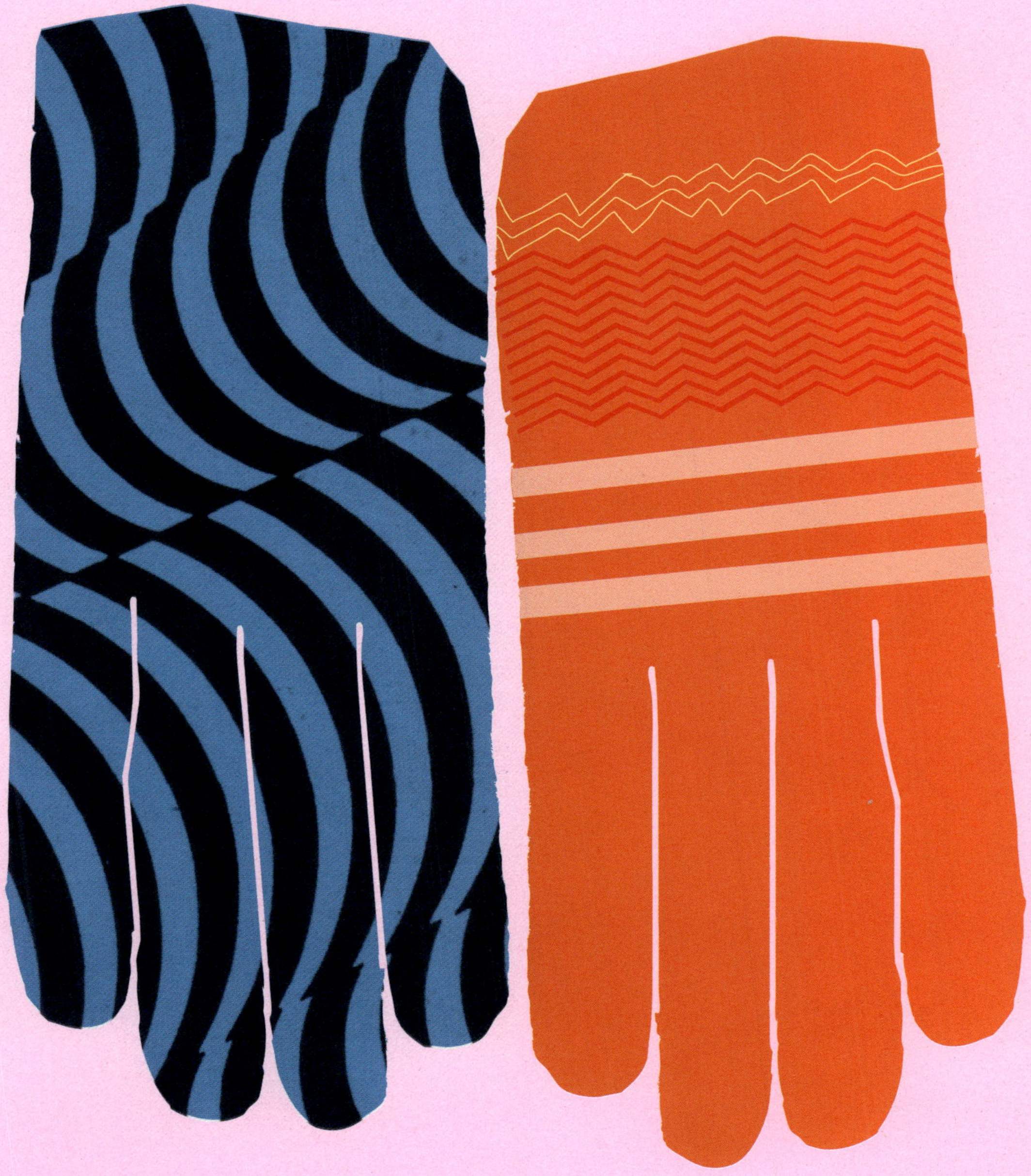

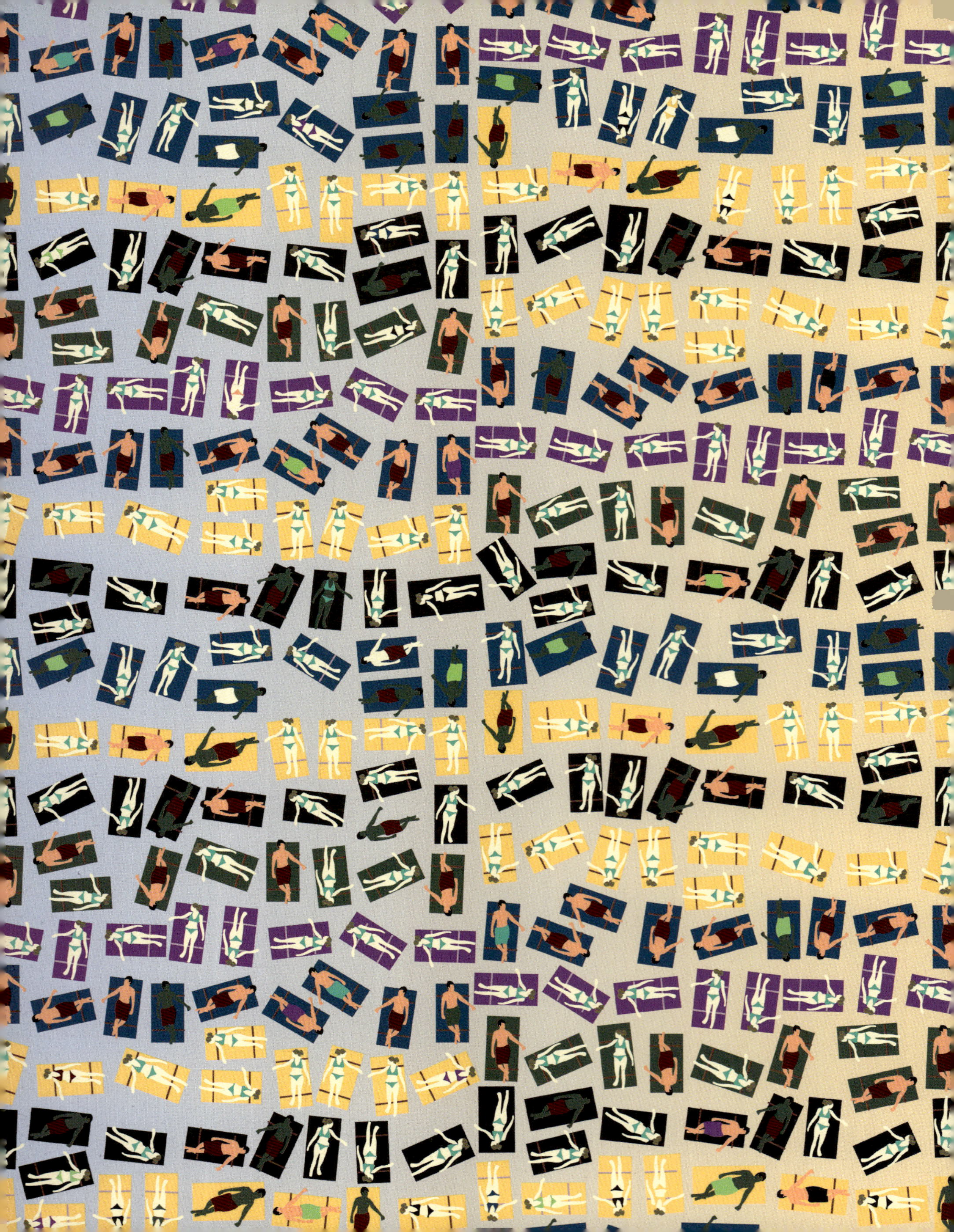

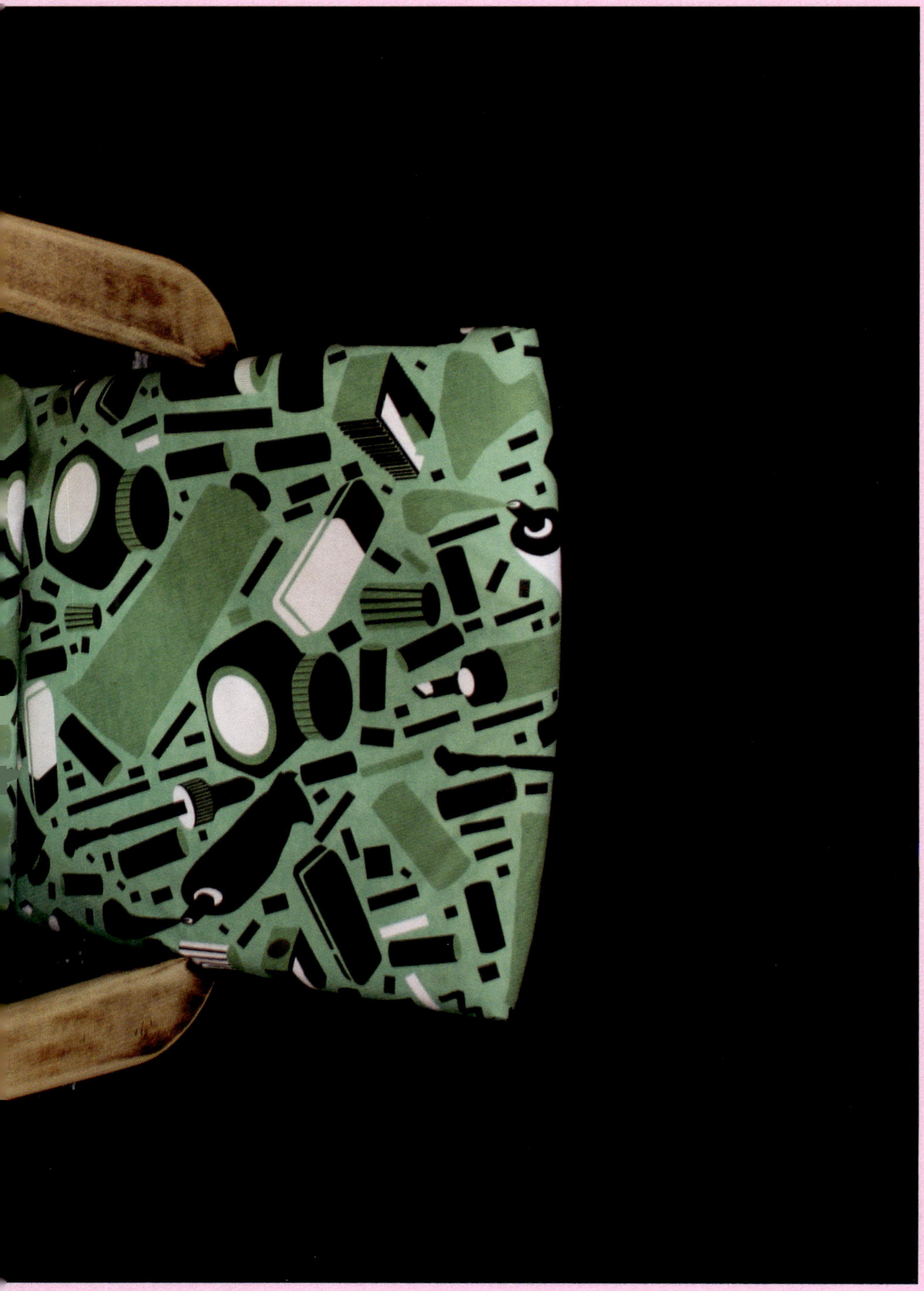

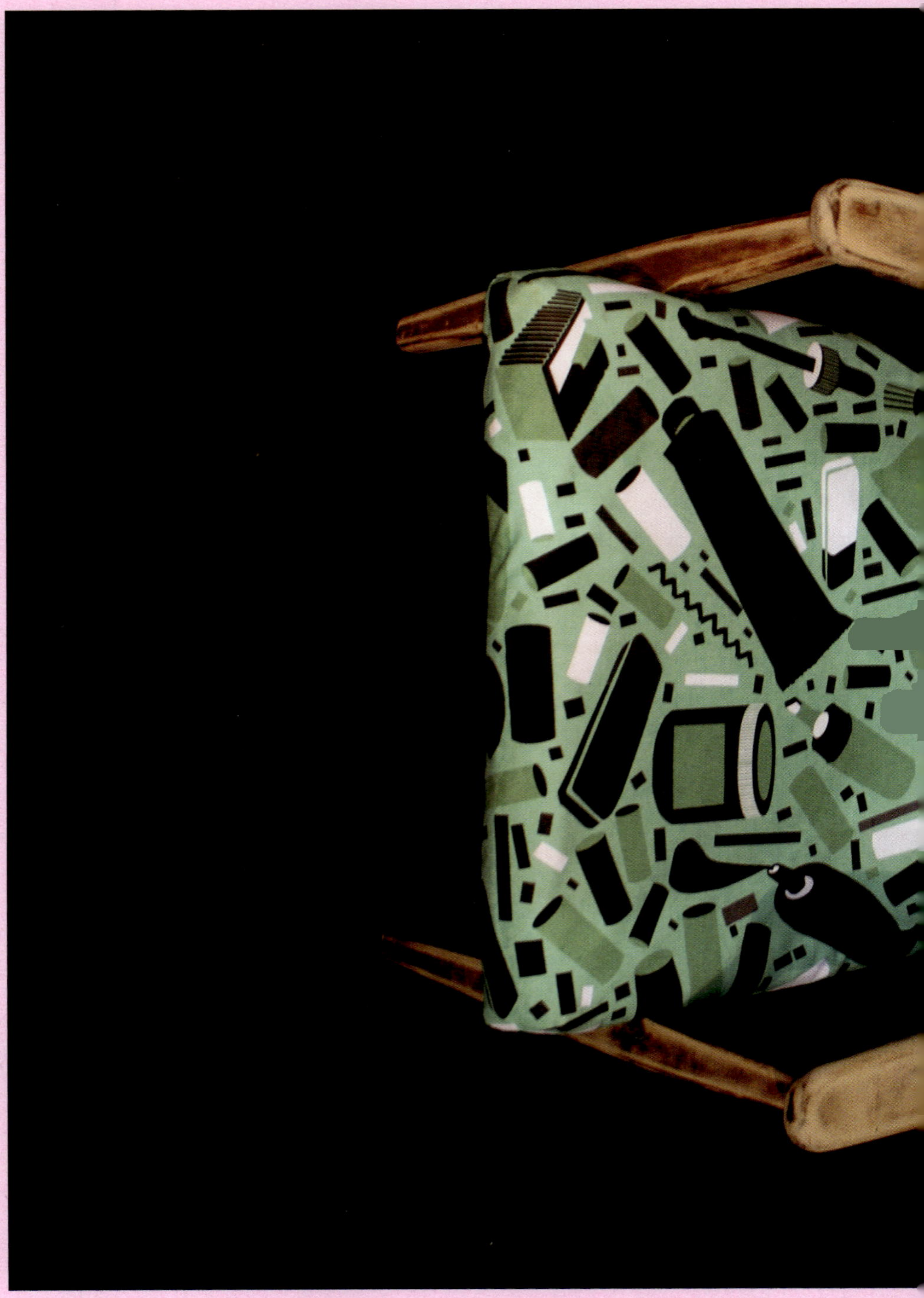

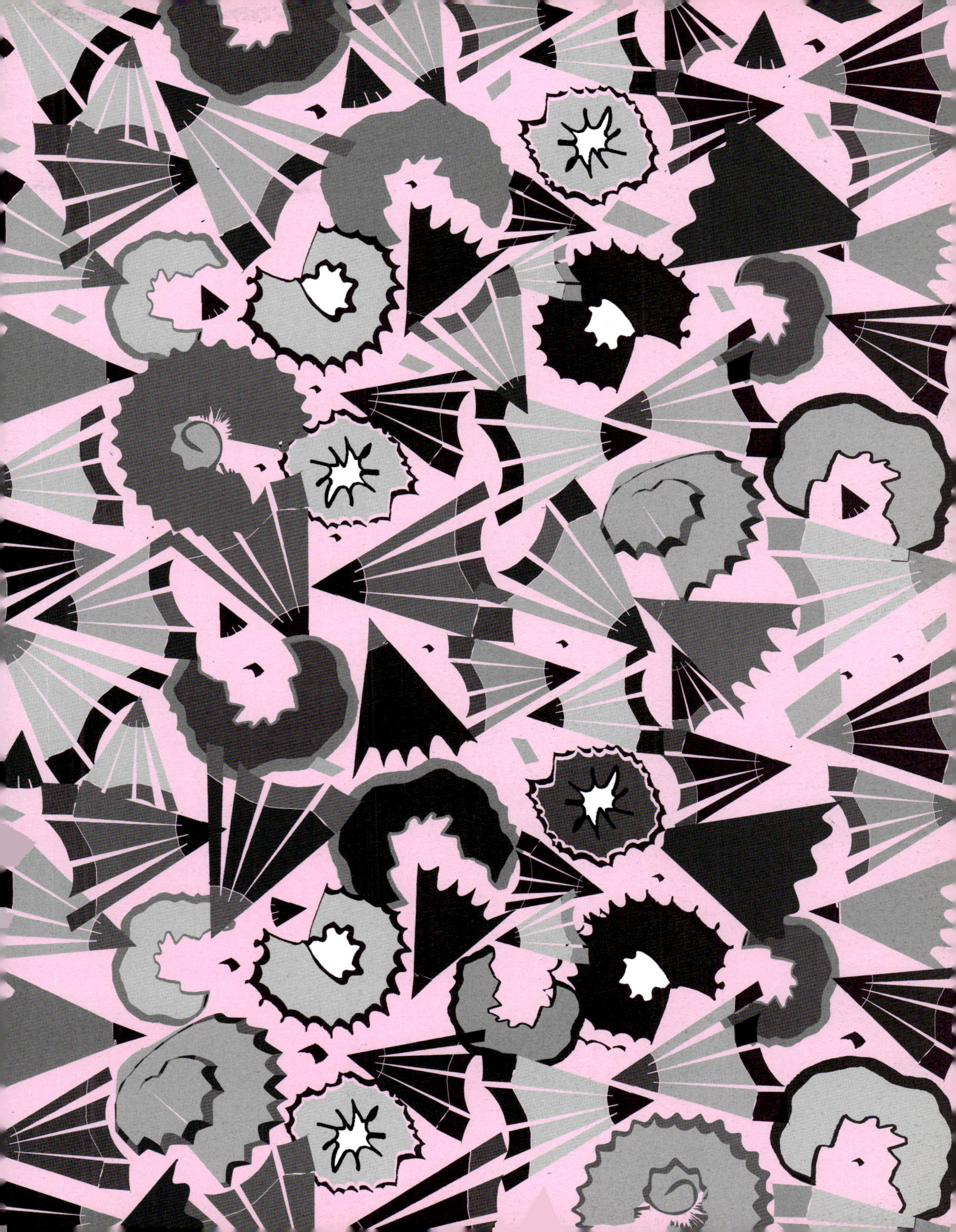

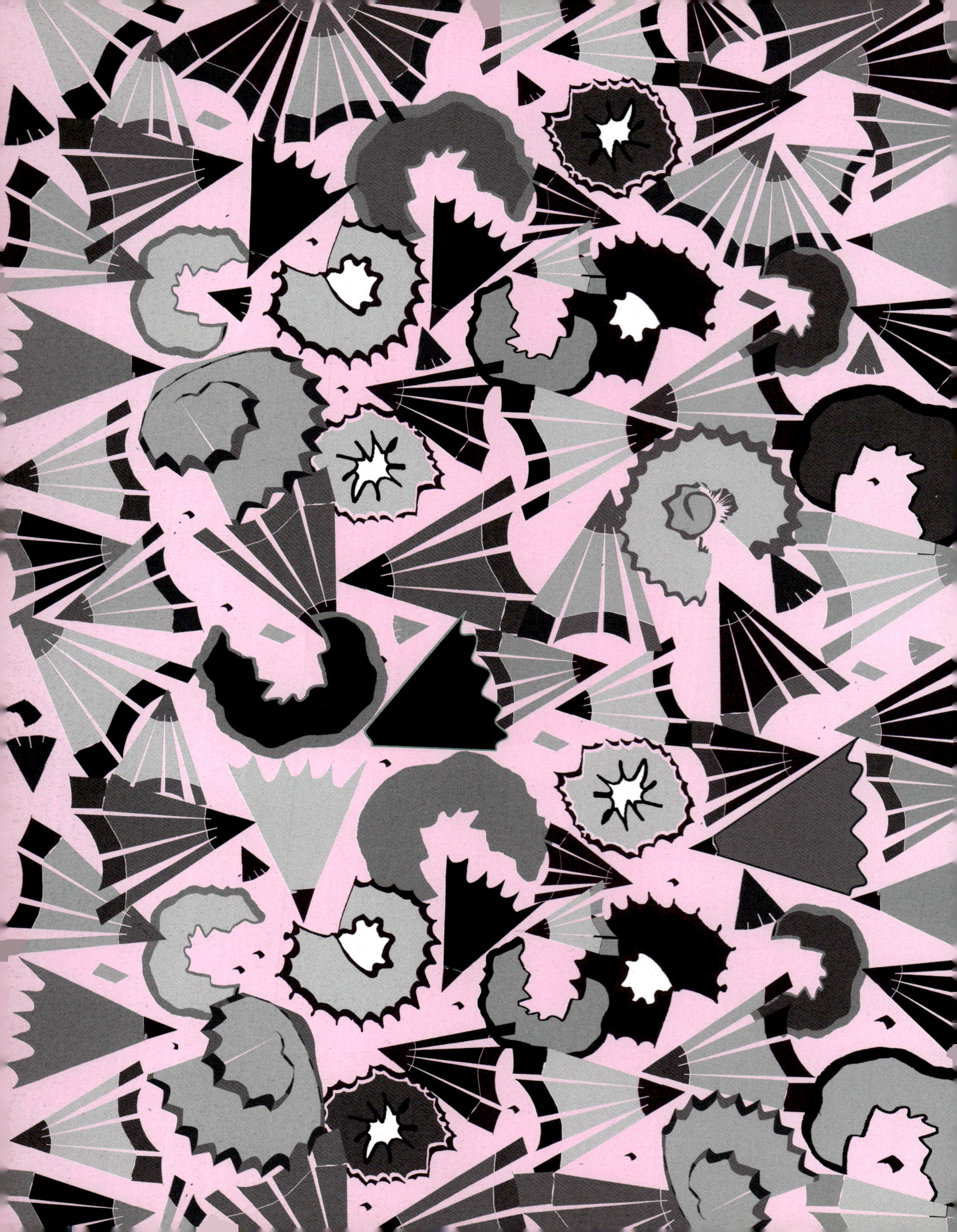

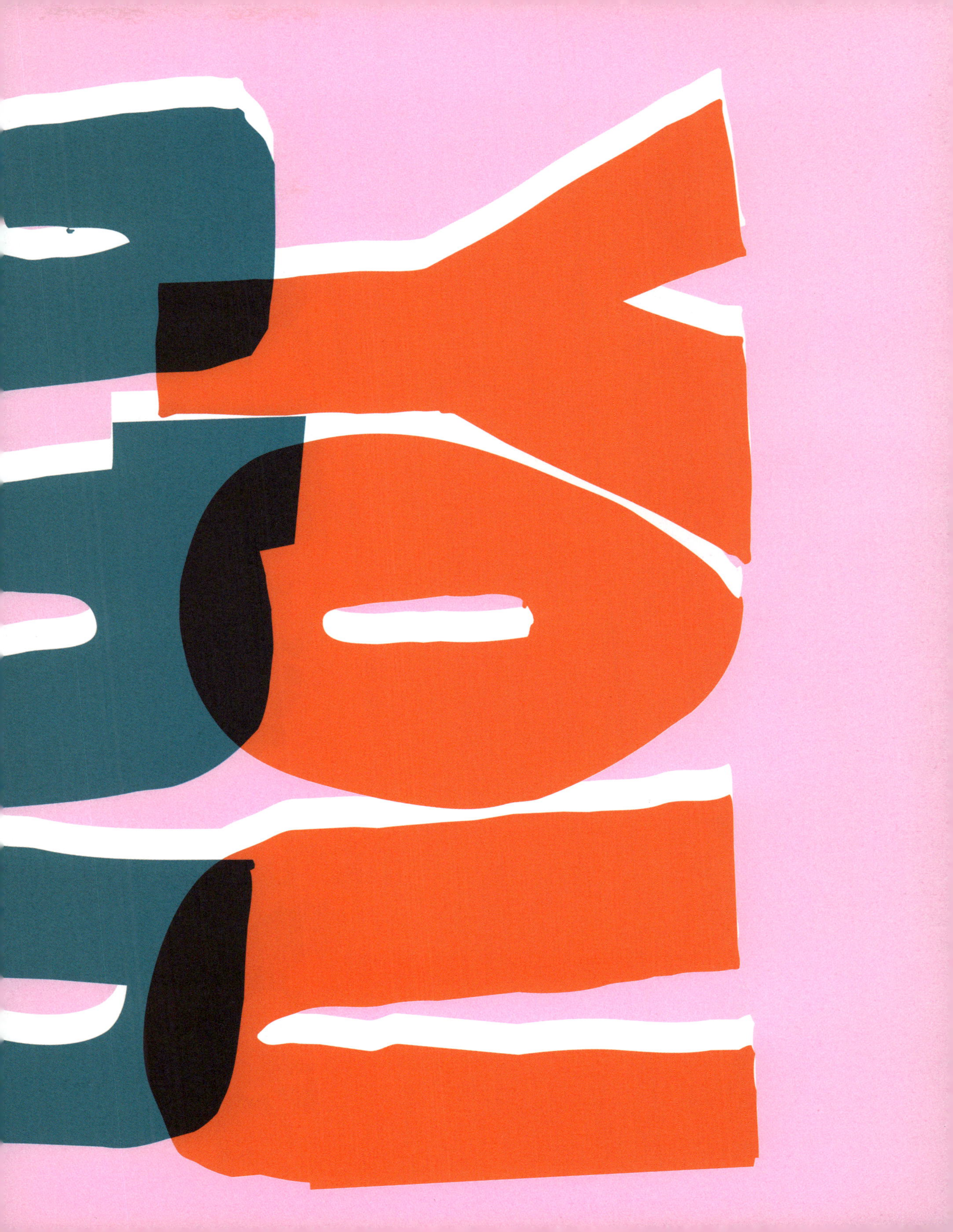

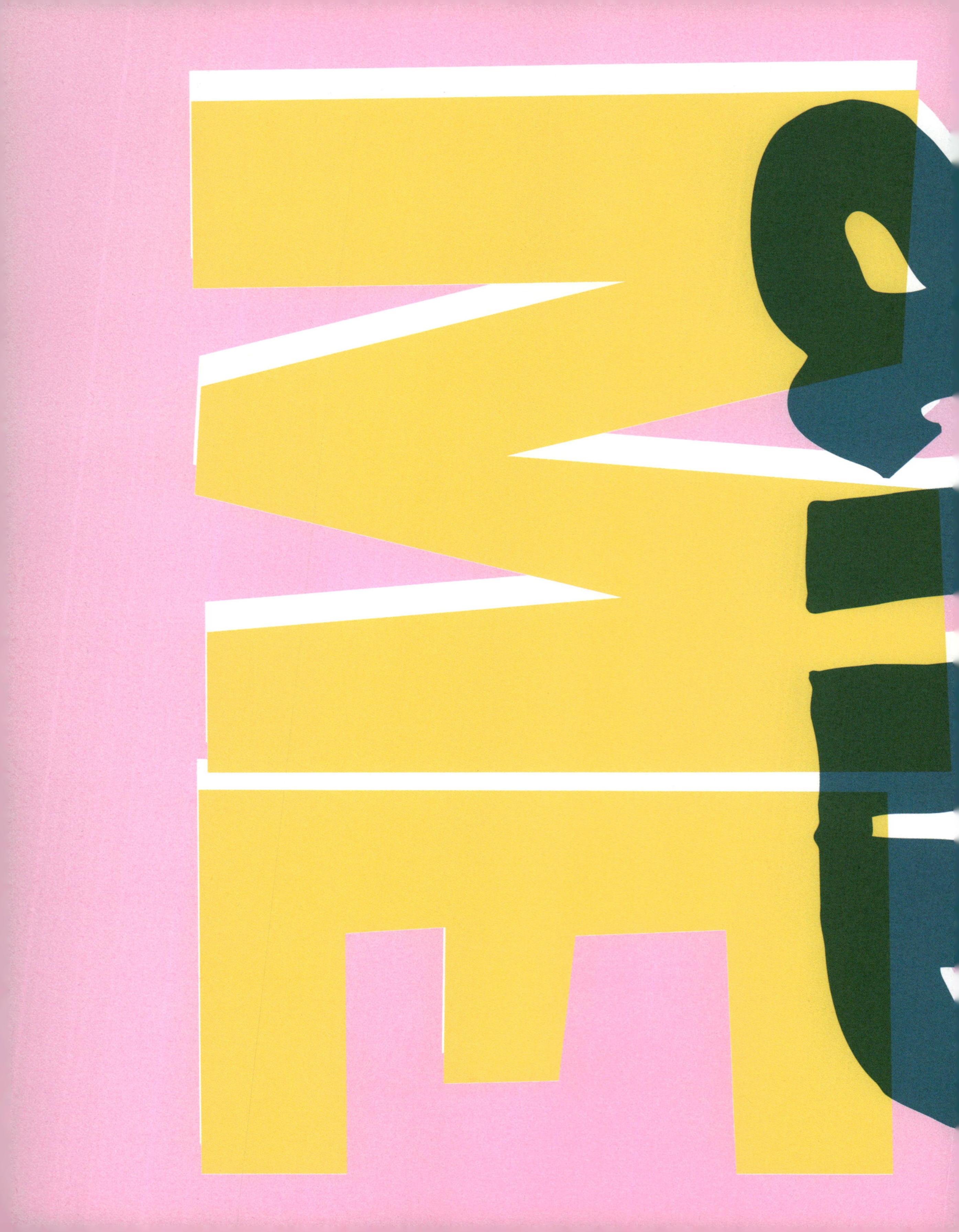
ME

2009—2014

1999 – 2008

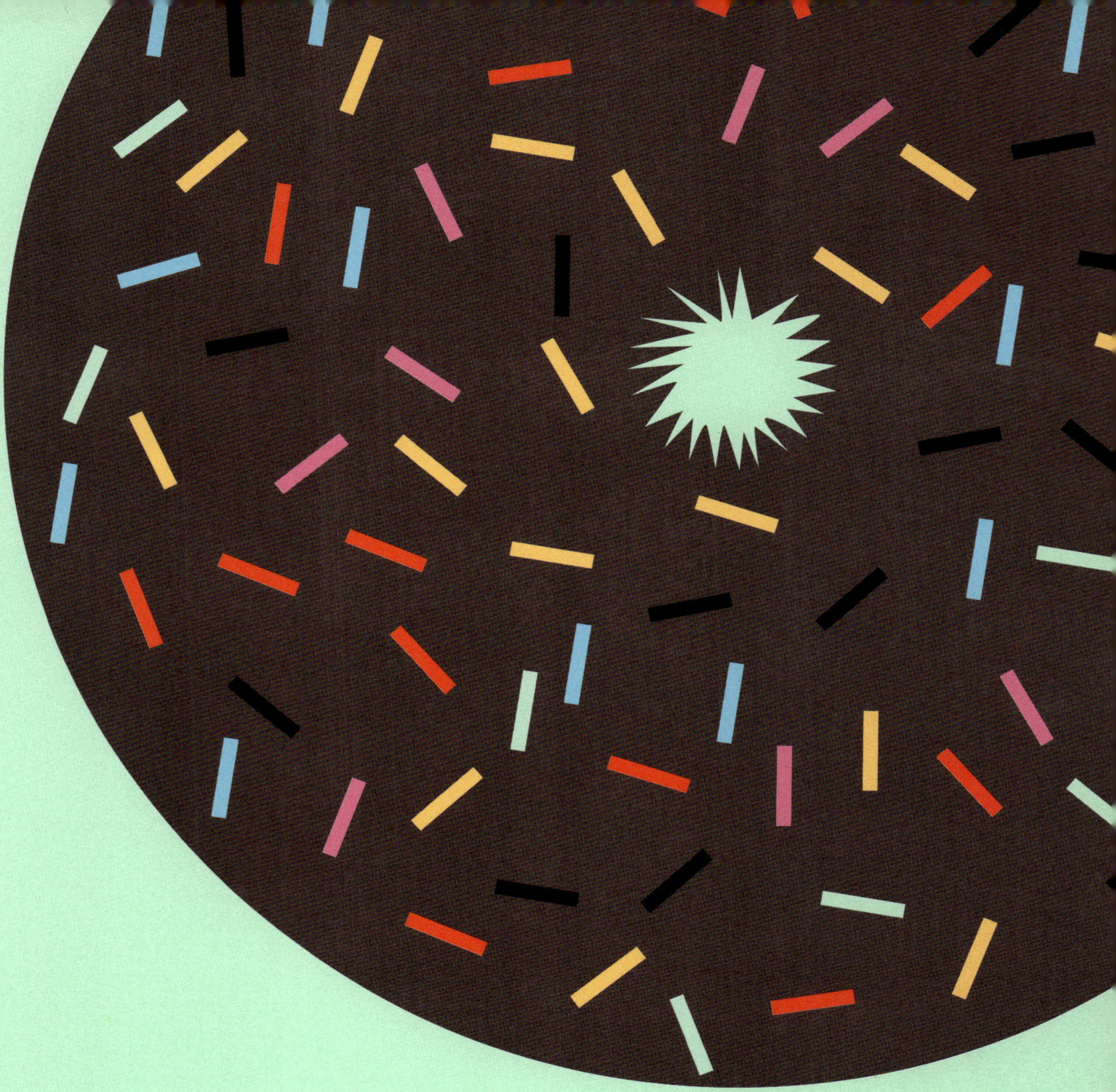

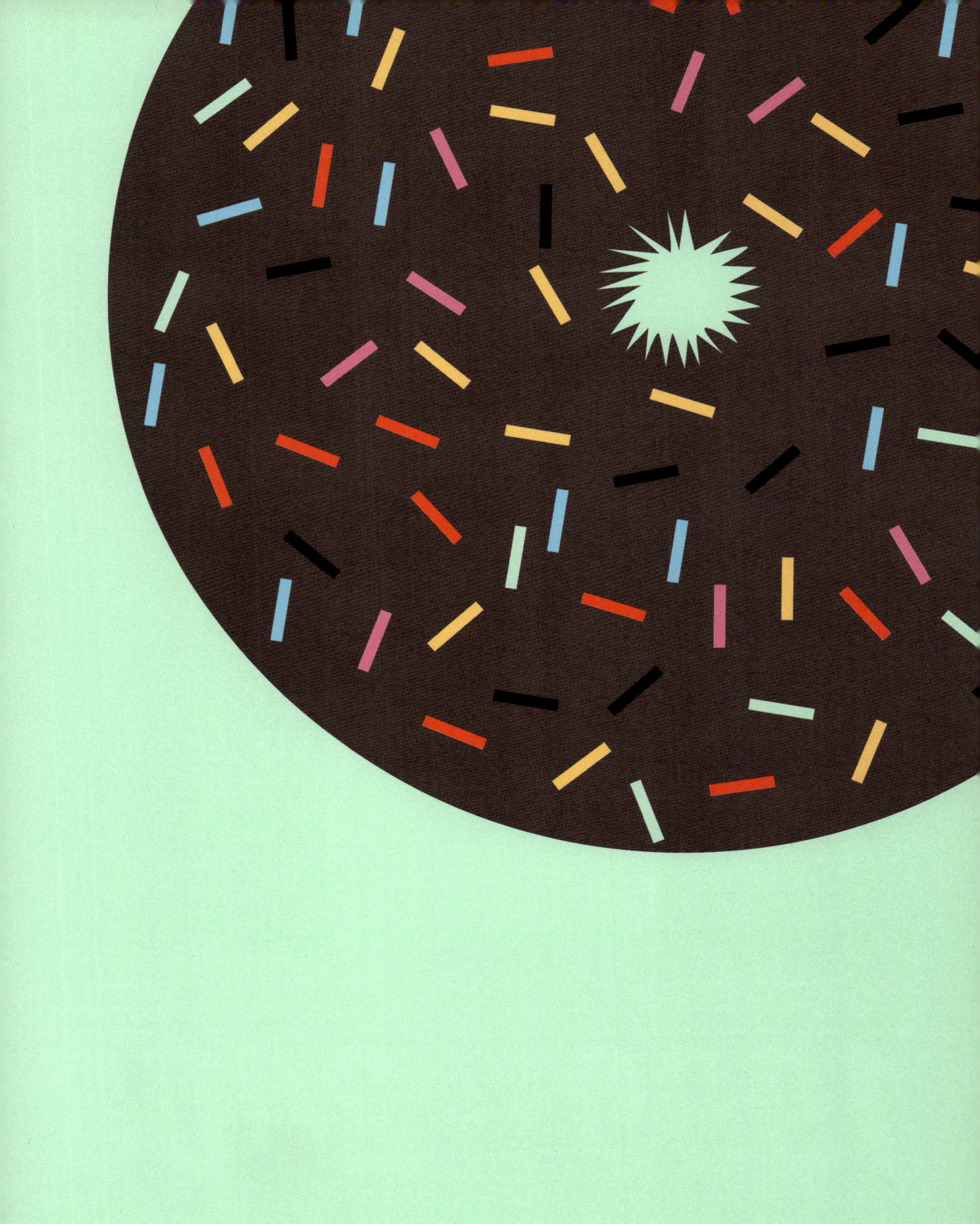

LOVELY PEAR

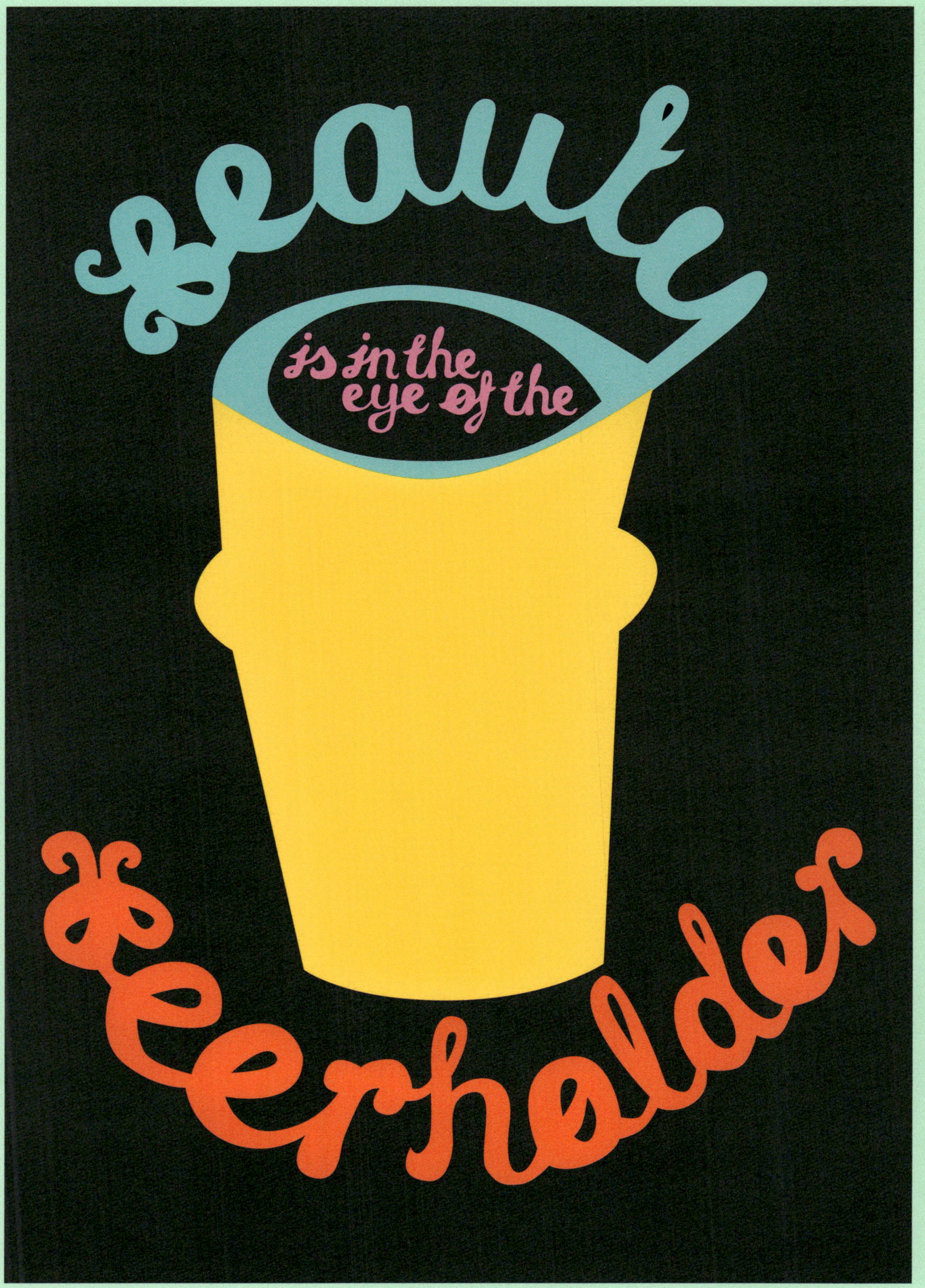
beauty
is in the
eye of the
beerholder

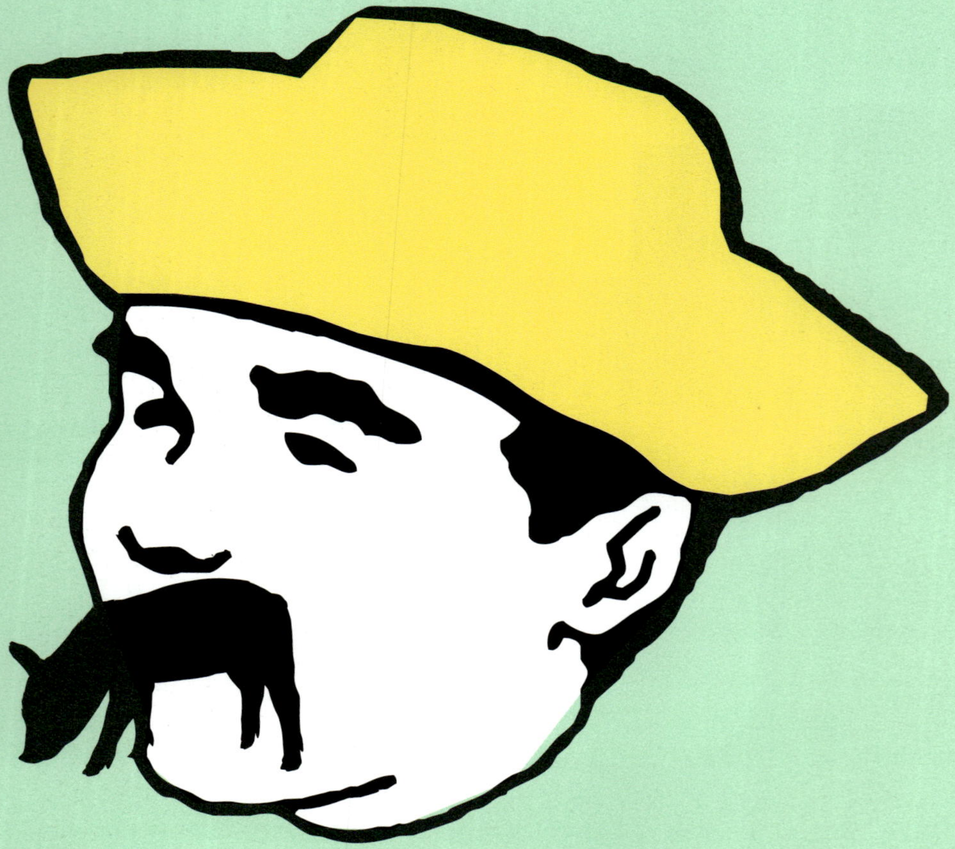

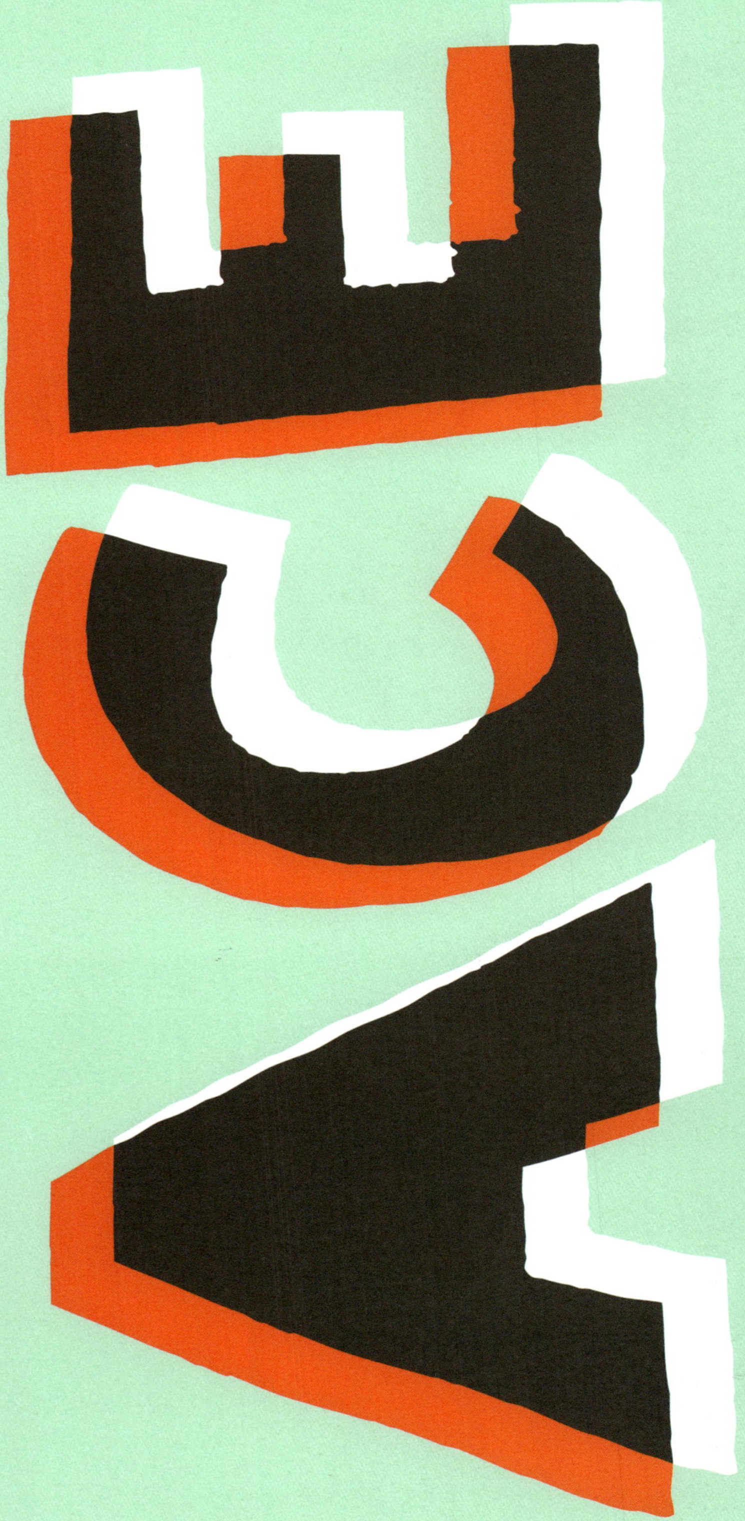
ACE

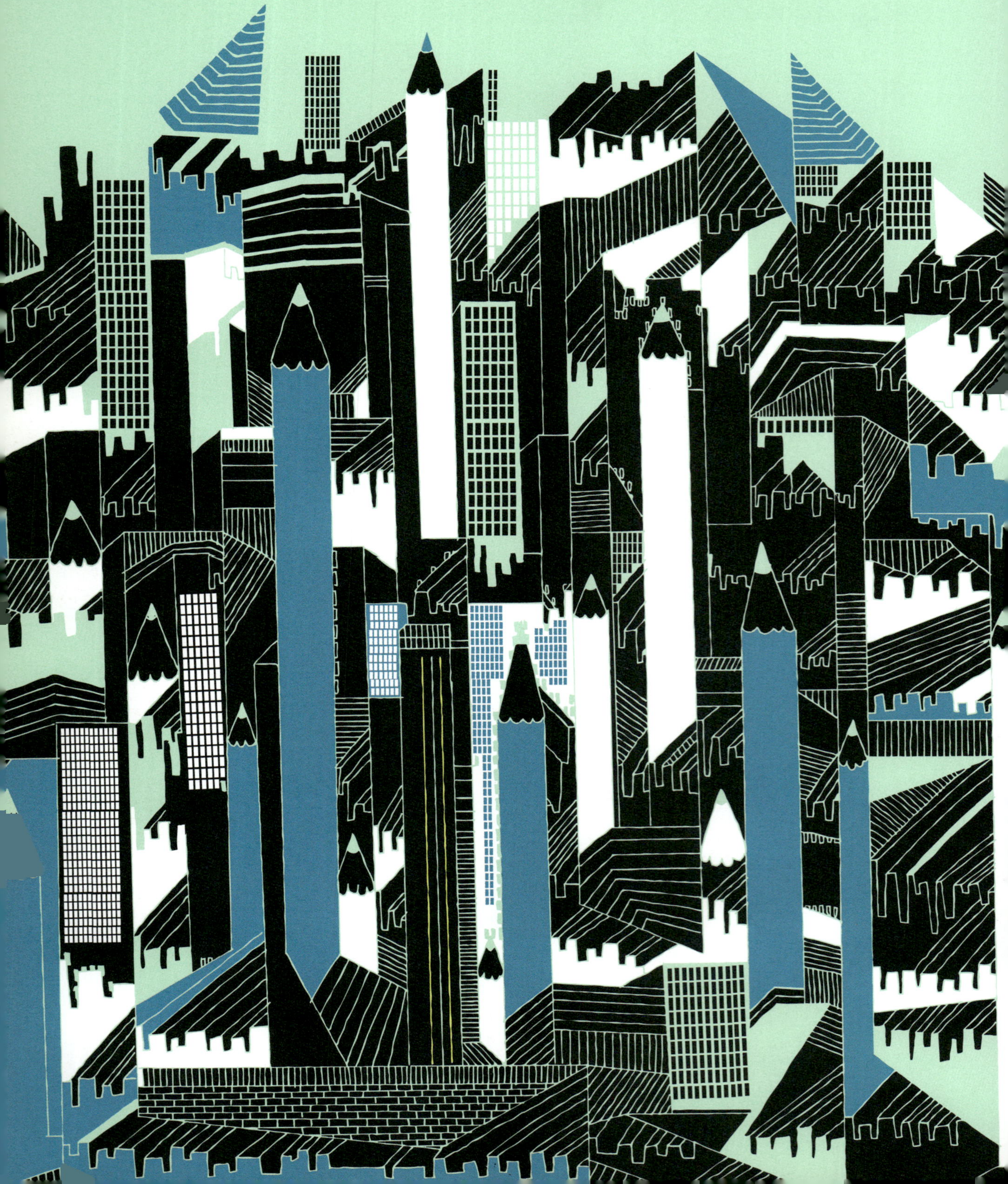

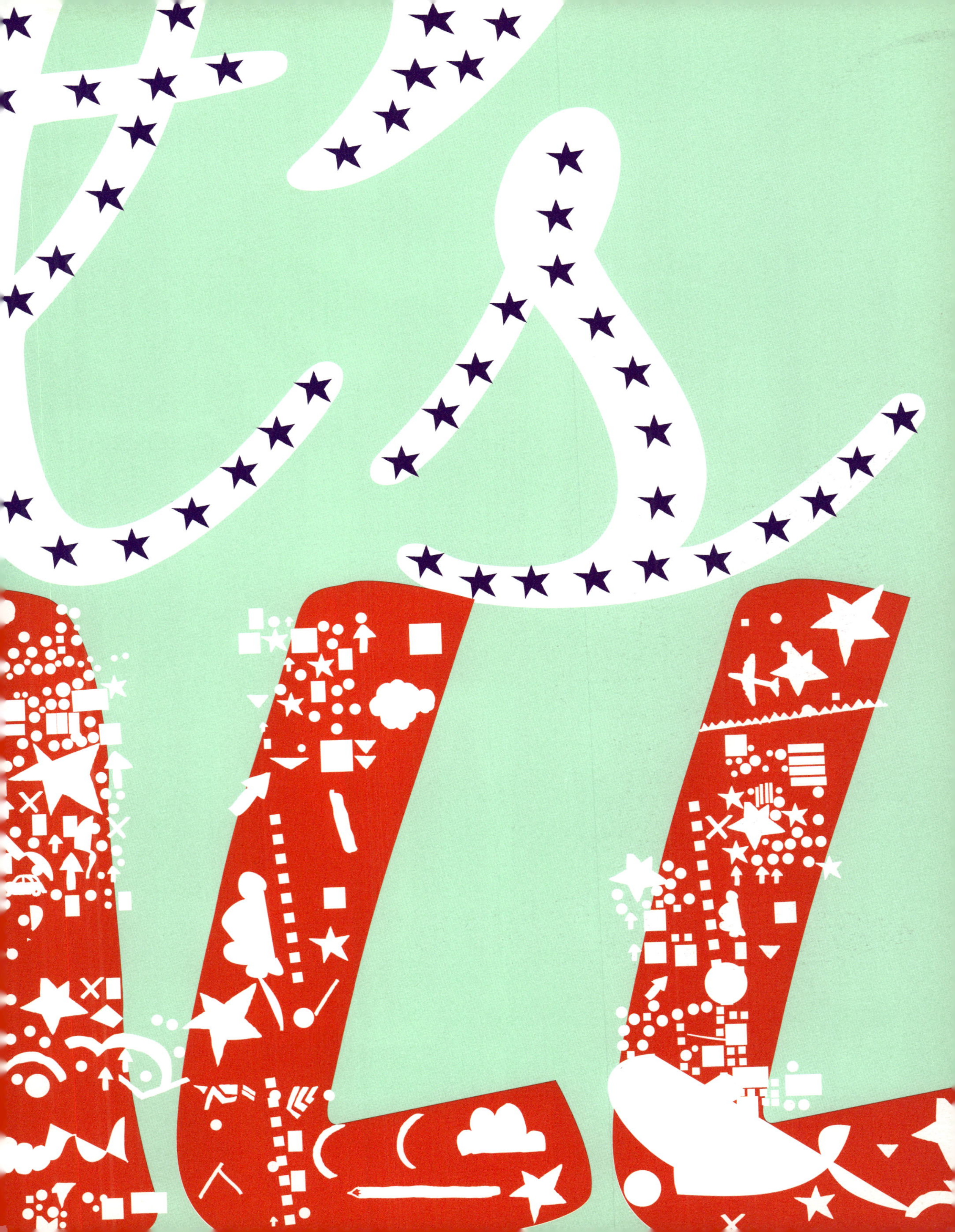

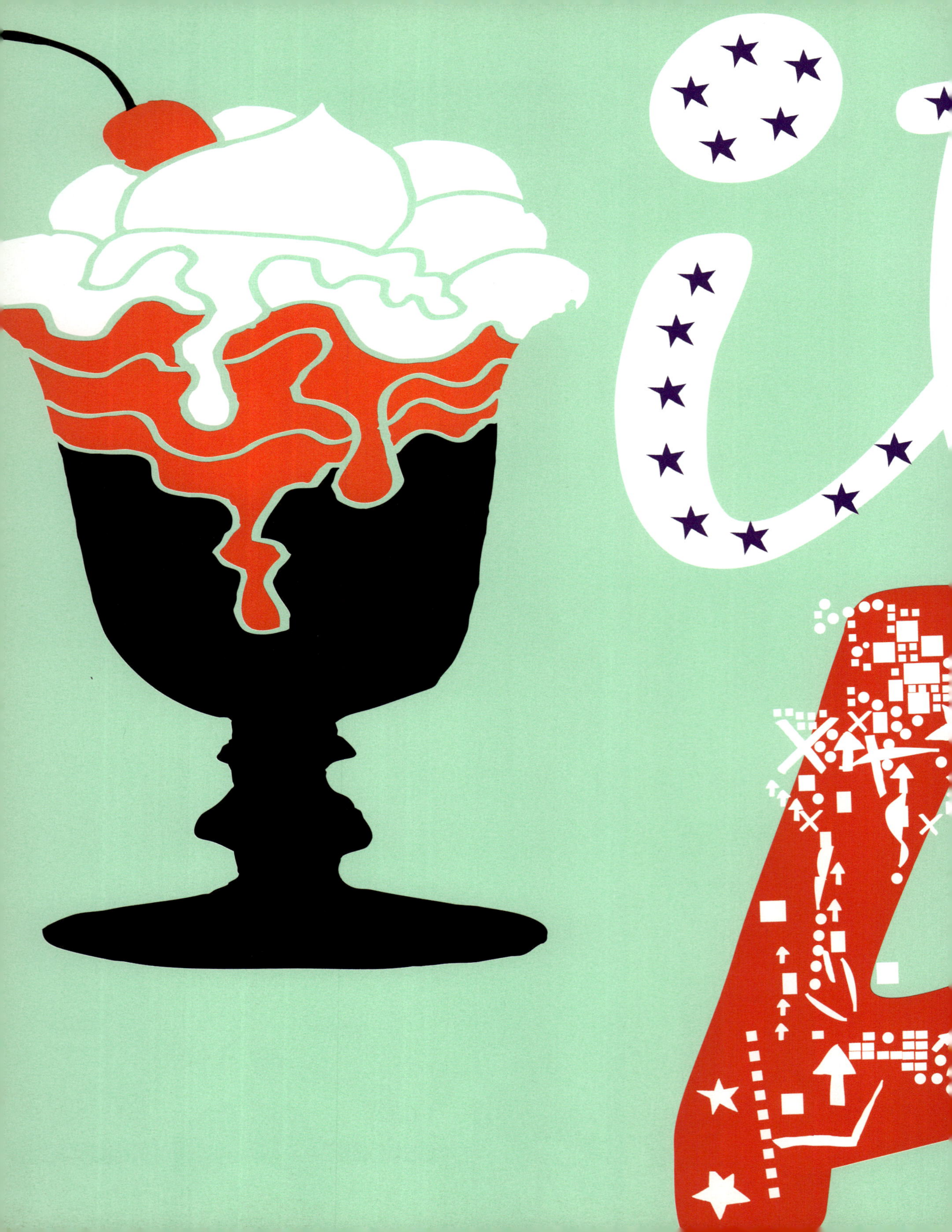